Teaching Assistant's Handbook

S/NVQ Level 3

Heinemann Educational Publishers,

Halley Court, Jordan Hill, Oxford OX2 8EJ

Part of Harcourt Education Limited

Heinemann is a registered trademark of Harcourt Education Limited

OXFORD MELBOURNE AUCKLAND JOHANNESBURG BLANTYRE GABORONE IBADAN PORTSMOUTH NH (USA) CHICAGO

© Louise Burnham and Helen Jones 2002

First published 2002

2006 2005 2004

10 9 8 7 6

A catalogue record for this book is available from the British Library on request.

ISBN 0 435 46370 5

All rights reserved.

Apart from any fair dealing for the purposes of research or private study, or criticism or review as permitted under the terms of the UK Copyright, Designs and Patents Act, 1988, this publication may not be reproduced, stored or transmitted, in any form or by any means, without the prior permission in writing of the publishers, or in the case of reprographic reproduction only in accordance with the terms of the licences issued by the Copyright Licensing Agency in the UK, or in accordance with the terms of licenses issued by the appropriate Reproduction Rights Organization outside the UK. Enquiries concerning reproduction outside the terms stated here should be sent to the publishers at the United Kingdom address printed on this page.

Typeset and illustrated by ✏ Tek-Art, Croydon, Surrey

Printed and bound in Great Britain by CPI Bath

Tel: 01865 888058 www.heinemann.co.uk

Websites

Please note that the examples of websites suggested in this book were up to date at the time of writing. It is essential for tutors to preview each site before using it to ensure that the URL is still accurate and the content is appropriate. We suggest that tutors bookmark useful sites and consider enabling students to access them through the school or college intranet.

Acknowledgements

Every effort has been made to contact copyright holders of material reproduced in this book. Any omissions will be rectified in subsequent printings if notice is given to the publishers.

Contents

Acknowledgements

Louise Burnham would like to thank all the staff at Pickhurst Infant School in West Wickham, Kent, for all their support and advice, in particular Gill Mallard for finding time to look at Units 4 and 21, Margaret McWalter for looking through the chapter on special educational needs, Ann Golding for Units 18 and 20 on literacy and the curriculum, and Heather Mathews for Unit 19 on mathematics. Thanks also to Linda Holledge and Sue Mitchell for their help and advice with Units 10 and 11.

Special thanks must also go to all the teaching assistants at Pickhurst Infant School, for their inspiration and support.

I am also grateful to Alison Ballantyne from the Behaviour Management Unit in Bromley who gave advice on Unit 1, and Mandy King from Bromley EAL support unit for reading through the section on bilingual and multilingual children.

Special thanks go to Mary James, my commissioning editor, for giving me the opportunity to work on this project, and to Penny Tassoni for her continued support and advice. Thanks also to Rachel Gear at Heinemann for her patience and help, particularly during the final stages. Finally, a big thank you to my children, Tom and Lucy, for their understanding and support at all times!

Helen Jones would like to thank Holly and Roger for their continuing support. Thanks also to Pam for giving me the opportunity to work with teaching assistants.

Photo acknowledgements

The authors and publisher would like to thank the following for permission to reproduce photographs:

Bubbles p.270
Gareth Boden p.67, 115, 133, 154, 157, 195, 202, 218, 281
Michael Dunning p. 48, 90, 91, 266
Martin Sookias p.242
Gerald Sunderland p.210
John Walmsley p.229

Dedication

This book is dedicated to my wonderful parents, Gill and Geoff Burnham.

Introduction

Welcome to this handbook for the National Vocational Qualification (NVQ) or Scottish Vocational Qualification (SVQ) for Teaching Assistants. If you are using this handbook, you will be setting out or have already begun to train for work as a Teaching Assistant. This handbook has been written for assistants in primary schools although if you are working in a secondary school you may find that many of the ideas and principles will apply to you as well.

You may find yourself referred to under the general title of 'Teaching Assistant' within your school, but you may also be called a 'Classroom Assistant', 'School Assistant', 'Individual Support Assistant', 'Special Needs Assistant' or 'Learning Support Assistant'. These different titles have come about due to different types of work which assistants are required to do within the classroom. For the purpose of this book we will refer to all those who assist within the classroom as teaching assistants.

As an assistant, you will be required to carry out many different jobs within the classroom. At the time of writing, assistants are being increasingly required to take on a more leading role alongside teachers and are being given more responsibilities. You may be one of a large team of assistants within a big urban primary school, or you may be part of a much smaller team of adults in a village school.

Some background information about the NVQ

The structure of the NVQ requires you to achieve **ten** units of competence from the national occupational standards. You will need to complete each of the four **mandatory units** and six of the **optional units**. The mandatory units are longer than the optional units as they contain more information. The optional units are divided into sets A, B, C and D, and you must choose one from each section plus any two others. This book will provide you with the knowledge you need for each unit of the award.

Each unit within this book is given a separate chapter, apart from Units 3–13 to 3–16 which have been written as one chapter. For each unit, we have identified what you will need to know and understand, and then given information and activities related to these items of learning. At the end of each unit, there is a unit test which you can use to check through your understanding. As each unit stands alone, this will also mean that you will be able to use them in any order. There are places in which information overlaps, and you will find cross-references within the book for these. Throughout each chapter, there are a number of features to help you with your studies:

Knowledge into action

These are activities which ask you to check or try out ideas within your own workplace. They will help you to link your ideas with what happens in practice.

Find out about...

These activities help you to think more deeply about key issues and encourage you to carry out your own research.

Keys to good practice

These are checklists of the most important aspects of what you have just learned.

Think about it

These activities encourage you to apply theory in a practical way.

Case studies

These are examples within real settings where you can apply what you have learned to particular situations.

Consolidation activities

These are to help you to check your understanding and will give you an idea about the kind of questions you may be asked.

Throughout the book, you will need to think about how the theory fits in with your experiences in the classroom. As you gain experience and expertise in your work with children, you may also find it a useful reference, particularly with reference to specific issues such as working with bilingual children.

There are some items of knowledge and understanding which are relevant to all the units. These are:

▷ awareness and appreciation of the rights of the child

▷ understanding of the need for confidentiality when working with children

▷ understanding for high standards of behaviour, commitment and reliability when working with children

▷ understanding your role and responsibilities towards children, their parents/carers, your colleagues and other professionals

▷ understanding and appreciation of the wide range of parenting styles, customs and cultures which co-exist in society.

You will need to consider these in relation to all the work you undertake within a school.

Mandatory units

Contribute to the management of pupil behaviour

This unit outlines your role when dealing with pupil behaviour. It will show how you need to work alongside the class teacher to support pupils and give you strategies for managing behaviour, through support which is available in school and also through other agencies. You will need to have an understanding of the behaviour which is expected of different ages and be able to recognise those children whose behaviour is more challenging. As an assistant, you should also be aware of how to promote good behaviour in schools and the ways in which you can do this.

This unit contains two elements:

3-1.1 Promote school policies with regard to pupil behaviour
3-1.2 Support the implementation of strategies to manage pupil behaviour

Element 3-1.1 Promote school policies with regard to pupil behaviour

For this element you will need to know and understand the following:

▶ the stages of social, emotional and physical development of the children you work with

▶ factors which may affect children's behaviour

▶ how to identify behaviour patterns which may indicate problems

▶ school policies for rewarding positive behaviour and managing unwanted behaviour

▶ how to work in line with local and national guidelines and policies.

Stages of social, emotional and physical development

It is important for all adults who have contact with children in early years and primary school settings to be aware of the different stages of children's development. Assistants will need to understand the way in which children learn and develop socially, emotionally and physically. In this way they will be able to support and enhance the learning process through a wider understanding of children's needs.

Physical development

As an assistant, you will be working with children who are developing skills through a wide range of physical activities. These may be gross motor skills such as beginning to walk, or fine motor skills like holding a pencil. You will need to know the order in which children develop these skills, although the age at which they achieve them may differ from one child to another.

Children will undergo health checks at some of these stages to check that they are developing normally and to draw attention to any potential problems. If a child is not reaching the milestones which are expected, these can then be investigated straight away and any action taken.

▷ **Gross motor skills** – these are skills which involve large movements through the use of children's arms and legs and may include running, hopping and skipping, and starting to use large apparatus such as climbing frames and other playground equipment.

▷ **Fine motor skills** – these are manipulative skills which involve finer hand control. They are vital for activities such as writing a child's own name, starting to draw recognisable pictures and colouring them in, cutting with scissors and completing jigsaws. These finer skills are vital for being able to learn to write.

Basic stages of physical development

Age	Stage of development
0–3 months	Infant will start to have control of head.
3–6 months	Babies will start to roll from side to side and push themselves up with their arms when on their front.
6–9 months	Babies start to grasp objects and sit unsupported. They may start to move by trying to crawl or shuffle.
9–12 months	Babies will have started to crawl or even walk. Starting to reach for objects.
1–2 years	Starting to build using blocks, make marks with a crayon, turn pages in picture books. Gaining confidence. Enjoying repetitive play and games and songs with a known outcome, for example 'Pat-a-cake', or 'Round and round the garden'.
2–3 years	Uses a spoon, puts on shoes, begins to use a preferred hand. Walks up and down stairs with confidence.
3–4 years	Turns pages in a book, puts on coat and shoes, throws and kicks a ball, washes and dries hands with help.

Age	Stage of development
4-5 years	Draws a person, cuts out simple shapes, completes simple puzzles, starting to hop.
5-6 years	Forms letters, writes name, dresses and undresses, runs quickly, uses large apparatus.
6-7 years	Handwriting evenly spaced, ties laces, can complete more complex puzzles, chases and plays with others.
7-11 years	Refining physical skills such as running, jumping and skipping.

Physical needs of children in the early years

When children first arrive in school, most of them will possess a number of physical skills. These will have been developed through a range of physical activities which they have will have experienced by this age – for example, walking, running, riding tricycles for their gross motor skills, and holding a knife and fork, or a pencil, for fine motor skills. While children are learning to control their bodies, they need to be able to gain control of these two types of movements. They will need to have opportunities to play and develop these skills within the learning environment, through a selection of indoor and outdoor activities.

Activities which may be used within the early years to promote physical development
Gross motor skills: running, skipping, balancing, riding a bicycle, throwing and catching a ball.
Fine motor skills: threading, painting, sand and water play, simple handwriting skills, cutting with scissors, puzzles.

Social and emotional development

The social and emotional development of children is directly linked to the way in which they begin to relate to others. Children need to interact with others so that they have opportunities to gain confidence. If there are physical difficulties, for example a hearing problem, these may affect the way in which children relate to others and cause a delay in their overall development. For example, they may withdraw socially, find communicating difficult or suffer a language delay. All of these could have a negative effect on their developing self-esteem.

Stages of social and emotional development

Age	Stage of development
0-12 months	Babies start to communicate through smiling and making eye contact with their families. They will enjoy being cuddled and played with.
1-2 years	Children start to gain a sense of their own identities. They will respond to their own names and start to explore independently. They will start to show anger if their needs are not met and they do not yet recognise the needs of others. Children start to play with others.
2-3 years	Children will start to show concern for others but will still have strong feelings about their own needs being met. They will be starting to come to terms with their own independence.
3-4 years	This is a more settled year and children will be growing in confidence and social skills. They may still have tantrums as they will still feel strong emotions, but will be starting to play independently for longer periods.
4-6 years	Children will generally feel much more confident in themselves and start to be proud of their own achievements. Close friendships are increasingly more important to them.
6-8 years	Children start to develop a sense of fairness and are more able to share items and equipment. They have a greater self-awareness and can be critical of themselves. They may start to compare themselves to their peers. Friendship groups can start to be problematic if children fall out with one another. Children will also make some gender friendships in this age group.
8-11 years	Children will be settled in their friendships and may form more stable 'groups'. They will continue to compare themselves with others and will need to 'belong'.

Children who are entering school will be at an age where they are just beginning to gain confidence and become independent. They will still be developing their ability to show desirable behaviour and will be learning how to share and think of other people. Adults need to give children as many opportunities as possible to allow them to feel independent and to praise them as much as they can for good behaviour. In this way, children will start to develop a positive self-esteem. The development of self-esteem may be high or low, positive or negative. Self-esteem is how we feel about ourselves and leads to our self-image, that is how we think about or perceive ourselves. Children develop a positive self-esteem when they feel good about themselves and when they feel valued. The way in which we treat children has a direct effect on this so it is important that we encourage and praise them, value each child as an individual and celebrate differences and similarities.

The rate at which a child will develop socially and emotionally will depend on the opportunities which have been given for them to interact with others. Where a child has come from a large family, for example, there may have been many more opportunities to play with others and form relationships. If a child has had very little contact or social interaction with other children, it may be more difficult when starting at a school or nursery to understand how relationships with others are formed.

The DfES document *Curriculum Guidance for the Foundation Stage* gives a breakdown of the ways in which settings can give children the best opportunities for personal, social and emotional development. Indeed, this document places a great emphasis on the importance of children's emotional development and the need to create environments that value all children along with their different cultures, backgrounds and abilities or disabilities (see *Curriculum Guidance for the Foundation Stage,* pages 28-43).

Knowledge into action

Identify two different children in your class. How does each of them behave? Is this 'normal' for their age and stage of development?

Case study

Imran is a Reception child who often finds it difficult to leave his mother in the morning. He is easily upset and is unable to organise himself when putting away his lunchbox, his book bag and his coat. He has one or two close friends.

Vijay is settled in the Reception class and does not have any difficulties with organisation and behaviour. He has several friends and is able to settle to tasks quickly.

1 Compare these two cases. How does the behaviour of these two children fit in with their age and stage of social and emotional development?

2 Are either, or both, 'normal'?

Factors which may affect children's behaviour

Background

Children will enter schools with a variety of backgrounds and experiences, all of which will have affected the way in which their individual personalities react to others. Some children may come from a secure and loving family background while others may have had very unsettled experiences or a series of different homes and carers. Some may have experienced many social situations while others' experience may be limited to family members or friends. These experiences will affect the child's ability and confidence when socialising with others.

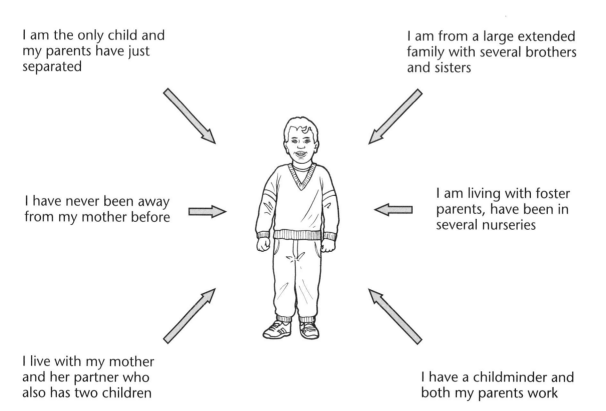

I am the only child and my parents have just separated

I am from a large extended family with several brothers and sisters

I have never been away from my mother before

I am living with foster parents, have been in several nurseries

I live with my mother and her partner who also has two children

I have a childminder and both my parents work

There are also other factors which will have an effect on the way in which children behave.

Age

The child may develop physically or socially particularly quickly or slowly for their age. This can affect the way that others see them, which in turn will impact on their behaviour. For example, a child who is particularly small for his or her age may have been 'babied' at home and find it difficult when faced with the need for increasing independence.

Gender

It may be that a child enters school with limited experiences due to gender, for example parents who have not allowed a boy to experience sewing or cooking. As a result of this, the child may not expect that both sexes may be able to participate in all tasks at school.

Medical

A child who was premature at birth may have delayed physical development and this can also be the cause of immature behaviour. Some children who have medical intervention for specific problems such as poor hearing may be less confident about becoming involved with tasks within the classroom. At an early age, some physical problems may be as yet undiagnosed so it is important to be aware that these children may not be picking up on various cues or be aware of what is expected of them.

Disability

It is now a statutory requirement to encourage the inclusion of children with disabilities into mainstream schools. According to the Disability Discrimination Act (1995), a person has a disability if 'he or she has a physical or mental impairment that has a substantial and long-term adverse effect on his or her ability to carry out normal day to day activities'. The inclusion of disabled pupils is to encourage more positive integration of disabled people into society, and to give children a greater understanding of the needs of others. The impact of inclusion will mean that there are more pupils in mainstream schools who may have disabilities.

Culture

Children may enter school from a variety of cultures. Some of these may encourage particular behaviours from men and women which differ from those in school. For example, some cultures may not encourage women to go out to work. In early years settings, teachers and assistants are predominantly female.

Self-esteem

All children's self-esteem, or how they view themselves, is directly affected by whether they feel valued by others. A child whose self-esteem is low may display behaviours which are disruptive or may also withdraw and be timid in class. There may be several reasons why a child has low self-esteem. These could include poor relationships at home, or a family who spends little time with the child.

Case study

Richard has been in school for a year. He is very able orally but has trouble with recording his ideas, as his written work is not of the same level as that of his peers. He often starts trying to write things down and quickly becomes frustrated, saying that his work is no good and wanting to tear it up and start again.

1 Why might Richard say that his work is no good?

2 Can you think of a way of helping Richard?

Stereotyping

Adults need to be aware of their own assumptions and opinions about pupils' behaviour, for example stereotyping of children when giving them tasks within the school. 'I need some sensible girls to take this message for me' may sound to the boys that only girls can be sensible. Care should also be taken in other situations: it should not be assumed that a child with a disability should necessarily be excluded from activities, he or she should be included wherever possible.

Learning difficulties or inappropriate task given

If a child feels unable to complete a task, poor behaviour may result as the child will not be able to focus attention on the activity. This may be due to the teacher giving the child an inappropriate task for his or her ability, but could also be due to an undiagnosed learning difficulty.

Behaviour patterns which may indicate problems

Learning how to behave is an important part of a child's development. This is because it is a learned skill which affects the way in which children will interact with others. Children must learn to be able to listen to others, take turns, share and show good manners. Some children may enter schools with less experience than others and need to have more guidance from staff.

Children may start to show signs of behaviour which are significantly different from those of other children immediately, or it may not be apparent until later.

▷ **Child is timid or withdrawn** – this kind of behaviour may be due to shyness, and some children may take some time to settle into new surroundings, especially if they have had an unsettled home life. However, children will usually start to make friends and join in with activities fairly quickly, even if they remain shy with adults.

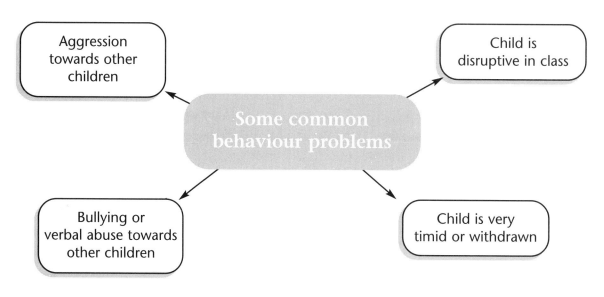

Aggression towards other children

Child is disruptive in class

Some common behaviour problems

Bullying or verbal abuse towards other children

Child is very timid or withdrawn

▲ Behaviour problems can take different forms

If a child is very timid with parents but not within the setting, staff should be aware that this could be an indication of problems at home or even of child abuse.

▷ **Child is very disruptive in the class** – this could take the form of calling out or disturbing other children. It can be caused by the child seeking attention from adults within the setting. This may be because the child receives a lot of attention at home and has become used to it. Children who do not receive much attention from adults at home may also resort to being disruptive, even though the attention they will receive is negative.

▷ **Child is aggressive towards other children** – this may be another attention-seeking device, or the child may not have had many social experiences with other children before starting school. It takes time for children to learn social skills such as turn-taking and sharing with others. Some children take longer to adapt to waiting their turn and being one of a group and may find it difficult.

▷ **Child bullies others** – bullying can be either physical or verbal, over a period of time, possibly leading to the victim being reluctant to come to school. The bully will feel a need to have control over others, perhaps because of their own insecurities. A child may verbally abuse others, including racist/sexist/religious comments, personal abuse or bad language. This is not common at an early age but it does happen within primary schools. Some children may have heard some verbal abuse at home or on television and use it on others, copying poor role models. It is important that such behaviour is challenged and that positive role modelling occurs within all schools.

Children who have been abused

Children may display behaviour to indicate that they have been abused in some way. Abuse can be physical, emotional, sexual or caused by neglect. A child could also be the victim of more than one of these.

Examples of behaviour which may give cause for concern including the following:

▷ Child is reluctant to change for PE or remove clothing. While this is perfectly normal for some children it may also be a sign that the child has been the victim of physical abuse and is aware that the abuse will be visible. Look for marks, bruises or burns which may not be caused by accident.

▷ Child displays uncharacteristic behaviour patterns from those normally shown. If a child suddenly starts to behave very differently and is particularly 'clingy' with adults or is reluctant to go home, this should be reported to the adult in charge of the class. This may indicate physical, emotional or sexual abuse.

▷ Child is unusually tearful or attention seeking. Where parents or carers emotionally abuse a child, the child may become insecure and need more attention.

You may also find yourself in the position of suspecting that a child has been subjected or exposed to some form of substance abuse. This could be through parents or older brothers and sisters. The main indicators would be health and emotional problems, or the child may not relate to others, either children or staff, as before.

Where adults have any suspicion of child abuse or neglect, they should immediately inform the teacher or supervisor with whom they are working. In this way steps can be taken to monitor the child and keep a record of any signs of abuse. When recording incidents, note should be taken of the child's name, any other child involved, the date and the exact behaviour shown. It is also important to reassure and listen to children if they are able to talk about what has happened to them, while taking care not to make promises to not tell anyone else or keep secrets. (There is more on this in Unit 9 on page 165.)

Case study

Melissa has always behaved well at school, although she is extremely quiet and has not socialised much with other children or adults. She has recently started to become more interested in the group and mix more freely with the others, although she is still reluctant to talk to adults. When her mother comes to collect her from school one day, she says that she does not want to go home.

1 Why might Melissa have initially been so shy to join the class?

2 What would you do if this happened in your school?

3 What might be the problem in Melissa's case?

School policies for rewarding positive behaviour and managing unwanted behaviour

Theories about behaviour

There are three main theories about behaviour and how children learn.

▷ **Social learning theory**, developed by Albert Bandura in the 1960s, suggests that children will learn by copying the behaviour of those around them. They will tend to copy adults, and later their peers. This means that it is important that children have good role models for behaviour so that they learn appropriate behaviour themselves.

What this means for the adult: adults should remember that they will be teaching children not only by what they say, but also by what they do. Where children see an adult being courteous and kind to others, it will encourage them to behave in the same way. Similarly, if children usually witness loud or aggressive behaviour, they will learn that this is the way to behave. Adults should therefore remember that they need to be good *role models* for children.

▷ **Behaviourist theory**, developed by B.F. Skinner in the 1940s, suggests that children will respond to praise and so will repeat behaviour which gives them recognition or praise for what they do. This kind of praise may take the form of rewards such as stickers, charts, or adult attention. Children who receive praise or attention for positive behaviour, such as kindness towards others, are more likely to repeat this behaviour.

What this means for the adult: adults need to remember to praise positive behaviour wherever possible, as children will also try to get their attention through undesirable behaviour. Where we can, we should ignore this kind of behaviour and instead give attention to those children who are behaving well.

▷ Another view widely held in psychology is the **self-fulfilling prophecy theory** – which states that children will be influenced by the way in which adults think about them. Children want to be noticed by adults and approved of. In this way, when adults believe a child is 'good', their opinion will encourage and influence the behaviour of that child. If adults think that a child is 'naughty', the child will live up to this expectation.

What this means for the adult: when speaking to children about their behaviour, we should always label the behaviour rather than the individual: for example, 'That was a silly thing to do,' rather than 'What a silly girl you are'.

? *Think about it*

On the first day of term, you are helping the new children into a Reception class. One of the mothers says to you, in front of her child, 'This is Natalie – you will need to watch her because she is a naughty girl'.

How do you think this will make Natalie feel?

What sort of behaviour might Natalie display?

Using strategies to manage behaviour

In any early years setting or school, staff will need a series of agreed strategies to use both for managing unwanted behaviour and rewarding positive behaviour. They may even have their own classroom rules for behaviour, which the children can devise themselves with a little help. In this way, children will be able to take responsibility for their own behaviour and understand the results of their actions. Where children are showing unwanted behaviour, it is important for staff to know when to intervene, especially where children are a danger to themselves or others.

Strategies for promoting positive behaviour

In any early years setting, it is important to manage children's behaviour well so that their learning takes place in an effective environment. All adults within the setting should have high expectations so that a pattern of positive behaviour is established.

Children need to be aware of what these expectations are, and there should be a behaviour management policy in the school with consistent adult expectations.

It is imperative in any early years setting for children to be aware of a set of rules or guidelines so that they have a clear understanding of how to behave. Children need to be aware of the boundaries within which to behave so that they understand what is expected of them.

Hawkwood Infant School

Golden Rules

1 I will treat myself and others with respect at all times.

2 I will treat all property with respect at all times.

3 I will play fair and friendly games in the playground.

4 I will work hard and always try to do my best.

5 I will walk quietly around the school.

These rules should be written in such a way that the children are given positive targets – 'I will walk quietly around the school' rather than negative – 'Do not run in school'. Where the language may be difficult for young children to understand, for example 'treating others with respect', it should be clear that they understand its meaning. The rules should be discussed frequently with the children, both in class and during assembly times, so that they understand and remember them.

As well as this list of school rules, pupils should be encouraged to behave in a positive way through watching the behaviour of adults. Children will soon notice if an adult is not acting in a way that they would expect, or there are not consistent expectations between adults. When a child is behaving particularly well, adults should remember to praise this behaviour so that it is recognised.

Case study

You are reading a story to the whole class when you notice some of the children are not listening and are talking amongst themselves. How could you show the rest of the class that you are valuing their good behaviour while preventing the children who are talking from continuing?

Adults must remember that young children need to be praised for work and behaviour genuinely and frequently for effort and achievement. This will reinforce good behaviour and build self-esteem.

Where there are cases of unwanted behaviour, staff will need to be familiar with the school's behaviour policy so that their responses and strategies tie in with whole school policy.

Below is the first page of a school's behaviour policy.

Mountfield Infant School
Behaviour Management Policy

At Mountfield School we believe that all children should be guided by a positive and professional approach to behaviour. This should be fairly and consistently applied by all adults (teachers, assistants, students, midday supervisors) who may have cause to discipline a child. It should establish the hierarchy for dealing with problems within school.

To work well, this policy must have the support of all members of the community, including the children, and should therefore be developed by them as a whole and be based on professional agreement. We have endeavoured to do this. This document therefore needs to be read and understood by all governors, teaching and support staff and midday supervisors.

Aims
The main aim of this policy is to help us to create an environment in which effective learning takes place. It should make us aware of the part our responses play in establishing a pattern of positive behaviour based on high expectations and mutual respect.

It aims to inform children, parents, governors and all teaching and support staff of our high standards and expresses our shared understanding of how we expect children to behave. It aims to inform all concerned of effective strategies that can be used to encourage positive behaviour and advise as to the consequences of misbehaviour. We will expect all children to know, understand and adhere to our school rules.

Objectives
The staff at our school will be encouraged to:
▶ Have a professional approach at all times
▶ Provide well structured environments to avoid disputes
▶ Create a working environment where children are able to achieve and where their work is seen to be valued
▶ Have high but realistic expectations of work and behaviour
▶ Praise work and behaviour frequently to reinforce good behaviour
▶ Be polite at all times to children and other adults to increase mutual respect and trust
▶ See parents as active partners and build positive relationships
▶ Make our expectations of work clear and consistent, ensuring our instructions are understood
▶ Intervene early so that misbehaviour does not escalate
▶ Be seen to be fair – try to establish all the facts

Your school's behaviour policy.

▶ What are the school's strategies for managing unwanted behaviour?

▶ How does the school ensure that all staff are aware of these strategies?

Where behaviour is undesirable despite modelling and encouraging good behaviour, you will need to have a scale of sanctions.

Keys to good practice
Managing unwanted behaviour

✔ Intervene early so that the problem does not escalate. If a situation arises where an assistant is the first to be aware of unacceptable behaviour, such as children misbehaving in the playground, it would be appropriate to draw the teacher's attention to it, or if this is not possible, to intervene.

✔ Give eye contact to the child who is misbehaving. Sometimes all that is needed is a stern look at a child so that they see an adult is aware of what they are doing.

✔ Remove items which are being used inappropriately. If a child is using an item, for example a pair of scissors or a piece of outdoor equipment, to hurt another child, these should be gently taken away. The child should then be told why they have been removed and when they will be able to have them back.

✔ Proximity – move closer to a child who is misbehaving so that they are aware of an adult presence. This will usually prevent the behaviour from continuing. Assistants can use this practice in whole class teaching time when the teacher is at the front to calm or prevent inappropriate behaviour by having an awareness of who to sit beside.

✔ Time out – this is sometimes used when older children are consistently misbehaving and need to be given some time to calm down before returning to a situation. It can be applied within the classroom or on the playground.

✔ Use a scale of sanctions which the children are aware of, for example:

    a time out

    b miss one minute or longer of playtime

    c send to deputy head

    d send to headteacher/speak to parents.

Your role and responsibilities and those of others when managing behaviour in school

As a teaching assistant, you will need to be aware of your role within the school for managing children's behaviour. If you have any worries or concerns about how to deal with children's behaviour you must always refer to the class teacher or supervisor. Teachers have the ultimate responsibility for managing behaviour of children within the class, and the headteacher has responsibility for all the children within the school. The school's behaviour policy will offer guidelines and school strategies for dealing with behaviour.

Some of the responsibilities of staff should include the following:

▷ Having high but realistic expectations of work and behaviour. Children will be aware of how they should behave and praised when they do. Adults need to give praise such as 'I know how sensibly you can sit on the carpet for a story' rather than, 'This class never sits quietly for a story'.

▷ Creating a working environment where children can achieve and where their work and efforts are seen to be valued, thus developing their self-esteem.
This can be done not only verbally but through displays of children's work and sharing with other children and adults in the school.

▷ Making expectations of behaviour and work clear and consistent, ensuring instructions have been understood. If children are unsure of what they need to do, it is very difficult for them to automatically behave in a way which adults expect.

▷ Working consistently as a staff so that the same expectations apply throughout the school. This is vital so that the children understand that all staff are working together throughout the school.

▷ Being aware of your own values and opinions. You should ensure that you do not make assumptions about people on the grounds of gender, race or disability.

Working in line with local and national guidelines and policies

It will be useful to be aware of how your school's policies fit in with local guidelines and policies. You may need to ask other members of staff when the behaviour policy was devised and whether they used a borough model or local guidelines.

On a national level, the DFES training for behaviour management outlines some core principles to help those who are working with children. Some of these are to:

▷ plan for good behaviour

▷ work within the 4 R's (Rules, Routines, Responsibilites and Rights) framework

▷ separate the (inappropriate) behaviour from the child
▷ use the language of choice
▷ actively build trust and rapport
▷ model the behaviour that you want to see.

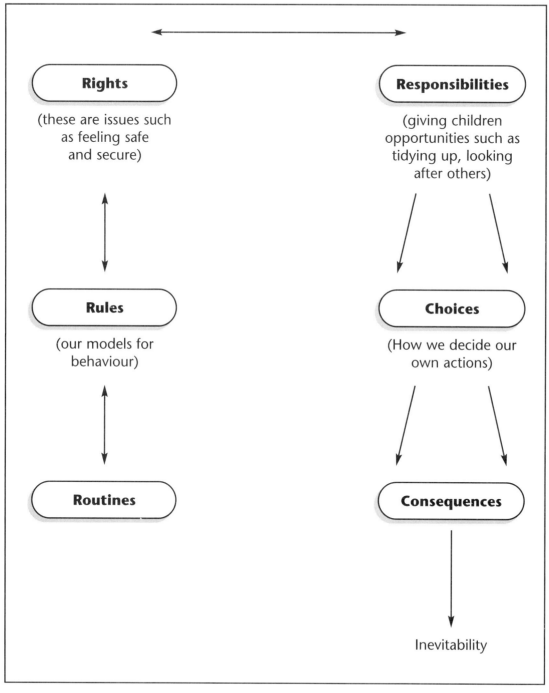

▲ The 4 R's framework

As can be seen, these fit in with the types of ground rules which are expected of children in most schools. Children will need to be aware of others' expectations of them and how they fit into the school as a whole. These guidelines give the choice to the individual as well as an awareness of the consequences of their actions.

→ *Knowledge into action*

Do you think that your school's behaviour policy draws on any of these principles? Make a list of phrases you could use to define behaviour using words from this model.

Element 3-1.2 Support the implementation of strategies to manage pupil behaviour

For this element you will need to know and understand the following:

▶ managing behaviour and the implications of the Children Act and child protection

▶ reporting behaviour or discipline problems to the teacher

▶ specialist advice for dealing with unwanted behaviour

▶ implementing behaviour support plans.

Managing behaviour and the implication of the Children Act 1989 and child protection

When looking at behaviour which is acceptable, adults should be aware that we all have different ideas and expectations. We should recognise that our ideas about what is acceptable or unacceptable will come from our own experiences and cultures. Children may therefore enter schools and nurseries with a variety of accepted 'normal' behaviour.

? *Think about it*

Read and think about the following statements:

▶ Children should always write thank you letters at Christmas and birthdays.

▶ Children should never leave the table until everyone has finished eating.

▶ Children should be required to fast during Ramadan.

▶ Children should always stand up when an adult enters the room.

▶ Children should not be allowed to address an adult by their first name.

Work in a group and consider which of these statements you agree with.

Do others in the room give the same answers as you?

We may therefore have conflicting ideas about the kind of behaviour we view as 'normal' and what we expect from children. For this reason, many schools and nurseries will have their own guidelines for behaviour. Parents should be informed of these so that they are aware of what is acceptable and not acceptable in school. Where parents and schools have conflicting ideas about acceptable behaviour, children will find it difficult to know how to conform.

As already mentioned, children should be aware and reminded of the school's expectations for behaviour so that they know how to conform in the classroom, playground and in other parts of the school. Where children are not conforming to the rules, they should know what the consequences are.

Find out about...

The different 'normal' behaviours which may be expected of children at various ages.

Examples of behaviour and consequences

Action	Consequence
Running in the school corridor	Going back and walking
Disruptive behaviour in class	Time out – working alone
Verbally abusing other children/adults	Apology/letter of apology
Aggressive behaviour in the playground	One minute by the wall

The school's policies on behaviour and equal opportunities should set out guidelines for managing the way in which pupils interact with one another. Where assistants are unsure of the kinds of sanctions or consequences that they are able to use, they should always clarify this with their class teacher or supervisor.

The Children Act (1989)

This Act was passed in 1989 and has had far-reaching effects on the care and protection of children. It aims to put children first and to make professionals and local authorities dealing with families and children think about their individual needs. The Children Act covers a wide range of issues including the registration and inspection of childcare services for children under eight. It also provides guidance for child protection issues and should therefore be considered when selecting and using behaviour management strategies.

▲ It is important to encourage good behaviour but sanctions may still be necessary

The main area in which the Children Act relates to behaviour in school is through its section on the care and protection of children, and the inspection of daycare settings for children under eight. All children who are placed in situations of care should be protected and the Act outlines the responsibilities of the local authority in ensuring that these needs are met. Where schools and nurseries are looking after young children it is important for all staff to know and understand the rights of children and how they should be protected – for example, that adults are not allowed to give corporal punishment. It is through the school's policies and guidelines for behaviour management that inspectors can see that all staff are aware of and adhere to these guidelines. Behaviour management strategies will need to take into consideration how we can encourage good behaviour and remain fair when applying sanctions for bad behaviour.

Reporting behaviour or discipline problems to the teacher

Working alongside the teacher to promote an effective learning environment

When working in partnership with the class teacher, assistants should be clear about their roles and responsibilities with regard to pupil behaviour. This is as important for adults in the school to know and understand as it is for children, since they are responsible for ensuring that school policies and rules for behaviour are maintained.

National guidelines for behaviour management

► Local guidelines

► School behaviour policy

► School rules

► Class rules

► Playground rules

► Rules for using the computer room/cooking room/apparatus in the hall/working in the school grounds/safety on school visits

Structure of the rules

Assistants may find it difficult to know when and how they should intervene when they are faced with issues of behaviour. It is important to be clear exactly what 'normal' behaviour is and to make allowances for children in different circumstances. Some examples of these circumstances might include the following:

▷ On the first day of a new school, there may be several children who are upset and do not want to leave their parent or carer. However, if this behaviour carried on over a long period of time, the teacher may find it necessary to impose some kind of strategy for managing the child or children.

▷ It is getting towards the end of term and the normal routines of school are slightly different due to end of term activities. The children in the class are very excitable and restless. In this situation, which is not normal, some children may find it difficult to conform to the rules.

▷ There has been a Book Week in school. The children have been able to meet authors and have seen a short play. They are finding it difficult to sit still and listen when they go back to class.

Teachers and assistants should also be informed if any individual children in the class have had any kinds of upheaval or distress at home. The teacher should inform any assistants as soon as a problem comes to his or her attention. Examples of these might be a parents' divorce, or a death in the family. Sometimes it may be the death of a pet or a parent going away on business which can make a child behave differently. The school should make it clear to parents that staff need to be informed of anything which may be distressing the child. If assistants notice a child behaving differently or out of character, this is worth mentioning to the teacher so that parents can be asked if there is any reason for it. When children are settled in school and are used to the rules and routines, they will know and understand what is expected of them. Where children display unwanted behaviours in a normal school situation, sanctions should be applied to control the behaviour.

Applying sanctions

As a teaching assistant, you should be aware of the types of sanctions or rewards which are available to you when managing behaviour. Usually if the teacher is present, your main strategies will be verbal or involve eye contact. If you are alone with the class for any reason, you should, as the responsible adult, be able to use any of those which the teacher would normally use. However, you should always clarify this with the teacher first. If you have any problems in implementing sanctions, or if the children do not respond to you as the responsible adult, you should also inform the teacher.

Case study

You have been left with the class for ten minutes as the teacher has had to speak to the headteacher urgently. You are reading the class a story but two or three girls at the back are not listening and are disturbing the others. You tell them to behave sensibly and listen to the story but one of them says that you are not the teacher and they don't have to do what you say.

1 What would you do in this situation?
2 What could the teacher say to the class before leaving to make sure that they behaved appropriately?
3 How could the teacher support you?

If sanctions are applied and the child is still consistently not responding, there may be a deep-rooted problem which should be investigated (see page 24 for specialist advice on behaviour management).

Think about it

You are working apart from the class teacher with a group of children who are undertaking some DT work using hot glue guns. One of the children has not behaved sensibly while using the glue gun and for health and safety reasons you have taken the gun away and asked the child to go back to the teacher. The class teacher has not seen what has happened and when the child goes back to her does not support you over your reaction. You feel that this is because she does not want the child back in the classroom. In group discuss how you would deal with this situation.

Safety issues

Other situations in which you may need to apply sanctions or strategies are those when you find yourself or others at risk. It is important to be able to respond calmly and quickly in emergencies and other potentially dangerous situations. This may occur either within the school and grounds, or on a school trip.

Examples of this could be:

▷ a child or parent who becomes violent

▷ a child who unwittingly puts others in danger

▷ a child who displays severe behavioural problems and needs full adult attention

▷ a group of children who are misbehaving and putting others in danger.

If you find yourself in a situation where there is no other adult present and you are faced with a risk, you will be responsible for managing the situation. You must always remain calm, as children will quickly panic if they sense this in an adult. If it is a single child who is misbehaving or violent and they do not respond to your authority, you must make sure that other children are kept away from them and send a responsible child for another adult. Similarly, when faced with an adult who is aggressive or violent, remain calm and reassure them that you will need to ask for assistance from another member of staff. It is important that you seek adult help as soon as possible.

Specialist advice for dealing with unwanted behaviour

In some situations, where a teacher or supervisor has used all the ideas and strategies already available, it may be necessary to ask for extra help and support. If you are in a mainstream school, you should have a SENCo, or Special Needs Co-ordinator, on the staff. In a pre-school or nursery setting, the adult responsible for co-ordinating extra behaviour support will be the supervisor. There may be different situations which require the help of outside agencies, and as an assistant you will not be asked to contact them, but you should have an awareness of the support that is available.

▷ **SENCo or supervisor** – this should be the first point of contact for behaviour support and devising additional strategies for use within the classroom. They will also contact other professionals outside the school.

▷ **Behaviour Unit** – this unit is usually run by the local authority and will offer support and suggestions for dealing with pupils who have behaviour problems. They may also come into schools to observe or work with specific children.

▷ **Educational psychologists** – these professionals visit all schools regularly to support children and the adults who work with them. They offer help and advice on a variety of Special Needs problems, and may assess children and devise individual programmes. They are also involved with assessing those children who may need a statement of Special Educational Needs.

Implementing behaviour support plans

The SENCo will be the first point of contact for teachers and with their help, teachers may devise an Individual Education Plan for children with learning difficulties, or a Behaviour Support Plan for those who need it. This should set realistic targets for work or behaviour, which should be Specific, Measurable, Achievable, Realistic and Time bound (SMART). It is vital that pupils have achievable targets, so that they are able to experience success and start to build positive behaviour. If you are an individual support assistant and responsible for supporting a specific child in the class, it is likely that you are familiar with setting targets for the child with whom you are working.

? Think about it

Have you been involved with the development of a Behaviour Support Plan, or a behaviour target on an Individual Education Plan? Were you also involved in the review of the plan? What kinds of targets have you set for children with whom you have been working?

Below is an example of a Behaviour Support Plan. There should not be more than three or four targets on any one plan.

Behaviour Support Plan

Name: James Fraser

Class: 1SW

Date set: March 2002   **Date for review:** May 2002

Targets: **Review:**

1. To sit close to the teacher when   James has stopped calling out
    on the carpet to encourage   although still finds it difficult to
    him to listen carefully and   listen. Ongoing target.
    prevent calling out.

2. To encourage good behaviour on   This has worked well – target
    the playground through teaching   achieved. Now teaching games
    some playground games.   to others.

                                        Reviewed by: L. Clark

---

No more than 3 targets – easier to achieve

At the review, you and the class teacher should discuss the success of any strategies used

The review column should contain comments and include next steps

▲ A Behaviour Support Plan

End of unit test

1 What are the main areas of social and emotional development for 4 to 5-year-olds?

2 List some common behaviour problems and how you might deal with them.

3 How could you reward positive behaviour?

4 True or false – a child who witnesses adults swearing and being aggressive will copy this behaviour.

5 How would you define your role as an assistant when managing behaviour in school?

6 What kind of specialist advice is available in schools to help support behaviour problems?

7 When would you provide feedback to the teacher about any pupils who have a Behaviour Support Plan?

8 Which of these would be effective school rules?

    a Always show good sitting when in assembly

    b Don't run down the corridors

    c Treat others in a way which you would like to be treated

    d Don't hurt other children in the playground

9 What would you do if a child in your class showed uncharacteristically aggressive behaviour towards another child?

10 What are the main aims of the Children Act 1989?

References

Index for Inclusion (CSIE, 2000)

Curriculum Guidance for the Foundation Stage (QCA, 2000)

Websites

CSIE: http://inclusion.uwe.ac.uk

www.qca.org.uk

Unit 3-2 Establish and maintain relationships with individual pupils and groups

This unit contains two elements:

3-2.1 Establish and maintain relationships with individual pupils

3-2.2 Establish and maintain relationships with groups of pupils

Element 3-2.1 Establish and maintain relationships with individual pupils

As part of your work with children, you will need to be able to establish and maintain relationships with individual pupils. It is essential to pupil's learning that relationships are forged between them and the teaching assistant. With support children can gain skills and confidence, which may enable them to reach their targets. Vygotsky (1978) suggests that 'young children learn primarily through social interaction, through being with and interacting with adults' (Tilstone, Florian and Rose, 1998). In the case of teaching assistants, this dialogue will usually be through talking to pupils, thus encouraging and motivating pupils to achieve set learning outcomes.

For this element you will need to know and understand the following:

▶ how to communicate effectively with children

▶ how to support individual pupils in the learning environment

▶ how to deal with problems and build relationships with individual children.

How to communicate effectively with children

Communication is a two-way process. It involves speaking, listening, hearing, understanding and replying. Communication can be both **verbal** (speaking) and **non-verbal** (body language). Both forms of communication are powerful tools and can be used with great skill in our interactions with others.

Listening

Listening is essential in the communication process and is interactive as it involves:

1 hearing the person's words

2 thinking about their meaning and

3 responding – thinking of a reply and answering appropriately.

Active listening is important when working with children – in other words, it is important to make your question **open-ended**, where you will expect a reply. For example, 'What have you brought for your lunch today?' invites a description, whereas 'Have you brought lunch today?' requires 'Yes', 'No' or simply a shrug.

Apart from careful thinking and remembering what has been said, listeners need to ensure their non-verbal communication is appropriate too. It should involve displaying that you are listening, by use of eye contact or attentive body language, i.e. leaning slightly forward and wearing an interested expression.

Listening also involves:

1 looking interested
2 hearing what is said
3 remembering what is said
4 checking out your understanding.

This is called **reflective listening**. Checking out your understanding involves hearing what has been said and asking the other person questions. To do this you need to reflect or translate back what they have said in your own words, thus checking out your understanding. This also reassures the other person that you are listening.

As we listen to a child telling us something important we need to build up a mental picture of the information that the child is giving us.

It is fundamental to the relationships we build with children that we listen and remember what they tell us. By failing to remember, we may lose trust that is developing and the child might think, 'Oh, I won't bother to tell that person anything anymore, she/he doesn't listen, isn't interested in me'.

? Think about it

Do you actively listen?

a Individually, list on paper, six statements about yourself.
b In pairs, take turns in sharing these statements (without the use of paper and pens).
c Once this has been done, share the information with the whole group!

✓ Keys to good practice
Speaking and listening

✔ Remember to speak clearly.

✔ Face the child you are communicating with.

✔ Keep your face clear (a hand over your mouth will obscure what you are saying).

✔ Remember to use the correct tone of voice for the situation.

✔ If signing, make sure the child can see what you are doing.

✔ When being supported by a translator or communicator, remember to speak to and face the child.

✔ Use open-ended questions to create dialogue.

✔ Remember if gaining information from a child, the need to reflect on what is said, to clarify meaning.

✔ Look interested.

✔ Always think about what you say and the possible consequences.

Non-verbal communication (body language)

Using body language, we can interpret how a person is feeling without the use of words. We give messages using our eyes, facial expression, gestures, touch, stance (the way we stand) and the angle of our head.

Eye-contact

How many times have you sat in the carpeted area of the classroom and quietened a child, while the teacher is talking, merely by having direct eye-contact with the child, looking directly at them and raising your eyebrows?

Eye-contact is a very powerful indicator of emotion: staring can be threatening; making friendly eye-contact and looking away is effective.

Gestures

These are finger, hand and arm movements that can be an effective way of helping us to understand what a person is trying to say. Shrugging the shoulders indicates, 'I don't know', thumbs up sign communicates that all is going well and shaking a fist and wagging a finger is threatening and aggressive. Arms folded in front of the body acts as a barrier and may indicate some mistrust or a resistance to respond.

Touch

All schools and early years setting should have a policy on touch and you need to know yours. In general, touching should be avoided where possible because it may be inappropriate or misinterpreted. However, there are some situations such as comforting a child, or attracting a child's attention, where it may be necessary.

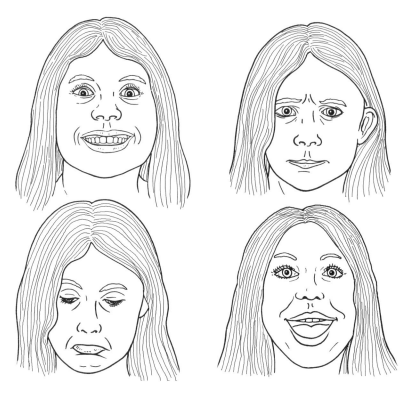

▲ Non-verbal communication can give us a lot of information

Think about it

What would you do in these circumstances?
1 A child sits quietly crying in the classroom…
2 Two children collide in the playground, one of them has hurt himself and is holding his head and crying noisily.

Stance

Stance, also known as body posture, is a communicator. Looming over a child with hands on hips can be very threatening, whereas adapting your height by bending, crouching or sitting is far friendlier. Always sit if you can, as continually bending can be harmful to the lower back!

Knowledge into action

In small groups take turns in demonstrating non-verbal communication using eye-contact, facial expression and body language. Individually and randomly role play the statements below.

1 I've had a tiring day.

2 I'm really pleased with your progress.

3 No, don't do that!

4 I really don't think you should.

5 Well done, keep on going.

6 Come here now!

Being aware of differences

To have a caring relationship is a two-way process. Friendliness and warmth create a positive environment and will be useful in cementing a good working relationship, so helping the children to reach their potential. Where children feel 'different' from others, it is vital that you are able to make them feel part of the class so that they can achieve their potential.

Acceptance is essential, we must always look beyond the difficulty, cultural difference, problem or disability and recognise that the child comes first. It is important that all staff treat each child as an individual. You should refer to your school's equal opportunities and disability policies to find out ways in which your school ensures non-discriminatory behaviour and values cultural diversity.

Case study

Ashima is the only Indian child in your class. She is quiet but has many friends within the class and is happy and settled at school. During an RE lesson, the others start to ask her about her home life and so one day she brings her sari in to show them.

1 Why do you think that it is important to encourage Ashima to talk to the others about her sari?

2 How will this also help the rest of the class?

It is 'normal' for individuals to expect eye-contact while engaged in conversation with each other. If the person with whom you are speaking tends to look down and not make eye-contact, this can be interpreted as a sign of dishonesty or maybe sadness, depression or rudeness. However, in some cultures looking down or away when engaged in conversation is a sign of respect and a way of showing that you are listening.

Knowledge into action

Practise your communication skills with the next child you are assigned to; consider the following:

1 How much relevant information are you able to find out from the child in a friendly way?

2 How long can you keep the conversation going?

3 Observe and reflect upon the child's listening and non-verbal skills (noting your responses).

4 How highly do you rate your skills?

5 List your strengths.

6 Are there any areas for improvement?

✓ Keys to good practice
Communication

✔ Be totally aware that our bodies can 'speak volumes'.

✔ Be aware of the body language of individuals; cultural differences must be valued.

✔ The use of non-verbal communication can be less disruptive in group work.

✔ Remember the school's policy regarding touch.

✔ Always reach the pupil's physical level.

✔ Think about personal space (the appropriate distance between you and the individual).

✔ Think of the child first and any problems they may have as a secondary issue.

✔ Be caring and friendly, not friends.

✔ Reflect upon your practice of non-verbal communication regularly.

How to support individual pupils in the learning environment

Teaching assistants often work in a variety of settings within the learning environment – classroom, playground, dining hall, gym, school trips, etc. In order for teaching assistants to work to their full effectiveness, it is important that they know in advance what they are need to do in each lesson or session where a child is being supported. Assistants will need to be aware of children's learning outcomes and individual targets so that they can help them to achieve their full potential.

How to plan for desired learning outcomes

Each year curriculum areas are planned and this is a **long-term** plan known as the learning framework. Each term and half-term's teaching is planned and teachers will devise schemes of work, which illustrate week by week the outline of lessons for the term/half term. This is known as **medium-term** planning.

Lessons are scheduled on a weekly plan and are organised in greater detail. These will appear on individual lesson plans. The **lesson plan** will include the aim for each lesson and the objectives (steps in how to achieve the aim). These will include the **learning outcomes**. This is **short-term** planning.

(Note: see also Unit 3-3, page 65, Support pupils during learning activities.)

Below is an example of a lesson including learning outcomes.

(Year 3 Literacy) Learning outcome – for children to use more descriptive words

First part of the lesson to focus on shared writing following discussion of big book the previous day. Children to think about adjectives and how the text is made more interesting by using descriptive words. Groups then to go and work on their own activities.

Red group: working on their own independent writing, thinking about using descriptive words.

Blue group: sitting with assistant at computers in pairs, using program which encourages use of descriptive words.

Green group: completing worksheet offering a choice of adjectives.

Yellow group: working with class teacher on shared reading activity.

Plenary (end of session): for the children who have been working on independent writing to read some of their work to the others.

Importance of teaching assistant's input during planning

If the teaching assistant has seen the lesson plans, or indeed has been part of the planning, from the medium-term to the more detailed and specific short-term planning, then they will know what the children's learning outcomes will be. If not privy to planning then the teaching assistant will only be aware of the learning outcomes once they enter the lesson.

The DfES is asking teachers who deliver the National Literacy Hour, for example, to use the support available within the classroom to deliver the strategy effectively. It refers to assistants by saying that 'These people have a key role to play in the NLS (National Literacy Strategy), which should give them an enhanced sense of responsibility for the pupils they work with, and help them to focus on short term learning targets' (DfES, 2001). The NLS points out that everyone involved in the Literacy Hour *should be aware of the objectives for the day* and should be involved in the planning process. The Literacy Hour is designed to challenge the most able pupil while allowing the less able to participate and understand, which is why you work with individual pupils using a variety of teaching approaches to match the child's learning style. All lessons should be planned by the same method.

Individual learning targets

Children will now usually have individual learning targets, which are set by the teacher on a termly or half termly basis. They will usually include a target for numeracy and for literacy and the child will be aware of these targets and encouraged to work on them. They may also have behaviour targets within the class or around the school. Parents should also be encouraged to help the child to know and work on their targets. They will have these targets from Reception.

> The behaviour targets which children may have could include:
>
> 'I will remember to walk sensibly around the school'
>
> 'I will sit quietly and listen on the carpet'.

In order to support individual children effectively, all those working with them will need to know both the desired learning outcomes and individual targets. One way of remembering them may be for children to have targets for their groups which are on the wall, or for them to have a reminder inside their folder or exercise book.

Careful planning between the teacher and teaching assistant enables teaching at a level to match the pupil's individual needs. It is important to recognise there is a close relationship between teaching and learning and if this is established then a good match is made.

How to support children to achieve the desired learning outcomes

Some children need to work on the development of particular skills or practise them for longer than the rest of the group in order to gain access to the objectives in the framework that are being taught to the whole group. For example, pupils with speech and language difficulties will need to work on programmes devised by a Speech and Language Therapist or Specialist Language Teacher, to fit the teaching of the rest of the group.

Pupils may need intensive training in the use of signing, symbols, Braille, radio microphones or electronic communicators, to give them better access to activities in the whole class and in small groups. Look at this example:

> Six-year-old Susan had a hearing loss in her pre-school years and as a result has difficulties with words with several syllables. Susan was assessed by a Speech and Language Therapist and a programme of relevant objectives was organised in conjunction with the SENCo, class teacher, teaching assistant and parents. During group work in Literacy Hour the teaching assistant is able to create opportunities for Susan to focus on phonic work. Once a week the teaching assistant spends 20 minutes working with Susan on an individual basis, while the rest of the group are working independently.

Teachers often use 'big books' for shared text work. Some assistants may need to support children who lack concentration in a whole group situation. Pupils may benefit from a range of resources to help them follow the text, such as picture cards, word cards, appropriate objects, etc. Assistants may need to sit close to individual children where they have these difficulties to help them to stay on task during whole class teaching. It may also be necessary for the teacher or teaching assistant to sign, or use tactile cues, to support children with visual or hearing impairments.

Craig is 7 years old and has Attention Deficit Disorder which has caused problems with his reading, writing and with mathematics as he is unable to stay focused on his work. He has five hours of support each week and it is recommended that this be used to help him to stay focused during whole class teaching of the Literacy and Numeracy sessions. He sometimes needs to be taken out of the class so that his calling out does not distract the others.

Valuing individuals

Giving pupils attention when misbehaving can cause the behaviour to be repeated again and again, even if the attention is one of disapproval. Attention of any type is still attention to a child who craves it. Adults in the classroom cannot always ignore misbehaviour as it could be dangerous and if unnoticed may escalate.

There are two strategies – **giving rewards** and '**catching them being good**' (Montgomery, 1990). Rewarding may seem unfair to pupils who 'get it right' most of the time. The rewards may need to get bigger and be given more often to encourage reasonable behaviour or accomplishment of a task.

However, long term 'catching them being good' has greater effects on the building of self-esteem. Quietly say as you pass the child working appropriately, 'You're working really well'. Positive eye-contact and gesture also works. It is a sincere way of praising and works right across the age range. The older the child, the less 'cool' it is to be praised publicly but their self-esteem requires it, so the quiet and/or non-verbal approach is effective. If you are insincere then this method will not work.

It is surprising but useful to know that this strategy works with the most unlikely pupils. It is harder than giving rewards because you do need to be ever-vigilant in 'catching them being good'.

Montgomery (1990) reveals a **pattern of teacher behaviours** which also may reflect some practice by teaching assistants.

▷ **Support** – verbal or gesture (nod, smile, etc.), this communication is positive.

▷ **Approach** – the adult in the group responds favourably, use of posture indicates that they are giving attention.

▲ It is not always possible to ignore bad behaviour

▷ **General verbal behaviour** – short explanations and simple instructions keep up interest and motivation.

▷ **Desist or disapproval behaviour** – either by gesture or word, asking a pupil to desist or stop an activity. The adult's behaviour is clearly designed to control a situation, e.g. moving pupils who are sitting next to one another because they keep chatting.

Research has produced findings that lengthy verbal **desist** behaviour generated a negative response from the children. However, 'sharp looks' and 'sharp gesture' were successful in acquiring appropriate behaviour. Verbal criticism caused a negative response, in particular if it was lengthy and even more if it included satire.

Once again Montgomery (1990) reports what she feels are the most powerful reinforcers and rewards, and good practice for teaching assistants. These are:

1 social approval of peers

2 social approval of teachers (and teaching assistants)

3 getting something right

4 succeeding in an overall task

5 taking responsibility for work

6 taking responsibility for others.

As a teaching assistant, you can be instrumental in supporting individuals and groups of children in achieving these goals, which all contribute to raising self-esteem and are motivational.

How to deal with problems and build relationships with individual pupils

Teaching assistants can be the true professionals when it comes to motivation. With the communication skills you have, you should be able to establish and maintain relationships with individual pupils. There are three sides to this: being interested in the child as an individual, understanding how a child learns best and overcoming barriers to building relationships.

1 Be interested in the child as an individual

You become the 'expert' on the particular child you work with as they put their trust in you for the support they need. You have the 'inside' information into what motivates that particular child, an understanding of their interests, capabilities, attention span and so on. This is why it is so important that you should have all the relevant information about the children you work with, including the medical history if there is one, the Statement of Special Educational Needs, the IEP, Record of Support, in conjunction with teachers. Your experience with an individual child will help you to find out how they best learn.

Keys to good practice
Being interested in the individual

✔ Never compare them with others.

✔ Ask about their own interests – maintain a conversation.

✔ Know about their family.

✔ Remember their name and preferences.

✔ Find out about any conditions or disabilities they may have.

✔ Praise them for their own specific achievements.

✔ Be sensitive to cultural differences – find out about their culture or language.

Local Education Authorities will have a variety of courses for school staff to attend. Often the book containing such details will be available to all members of staff. Sometimes the headteacher will suggest certain courses for certain members of staff.

The information that you find, coupled with all the information you have discovered through your ongoing polite and sensitive questioning, builds up an entire picture of the child and puts you in the primary position in motivating them.

Relationships with children will vary because you may have long-term or short-term time with them. If you have only one session a week with a child, to an extent you have to renew your relationship each time, and this is where your listening skills come to the fore. If you have remembered 'where you were up to' with the child the week before, then you are at an advantage. The child will feel valued and will have raised self-esteem, which is a very positive place to start a session. Long-term relationships mean greater constancy but also can be a disadvantage as 'familiarity breeds contempt'; this will largely depend upon personalities and just how challenging the child's behaviour can be.

2 Understanding how a child learns best

In order to help individual children to learn, you will need to be aware of the different ways in which they may do this.

Different methods of learning.

(See also Unit 3-3, page 78 for fuller definitions of these.)

Repetition is where a child is given an activity which repeats the task several times, e.g. practising pencil control by following the dots that form the letter 'a'.

Facilitation is the method by which we give children resources to carry out an activity and allow them to experiment for themselves to reach a learning outcome.

Instruction is where a child carries out a task by following a set of step-by-step instructions, e.g. making a small box out of paper.

Collaboration involves a group of children who work together in discussing ideas and solving a problem. Children will learn how to work as a team, taking turns in listening and speaking, valuing the opinion of others.

You will need to monitor the child's response to these different methods of learning and where necessary work with them to ensure that the desired learning outcomes are achieved. If you need to modify the way in which you are working to do this, you will need to tell the teacher. It is also vital within all these methods of learning that you use praise and encouragement with children.

? Think about it

Think about ways in which you find it easier to absorb and learn information. This may help you to empathise with children in the learning situation.

3 Overcoming barriers to building relationships

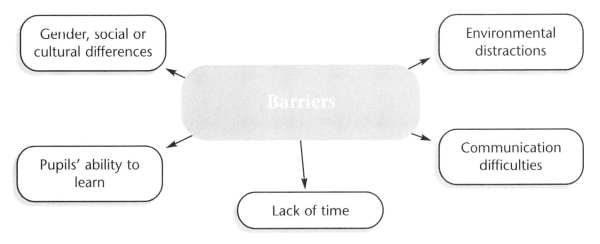

▲ There can different factors which create barriers to relationships

Environmental distractions

There may be a variety of reasons that you find it difficult to form positive relationships with pupils. If there are distractions when pupils are trying to focus on a task, this will make it difficult to reach the learning outcomes required.

Noise may be an environmental issue that is a barrier to learning. For example, during spring and summer, the lawns and/or playing field might be mown every Wednesday – causing noise and distraction.

Sometimes groups have to work in corridors and these can be distracting, uncomfortable and/or noisy. They can also be cold or draughty places to work. Working in part of the dining hall can also be distracting, because of the noise of people working in the kitchen, setting up tables, etc., together with the smell of cooking.

Split sites can be problematic, such as extra classrooms, which may be in 'portacabins', away from the main school. These are often too hot in the summer and too cold in the winter. The split site may be a problem for those with poor mobility.

Gender, social or cultural differences

You may find it difficult to form relationships with individuals where there are gender, social or cultural differences. For example, some children may find it easier to form positive relationships with an adult who is of the same sex. If there is a male teaching assistant, this may also help to form a positive relationship with a child who does not have a male role model.

Case study

Ashim is a very quiet child in Year 4 who has a female teacher. He does not find it easy to relate to her and she asks you if you could so some extra work with him since you are a male assistant.

1 Why do you think this might help Ashim?

2 How else could you encourage Ashim and develop his confidence?

Communication difficulties

Where children have communication difficulties, you will need to find out how best to support and encourage them through advice and help from the school and outside agencies. It the child has autism, for example, you may have to work on set targets for short periods.

Lack of time

You may find that it is difficult to form effective relationships with children because there are so many constraints on time. It is important that you are able to give as much time as is needed to your work with children so that they do not feel you do not have time for them. If time runs out when working on an activity with a child, make sure that you go back to it later.

Pupil's ability to learn

Where pupils find tasks difficult, they will look to you for help, so you must do all you can to motivate and help them through praise and encouragement. You must always tell the class teacher if the child or children are struggling with a task or concept.

Think about it

Gavin is supporting a child who speaks English as a second language. How could he go about building a relationship with the child?

Element 3-2.2 Establish and maintain relationships with groups of pupils

For this element you will need to know and understand how to work with groups of children. A teaching assistant often works with groups of children who find it difficult to keep up or to concentrate. They may also be general low achievers who for a variety of reasons, disability or language differences, find tasks difficult, or those whose social, emotional, intellectual, physical skills are not developing well. These difficulties often manifest themselves in poor behaviour, low self-esteem and a lack of motivation and your remit is to enable and support the group to meet a particular learning outcome.

Teaching assistants, as described in 3-2.1, may work in a variety of areas within the learning environment such as the classroom, dining hall, corridors, gyms, etc., and support pupils on school trips.

For this element you will need to know and understand the following:

▶ how to work effectively with a group of pupils

▶ how to monitor and evaluate the dynamic of the group

▶ how to deal with difficulties within the group

▶ how to maintain fairness and authority.

How to work effectively with a group of pupils

The benefits of group work

Group work has been identified as beneficial to learning as recognised by Ainscow (1999). Galton and Williamson (1992) classified a range of small groups, which are commonly developed in classrooms, and you may find these familiar.

Different groups in the classroom
▶ Seating groups: pupils sit together but are engaged in separate tasks and produce separate outcomes, e.g. children who are working on the same maths activity may be working at their own pace, and will therefore achieve differently.
▶ Working groups: where pupils tackle similar tasks, which result in similar outcomes, but their work is independent, e.g. measuring different objects in the playground.
▶ Co-operative groups: where pupils have separate but related tasks which result in a joint outcome, e.g. a wall display of different paintings but all in the style of Monet.
▶ Collaborative groups: pupils have the same task and work together towards a joint outcome, e.g. a giant dragon for Chinese New Year.

The main benefits to the child are the social exchanges which are encouraged to take place through these types of group work. Bruner (1972) and Vygotsky (1978) believed that a pupil's potential for learning is often realised while engaged in interaction with someone more knowledgeable within the group. This may be the teaching assistant but could equally be another child. Therefore, group work encourages pupils to share their ideas through discussion and also provides mutual support in a safe environment. This may lead to personal success and a raised self-esteem, while fostering a sense of fairness to all parties.

Short- and long-term groups

You may work constantly with one particular group, as indicated in the introduction to this element, which is working **long term**, or you may move from class to class seeing various groups in the course of a day. You may stay with one key stage or span them, or you may work with a group for a specific purpose, such as a visit to a local museum and support the completion of a work sheet. This is working together **short term**.

You may work **long term** within a large Year 1 class with a small group who all need a similar level of support. None of these children need close supervision and your role in the class has been negotiated with the class teacher. You position yourself near to your group and prompt reticent pupils in whole class activities, and work with the small group in translating vocabulary and phrases, helping with resources to find answers, e.g. number lines, IT resources as identified in IEP's, and observe their responses.

▲ You might work with a group for a visit to a museum

Small groups

Often teaching assistants will work with small groups outside the classroom in less than ideal circumstances – cramped spaces which are uncomfortable, in hall areas where disruption is inevitable and the noise level is less than conducive to working. These conditions, together with the behaviour that can follow as a result of a pupil's lack of ability to learn, can make your job a challenge.

Safe environment

It is important for children to have a safe environment when working. Both the area of work and the children's emotional health should be considered – for example, the children should feel safe to carry out their activities without any sense of failure or ridicule. (See also Unit 3-10.)

Working effectively with groups

Teaching assistants need to be interested in each member of the group. As described in Unit 3-2.1, you need to get to know each pupil – their likes, dislikes and interests, in and out of school. This can be a useful motivating tool, e.g. the use of a favourite cartoon character can be at the centre of an activity to achieve a learning outcome. Also you need to learn quickly the names of group members; most people feel more valued when their name is remembered 'correctly'.

Always be receptive – often we can have preconceived ideas from information we have received from others. Take each child at face value, look at what they can do and build upon it.

Always observe how the group works together, and who works best when sitting next to whom. Note the causes of any breakdowns in group work – that is, what triggers the disintegration? You will be able to diffuse situations if you are one step ahead by close observation.

? Think about it

Billy loses concentration before the rest of his group and he insists on distracting Grace, who he likes to sit next to. Once Grace loses focus, she becomes noisy which makes it impossible for others to continue. What can you do?

Strategies may be to:

a make sure that Billy and Grace are not sitting together

b start Billy on task after the rest of the group

c start a reward system encouraging all members to complete their tasks.

Sustaining attention

Teaching assistants need to keep an activity alive, and uphold attention. This is easier to manage when you know in advance what your role is for the session (as discussed in Unit 3-2.1). Praise and encouragement for the effort a pupil is putting into the task will help to sustain attention. It is also about having strategies in place for bringing pupils back to focus and getting the task complete. These can be verbal cues such as praising and then asking questions about completing, therefore keeping up the momentum. For example:

'You've completed the first bit, Sunita, which is really good. Look at Sanjay's section, what do you think it's going to do when everyone has finished, how fast will it go?'

Non-verbal communication may be open body language, positive gestures (thumbs up, nodding, etc.) facial expressions, such as smiling encouragingly, and looking enthusiastic and excited about the work being carried out.

Do you know what you should be doing?

Teaching assistants need to have sight of, or copies of, long-, medium- or short-term plans and should be part of the planning for the short term. A lesson will be far more effective if everyone knows their role and what activities they are expected to carry out in advance (see also Unit 3-8 page 141).

✔ Keys to good practice
Working with groups

- ✔ Be interested in the whole group.
- ✔ Be objective – do not have preconceived ideas.
- ✔ Be aware of any Statements of Educational Needs.
- ✔ Recognise the strengths of individual pupils.
- ✔ Sustain attention by praise and encouragement.
- ✔ Be enthusiastic.
- ✔ Be organised and flexible.
- ✔ Have positive verbal and non-verbal skills.

How to monitor and evaluate the dynamic of the group

Group dynamics

The mix of pupils make up the dynamic of the group; 'dynamics' being a *'force producing motion; forceful matter in motion'* (*Oxford English Dictionary*). Often in new groups there will be two or three (and maybe more) who are forceful, lively or attention-seeking individuals and these members often steer the main body out of general direction, causing a dynamic change.

Sometimes a group may make exceptions for a child who has a particular need and accept unwanted behaviour. For example, when a child's development is delayed in one or more areas, they may not have the language or social skills shared by the rest of the group and may find turn-taking and sharing very difficult. This may manifest itself in aggressive behaviour born out of frustration and result in throwing equipment, toys, biting or hitting others. When the child is absent, the dynamic or the energy alters and may become easier and more relaxed.

Sometimes the behaviour of individuals outside your group may be affecting your group's dynamic.

Case study

You are working with a pupil in an area outside the classroom, in a fairly spacious hallway, but there is always a steady flow of children for one reason or another. As they pass by they invariably politely speak to you and the children. 'Hello Mrs Jones, we're going to the hall', 'Guess what – I got a sticker this morning', 'See you at playtime, Joe'.

As you will see there is nothing wrong with this behaviour but it is affecting you and your group. What would you do?

▲ Coping with distractions

Development of groups

Groups tend to develop in a characteristic way, progressing through four stages, as can be seen below.

The different stages of groups
Stage 1: Introductory stage where individuals are polite and get to know each other. (Best behaviour away from home!)
Stage 2: Known as the conflict stage, where individuals start to fall out with each other. Getting to know each other and not liking all that is seen or heard.
Stage 3: This is the negotiation stage, where the group form unwritten rules of procedure.
Stage 4: This is the working stage, where the group starts to work together after sorting out individual differences.

These stages are universal and you may be able to identify with them when you have been in this situation yourself – for example, starting on a new course! You may also have heard of Tuckman and Jensen's ***Forming, Storming, Norming*** and ***Performing*** stages in the evolution of a team (see also Unit 3-21 page 279).With children, stage 3 usually becomes a written set of rules – see Hawkwood Infant School Golden Rules, page 14.

Monitoring a group

Monitoring the progress of a small group is easier to manage. If the pupils who seek attention through inappropriate behaviour have fewer people to 'entertain', they are less likely to misbehave because they are under closer supervision. They will also be kept on task and supported by the teaching assistant, along with peer pressure, and aims are more likely to be met.

You may like to consider the degree to which you like to work in groups. People act differently in groups than in a one to one situation and it is important to look at the following factors when arranging groups for group work.

Size

Generally, teachers make the decision over group sizes but once again, the teaching assistant with their experience may have some input into the membership of a group and the size.

Small groups are easier to observe and monitor, as you will know what all the children are doing, you have fewer children to work with and can give them more attention and be more aware of any underlying tensions and divert attention as necessary. In small groups children will feel more comfortable, gain confidence and take an active role.

▲ It is easier to control the behaviour of a small group

Purpose

You need to understand why this group has been organised in this way. What is your role and are you happy and comfortable with it, i.e. do you know what you are supposed to be doing and why?

Do the pupils know what their role is and what their purpose is? This will have been explained by the class teacher but inevitably you will 'break down' the task and may explain it in a variety of ways until the children are clear about their purpose and outcome.

An example of this may be: the whole class has been taught to extend number sequences – to count on or back in steps of 1 and 2. You work with four children who need to have demonstrated on a number line how to count on and back. You may need to break it down further, by using objects such as buttons, counters, etc., to help them grasp the concept.

Timing

As groups 'gel', the quicker they settle down and carry out work in order to achieve the target. They become more familiar with each other and are more likely to co-operate with each other and you.

▲ Group work can have a number of benefits

Physical

Children need to have easy access to resources, to be able to reach items on the table. For some children, activities may be better executed on the floor in a quieter corner of the room.

Language

Ensure the pupils understand the activity: verbal instructions should use appropriate language for the age and stage of the children, or may be by way of a translator, sign language and/or demonstration of the task, using verbal and non-verbal skills.

Intellectual factors

Children who are less quick to learn need to be encouraged and praised at each stage of the activity, to help build self-esteem and promote motivation. Brainstorming can be a useful vehicle for establishing what a group of children know and as a result, those with difficulties are allowed more thinking space.

What a child carries out with help from you today, they may well be able to carry out by themselves tomorrow. Lev Vygotsky (1896-1934) was keen that each child should achieve their own potential. This area/zone is the distance between what a child already understands and what they can understand with adult support and is known as the ZDP, or zone of proximal development.

Social and emotional factors

A child who struggles socially needs to be encouraged to join in and take turns. An activity such as a maths worksheet with different resources will help significantly when working in a small group for the pupil who will not take turns and the shy and withdrawn. Equally, a lively and disruptive child will learn by example and praise to take turns.

Working in small groups is of great benefit to children in encouraging working together as a team and fosters a sense of belonging. They have the security of the teaching assistant and just a few pupils to work with where they can feel safe and able to speak up. In time, with this safe framework around them, the child may be brave enough to join in with larger group activities.

Emotional difficulties may be the reverse of quiet and introverted. In many cases pupils can behave in a totally unacceptable way because they are slow to develop socially and emotionally, often as the result of a specific need.

? Think about it

Think about and evaluate a session during which you have worked with a group of pupils. Consider:

▶ How did the session go?
▶ What did the children learn?
▶ Did they meet the objectives?
▶ Did they enjoy the activity?
▶ Did anything go wrong? Why?
▶ Did I need to ask advice?
▶ Would I do it like that next time?

Sometimes it is necessary to evaluate formally, or write an account or report of events, especially in very challenging circumstances. Strategies for managing unwanted behaviour may need to be discussed with teachers and other members of staff. Certainly you may be asked to record achievements and behaviour on Individual Learning Plans and Records of Support.

✓ **Keys to good practice**
Monitoring a group

✔ Get to know your group, e.g. likes, dislikes, background, Records of Support, etc.

✔ Observe how the group works together.

✔ Act upon your observations to create the best learning situations.

✔ Be ready to deal with conflicts – a careful observer will see them coming!

✔ Have strategies in place.

✔ Reflect upon the session and discover how it went.

✔ Share thoughts and feelings.

✔ Never be afraid to seek advice.

How to deal with difficulties within the group

Tensions are difficulties within the group, which you must deal with, or pupils will lose confidence in you.

If you know that two of the children in your group aggravate each other, then you may organise the activity so that they are not sitting next to each other and you will be ready to divert and distract unnecessary behaviour which may force the group work in the wrong direction. If you are able to work with these two children as a 'pair', it is a valuable time to listen and observe the individual triggers which cause the unacceptable behaviour in each child. This information will be helpful to you in developing strategies, firstly for dealing with the behaviour, and secondly for a long-term plan of getting the children to accept each other's differences.

The tension and situation may not last long, but teaching assistants need to be aware that children may find difficulty in learning in the short term as a result.

→ *Knowledge into action*

Look at the diagram below on short-term factors which can cause tension in groups.

For each of the 'short-term' situations listed discuss in small groups

▶ how a child might be affected

▶ what type of behaviour may manifest itself

▶ how you could deal with the behaviour.

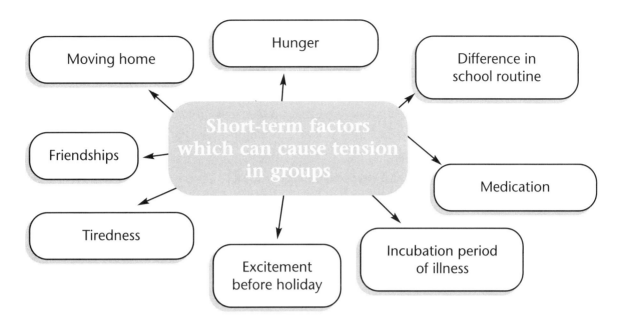

▲ What causes difficulties in groups?

Long-term situations that affect behaviour and learning can be due to:

▷ cultural differences
▷ divorce/separation of parents and/or the forming of a step-family
▷ severe illness or disability of family member
▷ foster care and/or adoption
▷ a succession of changes in home and school
▷ bullying.

Pupils who may be involved in one of these long-term situations may well require much more pastoral work in order to create stability for the child, in an environment where the child has a chance of developing their learning.

Common problems

Excitement in classrooms can cause problems, for example on the eve of the summer holiday, visits out of school, visitors in class or class teacher away. You will have experienced the change in behaviour in children who are normally 'in control' of their emotions.

You will need to be a constant influence for the children as they enjoy being part of a safe framework but where the boundaries on certain occasions can be a little flexible.

Case study

You are with a group of five children carrying out an activity planting cress seeds in containers. It is progressing well until Emily accidentally tips fertiliser over Soraya's hand and sleeve and laughs. Soraya, who has difficulty in controlling her temper, waves her hand and sleeve over Emily's head, showering everyone with soil, then rushes around kicking chairs.

Discuss in pairs how you would respond to this change in dynamic.

1 What would you do first?

2 How could you have prevented this from happening?

3 What will you do next time?

Compare your findings with others in your group

▲ Excitable behaviour can result in problems

It is most important that children understand that it is the *behaviour* that is disapproved of – *not* them.

Case study

Jamie is 6 years old and spends every other weekend with his father and his new family, which includes two step-brothers of 12 and 14 years old. After these visits Jamie's behaviour swings from clinginess to you and being very physically aggressive with the other boys in the small group.

1 What might be causing the behaviour?

2 How would you treat Jamie?

3 How would you treat the rest of the group?

4 Who would you share your concerns with?

Keys to good practice
Dealing with difficulties

✔ Anticipate potential sources of conflict and danger.

✔ Discriminatory behaviour should be dealt with immediately.

✔ Challenging or unwanted behaviour should be dealt with sensitively.

✔ Intervention needs to be calm and controlled.

✔ Wherever possible intervention should be positive.

Who to turn to when things go wrong

You will need to report promptly any problems in building relationships within groups. Changes in a child's behaviour should always be reported to the class teacher as this needs to be communicated with parents. It may be that a situation at home has created the different behaviour, e.g. illness causing a change in routine and a short-term problem. If the explanation is not so straightforward, it may need a formal record to be kept which needs to include:

▷ date

▷ time

▷ place

▷ incident

▷ action taken.

In this way you can build up a picture of the child's behaviour long term and observe if there is any form of pattern. Does the inappropriate behaviour occur after a weekend, when the child has eaten lunch or been out to play? There could be an underlying medical condition or social problem.

The importance of policies when difficulties arise

Policies are written by teachers, governors and parents from LEA guidelines. It is the responsibility of all adults in the school to share information with pupils and is the parent's role to uphold them too. All parents will have been given a school prospectus in which there may be copies of school policies or it will be stated where these policies can be located within school. Schools will also have Home/School Agreements which parents need to agree to and sign, therefore adhering to the policies. Governors regularly monitor schools to ensure that everyone works within the guidelines and that they are maintained and revised regularly.

For behaviour there will be a whole school policy and individual classes will have their own rules, which are generally the result of a class activity and reflect what the children believe to be important. These personalised rules will fit within the main policy (see Hawkwood Golden Rules, page 14). Upholding rules is easier if the class has made them and pupils may use peer group pressure to ensure their rules are kept.

Teaching assistants have opportunities to advise children on a variety of issues relating to many policies, such as behaviour, health and safety, anti-bias and non-discriminatory practice, in their everyday role. For example: 'Walk in the corridors please', 'That is not the place to play ball', 'That was an unkind thing to say, we don't say things like that here'.

Case study

You have noticed that each afternoon directly after lunch, Sarah's behaviour deteriorates. She is unable to sit still, is fidgety and unwilling to learn and annoys the rest of her small group. As the afternoon wears on Sarah seems to calm down.

1 Discuss in pairs what might be causing the problem in behaviour.

2 How should you treat Sarah?

3 How should you treat the rest of the group?

4 What will you report to the teacher and how will you do this?

5 Do you think the parents ought to know?

✔ Be friendly, not friends.

✔ Value each member of the group.

✔ Always observe your group to monitor what is happening.

✔ Always try to give equal time and attention to each group member (never favour one child over another).

✔ Listen to all members of the group.

✔ Ask children for their opinion.

✔ Explain why you have made a decision and stick to it!

✔ Make accurate notes of changes in behaviour and report to the teacher.

How to maintain fairness and authority

Teaching assistants need to have authority within the group if they are to succeed, and the teacher's respect for them gives the class a clear message of authority. To be seen as an important and integral part of the school team, in school entrance areas there are often photographs of all staff members – giving value to all, from the caretaker and cooks to the headteacher.

Most importantly, teaching assistants (as indicated in 3-2.1) must be good and active listeners. You will not maintain fairness and authority or communicate problems if you have not listened.

Case study

A squabble erupts because Jane has pushed past Kylie, causing Kylie to drop her lunch box on the floor and scattering its contents.

The teaching assistant intervenes by asking what has happened and helping to rescue the packed lunch. She suggests that Jane should be more careful when going into lunch and should apologize for causing the accident.

But Jane says, 'My mum says I don't have to do what you say, you're only Hayley's mum, you're not a teacher.'

How would you respond to this outburst?

Managing unwanted or challenging behaviour

Eye-contact

As discussed in Unit 3-2.1 eye-contact is a very useful tool. A warning look across the room is often enough to communicate that certain behaviour is unwanted and the child is stepping out of line, pushing the boundaries of the group. It may be necessary to hold the eye-contact until you are sure the behaviour ceases. This is a most appropriate form of communication if you do not want to stop the activity. You must always praise a child once they behave appropriately again.

Facial expression

A stern look together with the eye-contact, and raised eyebrows, 'what do you think you're doing' can achieve a lot.

These expressions and a shake of the head can be very effective and again will not disrupt a group otherwise working well with each other.

Explanations

Children need explanations; it is not always enough just to say 'No'. However, in a dangerous situation this undoubtedly is an essential word to prevent an accident occurring. If children are not aware of the consequences they will take a long time to learn why certain behaviour is inappropriate. Using a skipping rope around a child's throat, pretending she or he is a horse, is an imaginative game but one that is potentially very dangerous. 'You could hurt Gemma's throat really badly playing that game', tells a child of the consequence of the action. You may need to reiterate and add a condition 'I will have to take the skipping rope away, if you continue to misuse it' and you must stick to the condition. Do not be tempted to threaten a condition, and not carry it out as children will not believe you another time.

Time out

Time away from a situation can be a helpful strategy, if you can use that time to talk to the child about the behaviour and its inappropriateness. It may help the child to think before doing it next time, especially if you are on-hand to pre-empt the 'deed' with eye-contact and/or facial expression and/or shake of the head! Time out gives time for the child to step back from the situation and to calm down, it also gives the remainder of the group a chance to take breath. Listening skills are very important, so when you ask a child why they have behaved in a certain way, make sure you have understood by reflecting back to them what they have said. This is a very helpful tool, as often children realise by themselves how inappropriate their behaviour and attitude is.
It should not be seen as punishment or rejection.

The only time we are able to physically restrain a child is when they are in danger of hurting themselves or in danger of hurting others. The Children Act 1989 protects the right of children and physical punishment is an offence.

Encouraging pupils to take responsibility for their own group interactions

You may also need to help pupils if they are finding it difficult to work as a group and the group starts to break down as a result. Children will need to have practice from an early stage at working in groups, so that they are able to learn to work together. This may come easier to some children than to others, so your input may be to find ways of working through ideas or plans of action together, although you should try to ensure that the task remains child- and not adult-directed. In Key Stage 1 this may be mainly through discussions, while older children may need you to observe more and direct when necessary.

Think about it

You are working with a group of junior children during a drama activity. The children are all clear in what they have to do but they are being held up, as they all want to start in different places and are not listening to one another.

1 How could you help the group to take responsibility for the task?

2 How would you do this without taking over?

Keys to good practice
Fairness and authority

✔ Always explain carefully.

✔ Listen to all.

✔ Observe.

✔ Be objective (don't take sides).

End of unit test

1 Name two forms of communication. What does communication with others involve?

2 How can eye-contact and non-verbal communication be effective in the classroom?

3 What is the difference between long-, medium- and short-term planning?

4 How should assistants contribute to the planning process?

5 How can assistants help to raise children's self-esteem within the classroom?

6 What sort of problems might assistants have in forming positive relationships with children?

7 What types of groups might be found in a classroom? What are the benefits of working in a group?

8 What are the four stages of group development?

9 What differences might you face when working with a group?

10 What types of strategies could you use for dealing with unwanted behaviour in a group?

References

Ainscow, M., *Understanding the Development of Inclusive Schools* (Routledge, 1999)

DfES, *National Literacy Hour: Framework for teaching* (2001)

Galton, M. and Williamson, J., *Group Work in the Primary Classroom* (Routledge, 1992)

Montgomery, D., *Managing Behaviour Problems* (Hodder and Stoughton Educational, 1990)

Tilstone, C., Florian, L., and Rose, R., *Promoting Inclusive Practice* (Routledge, 1998)

Tuckman, B. and Jensen, M.A., 'Stages of small group development revisited' in *Group and Organizational Studies*, 2, 419–427 (1977)

Support pupils during learning activities

This unit contains two elements:

3-3.1 Provide support for learning activities

3-3.2 Promote independent learning

Element 3-3.1 Provide support for learning activities

This element examines how you can best support pupils when undertaking learning activities in school. You will need to understand how children learn and develop in order to implement a range of strategies for supporting them. As a teaching assistant you will also need to be able to manage problems within the classroom when supporting learning activities. This element will give you some idea of the types of problems you may encounter and how to deal with them. It is also important to be familiar with the Foundation Stage and Key Stages 1 and 2 and how different activities are planned within the framework of the Foundation Stage and the National Curriculum.

For this element you will need to know and understand the following:

▶ basic principles and influences on how children learn and develop

▶ understanding curriculum plans

▶ how pupils may be supported in learning activities

▶ the school's policies and practices for equal opportunities and inclusion, including supporting pupils with Special Educational Needs

▶ managing problems when supporting learning activities.

How children learn and develop

Theories of learning

There have been several theories put forward by educationalists and psychologists about how children learn and are influenced as they develop. There are other, inbuilt influences on children's learning which will be discussed on page 62, as they will also have a direct effect on how children learn. The two main ideas about how children's learning takes place are behaviourist theory and cognitive theory. By looking at these we are able to focus on different aspects of children's learning and consider how best to support them in an early years setting.

Behaviourist theory

This theory was first put forward by Burrhus Frank Skinner (1904-94). It states that as individuals we will repeat experiences which are enjoyable and avoid those which are not. This is as relevant for learning experiences as for behaviour itself. For example, a child who learns that it is enjoyable to work with construction toys will want to repeat the experience and do this again. If children are praised for working at a particular task, this may also reinforce their desire to repeat the experience. Skinner stated that good experiences are *positive reinforcement*. Many educationalists use the strategy of positive reinforcement when working with children – for example, by praising and encouraging them and by giving them tasks which they can carry out successfully.

We can ensure that children are gaining positive experiences when working by giving them:

▷ praise and encouragement
▷ enjoyable tasks
▷ manageable tasks.

Assistants will need to be aware of children's reactions to tasks as sometimes children may find it difficult to become motivated and lose enthusiasm quickly. It is important to recognise when children are not enjoying tasks and find out what may be the cause, so that we may encourage and motivate them. As assistants get to know children, it

▲ Adults will need to be aware when children are not able to focus on a task

will be more apparent when they are not 'themselves', or are unable to focus on what they are doing. Where children are not responding to a task, assistants should address them individually and try to find out the cause.

There may be a variety of reasons why the child is not motivated:

▷ Child does not understand the requirements of the task.

▷ Child is unable to complete the task as it is too difficult.

▷ Child finds the task too easy.

▷ Individual reasons why the child is not able to focus on the task, such as illness or anxiety.

Once the cause has been established, assistants may need to work closely with the child or speak to the teacher about the problem to decide the best way forward. Where the task is too easy or too difficult, it may be possible to put the child with another group of children and restructure their work for later. Children whose work is not enjoyable or manageable will be unlikely to want to repeat the experience.

Cognitive development theory

The second theory of learning is that which was put forward by Jean Piaget, (1896-1980) and is based on the cognitive model. This states that a child will need to pass through different stages of a learning process. He stated that children pass through stages of learning which are broadly related to their age, and that they cannot move from one stage to another until they are ready.

This theory has been criticised as all children learn and develop at a different pace and it is hard to say at exactly what age particular skills will develop. It is however accepted that children have individual learning needs and requirements.

Piaget's stages of learning

Age	Stage of learning	Characteristics
0-2 yrs	Sensory Motor	Babies are starting to find out about world around them and are discovering what things around them can do.
2-6 yrs	Pre-operational	Children are starting to develop thought processes, and are using symbolic play. They find it easier to learn when they can see and use practical examples.
6-11 yrs	Concrete Operations	Children are able to think on a more logical level. They can use more abstract concepts, for example a box can represent a car.

As an assistant, it is important to recognise that children's learning will be based on their own individual experiences, and that they will pass through learning stages, but that the age at which they reach them is not fixed.

Factors which influence children's learning

Children's learning is not only influenced by their stage of development. There are also a number of individual factors which will affect each child when it comes to their learning. These are based on their own experiences and personality so will be different for each child. An assistant will need to consider these factors when supporting children in order to understand each child's needs.

▷ **Intelligence and creativity** – each child will have their own talents and aptitudes, so will be more or less able at different tasks within the classroom. They may also perceive themselves to be better or worse than other children, and this may affect their motivation. For example, if they notice that another child is particularly good at a creative task such as art, they may think that their own work is not as good and feel inadequate. The adult will need to speak to and encourage the child so that they are able to continue. As children will always have strengths and weaknesses in different areas, the role of the adult will be to encourage children and instil an awareness that all of us are different and that this is a positive thing.

▷ **Social background** – children's background will have an influence on their learning as they may come to school with a variety of experiences. Some children may have had a wide range of social interactions, while others may have had very little. Where children's experiences are limited, they may lack confidence with others, find the setting difficult to adjust to or take longer to relate to other adults. This may affect their learning as they will take longer to adjust to the setting and to others before they are able to focus on tasks. They will need encouragement and praise to develop their confidence and skills when dealing with others.

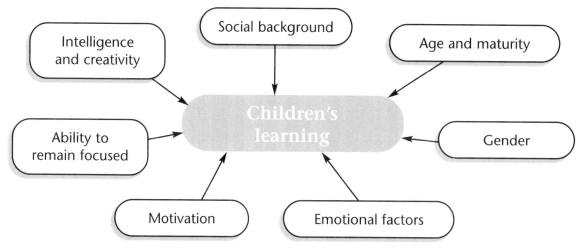

▲ Individual factors will affect each child's learning

▷ **Age and maturity** – as we have already seen, children will develop at an individual pace and so in any group of children there will be some who are more mature than others. Also, due to the way in which some schools have their intakes, there may be children in the same class or group who are almost a year apart in age. At an early age, this may make a big difference to the range of abilities which exist in the class. Adults should therefore be aware of this factor when monitoring children's learning.

▷ **Motivation** – this will directly affect the child's learning as it is the child's desire to learn and the interest which they have in a task. Where a child is not interested, does not see the purpose, or is unable to do a task, they may quickly become de-motivated. The adult should therefore be aware of this and make sure that the task is at the right level, is enjoyable, and makes sense to the child.

▷ **Emotional factors** – naturally, children will be affected by whether their home life is happy and settled. Some may have been living with parents who are going though a divorce, or they may have been bereaved. Sometimes children may be deeply affected by something seemingly insignificant to an adult, such as not saying goodbye to their mother or having an argument with a sibling. Any of these things may have an impact on the child's ability to learn. You may need to take them away from the situation and talk to them to find out what is upsetting them and give them reassurance before attempting to continue. If the child is too upset to work, it is not a good idea to try to force the issue.

▷ **Gender** – the sex of a child may affect their learning, particularly if they have been given greater or fewer opportunities owing to their gender. It is important that we do not favour boys or girls in school when directing questioning and do not have expectations of one sex over another. For example, research shows that girls are generally quicker to read, but this could be due to the expectations of adults (more on this on page 160).

▷ **Ability to concentrate** – children of different ages will vary in their ability to concentrate on tasks and to sit and listen when required, although children of the same age may have a similar concentration span. Teachers should be aware of the length of time the children in their class are able to focus on a task, so that the work given or the amount of time they are required to sit still is not too demanding for them. Where one child's ability to concentrate is markedly different from that of their classmates, this may affect the learning of both the individual and of the rest of the class.

Length of concentration expected of children at different stages of development

0-2 years: children are unable to concentrate for long on one activity and will copy adults and other children. They are easily distracted from what they are doing.

2-3 years: children will start to be able to concentrate for short periods although they will find waiting difficult. They may start to play alongside other children.

3-5 years: children will be able to sit and share a story for a short time. They will start to take turns and play more co-operatively with others.

5-8 years: children will start to be able to work independently for short periods depending on their maturity and ability.

8-11 years: children should be able to focus on a task for a given time without distractions. They will be able to work on activities that require them to read instructions and carry out set tasks.

➡ Knowledge into action

Ask the class teacher if you can observe a child for a short period of time.

Find out the age of the child. How long is the child able to stay settled and focused on a task? How does this compare with others in the class and with the expected length of concentration, as described above?

How to recognise when a pupil is losing concentration

A pupil who is not focused on the teacher or the task may:

▷ start to disturb other children

▷ be distracted and fidgety

▷ misbehave and try to gain attention

▷ start daydreaming.

Where pupils are not concentrating on a given task, the teacher or assistant must ensure that they try to engage them again as soon as possible. This can be done through re-involving them in the task. You can do this by:

▷ removing any distractions. This will refocus the child's attention on what they are doing.

▷ giving praise where possible for good work which children have completed, to give them encouragement.

▷ noticing the good behaviour or work of others so that you are giving positive attention to those children who are focusing on their work.

▷ making yourself available and approachable so that children are able to ask you for help if they are finding an activity challenging. You will need to develop a good relationship with the children so that they will respect and respond to you (see page 37).

▷ being able to manage spontaneous opportunities which may arise when children are working, and remembering to make learning fun!

▷ varying the pace of learning if pupils are finding a task too easy or too difficult. You may need to backtrack, to ensure children understand the task, or find ways of extending the task if they complete it quickly.

Think about it

You are working with a group of Reception children on a maths activity. They have been asked to describe and sort a variety of different materials and put them into trays. One of the children working with you has done some sorting but is now eager to move onto another table where he sees children are working with play-doh.

What could you do to try to re-involve the child in the task? Are there any other strategies that you could use to make sure that the child completes the activity?

Understanding curriculum plans

During the early years, that is when children are at the age of 3 to the end of the Reception Year, teachers will be working from the Foundation Stage curriculum. From the ages of 5 to 7, they will be working to the first stage of the National Curriculum, called Key Stage 1, and from 7 to 11 to Key Stage 2. For the purpose of this unit you need to understand that schools and classroom teachers will be working to curriculum plans, often based around a topic, which need to incorporate the six areas of learning at the Foundation Stage, and ten subjects under the National Curriculum. Your role as an assistant is to be able to interpret these curriculum plans and help the classroom teacher to deliver them.

The Foundation Stage

The Foundation Stage curriculum is divided into six areas of learning as identified by the DfES. At the end of the 'Stepping Stones' within these areas of learning there are goals for each child to achieve. These are known as the Early Learning Goals. The six areas of learning are:

▷ personal, social and emotional development

▷ communication, language and literacy

▷ mathematical development

▷ knowledge and understanding of the world

▷ physical development

▷ creative development.

The school should have an early years policy, which will give guidelines for planning the Foundation Stage, as well as information on assessment. Teachers will therefore be planning from the six areas, usually around a topic, to give the children more continuity and greater understanding in their learning, and to work towards the Early Learning Goals which are the basis of the Foundation Stage curriculum.

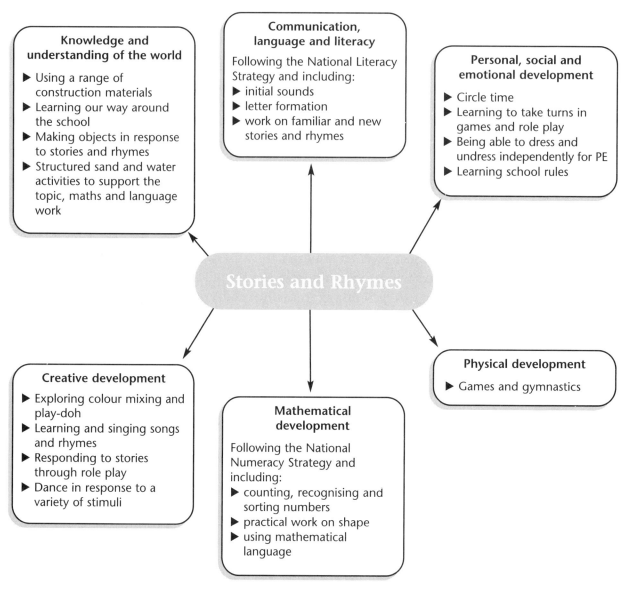

Knowledge and understanding of the world
▶ Using a range of construction materials
▶ Learning our way around the school
▶ Making objects in response to stories and rhymes
▶ Structured sand and water activities to support the topic, maths and language work

Communication, language and literacy
Following the National Literacy Strategy and including:
▶ initial sounds
▶ letter formation
▶ work on familiar and new stories and rhymes

Personal, social and emotional development
▶ Circle time
▶ Learning to take turns in games and role play
▶ Being able to dress and undress independently for PE
▶ Learning school rules

Stories and Rhymes

Creative development
▶ Exploring colour mixing and play-doh
▶ Learning and singing songs and rhymes
▶ Responding to stories through role play
▶ Dance in response to a variety of stimuli

Mathematical development
Following the National Numeracy Strategy and including:
▶ counting, recognising and sorting numbers
▶ practical work on shape
▶ using mathematical language

Physical development
▶ Games and gymnastics

▲ A topic web for the Foundation Stage using stories and rhymes

The above topic web gives an indication of how a topic such as Stories and Rhymes can be used to develop all six areas of the Foundation curriculum. As can be seen, the topic is used throughout the curriculum and links the areas of learning together, where possible.

Key Stages 1 and 2

From the end of Reception onwards, children will be learning through curriculum plans based on the National Curriculum document. This gives a more formal and subject-based approach to the way in which the curriculum is organised. The topic web opposite gives an example of how this has to link to a wider range of subjects.

▲ During the early years, children will be developing skills in all six areas of the Foundation curriculum

Year 1 Topic – Transport

Numeracy
Following the numeracy strategy
Maths from topic
Surveys
• Types of transport
• Ways of travelling
• Colours of staff cars
• Make sets, bar charts and graphs

History
Investigate how people used to travel
Changes to transport plus reasons
Find out about past from a range of sources
Famous men and women from the past
  related to transport stories, e.g. *Titanic*
Timelines

Geography
Views about street improvements
Design a housing area with regard to
  road safety
Maps

Science
Pushing and pulling (forces)
Investigating how vehicles move and work
Which factors affect movement, using ramps
Gravity
Unusual types of transport: canoes, hot air
  balloons, etc.

▲ Part of a Year 1 topic web on transport

By the beginning of Key Stage 2, the focus of teaching may be more on individual subject areas, although children will still have topics within subjects, for example they will learn about Victorians as part of their Year 6 History.

Each of the subjects should have a member of staff responsible for making sure that they are monitored throughout the school, to attend curriculum courses to remain up to date, and to offer curriculum support to other members of staff. These subject leaders will usually be called subject co-ordinators, or subject managers, for example 'Geography Manager'. They will also need to devise school curriculum policies for each subject which should outline the school's approach to planning and delivering the subject, and will tie in with National Curriculum guidelines. In this way, each subject is thoroughly monitored. In a large school, members of staff will have only one subject to manage but in smaller schools they will need to take on more than this.

Find out about...

Curriculum areas in your school.
▶ Who is responsible for English, Maths and Science?
▶ How do they monitor the curriculum within your school?

Long-, medium- and short-term planning

Where teaching staff devise topic webs for use over a term or half a term, these will then need to be broken down into medium-term (weekly) and finally short-term or daily plans which will give greater detail. For example, a medium-term plan for the topic of 'holidays' may include 'children to think about items they would need on holiday'. A short-term plan would then give more detail about which groups would be working on this at a given time and the exact task, so that the teacher and assistant know which individual or group of pupils they are working with at each time of day, and the learning outcomes for each session.

The headteacher will usually need to see all copies of plans and staff may discuss them at the long-term planning stage so that everyone's suggestions and expertise are included. When teachers' plans are at the medium-term and short-term stages, there should be consultation with assistants so that they are aware of their role, and have copies of plans so that they can refer to them. A weekly meeting with the class teacher should be an important part of the assistant's timetable, so that the teacher can be sure of involving the assistant for maximum benefit to the children. This should enable the assistant to put forward ideas and offer suggestions based on their own experiences. It will also ensure that the assistant is aware of any changes to the normal routine that are to take place during the following week.

Activities	Learning objectives	Assessment/ Evaluation
'Brainstorm' ideas about living things (children to make simple notes or key-words). Can split into people, animals, plants, etc.	**English**: Range of non-chronological writing **Science**: Relate knowledge about living things Group/sort information	Went very well – children developed sub-categories: i.e. animals into mammals/reptiles
Ask children to give examples of living/non-living things	**English**: Speak confidently. Include relevant detail. Listen to and respond to others.	Both discussions: children devised criteria that fitted both animal and plant
Discuss cues that let us know that something is alive	**Science**: Make simple comparisons Draw conclusions Does evidence support predictions/conclusions? Draw upon knowledge and understanding	

▲ Example of part of a medium-term plan for Year 2 – Life and Living Processes

'By the way, we are going on a visit to the local allotments this afternoon, is that all right?'

▲ Assistants should be aware of the teacher's plans

? *Think about it*

What opportunities do you have for discussion with your teacher or supervisor about short-term planning? How does this help you to organise your tasks during the week?

How pupils may be supported during learning activities

When supporting pupils for different activities, assistants may find themselves in a variety of situations. An individual support assistant, for example, will be assisting and supporting a particular child and will usually work alongside or close to that child. As that child may have a Statement of Special Educational Needs, they will need that adult support to ensure that they have full access to the curriculum.

Sometimes, teaching assistants will be asked to work with a group of children. In this situation, it is vital that all children are given the same opportunities to give their thoughts and opinions.

You may also find in the course of your work with children that, while working on a particular idea, other learning opportunities become available. You should always use these wherever possible so that the interest of the children is maintained and you capitalise on any ideas that they put forward. Assistants will need to use a range of strategies to support the planned learning activities.

▼ Strategies to support learning activities

Skills and strategies used	What to do
1 Instructing pupils	
Teacher may give you methods to teach specific concepts	Ensure that you are clear about the concept and understand the method
You may have the freedom to work on your own ideas	Give children a starting point so that they are able to focus
2 Questioning pupils	
Use open-ended questions	Who/what/why, rather than yes/no
Find out what they know first	Make sure children understand topic/are focused
Question all in group	Address pupils by name – ensure both quiet and enthusiastic are included

Skills and strategies used	What to do
3 Monitoring pupils Monitor pupils' response to learning activities	Ensure that the child is able to achieve Adapt the work so that the children maintain their interest
4 Explaining to pupils Make sure all children understand the task Make sure all children understand the concept they are required to learn	Before you start the activity ask the children what they have to do Talk to children to check their understanding – rephrase any difficult vocabulary

Effective use of praise during learning activities

As you will be working with children who are learning all the time, it is vital that you use praise and encouragement to keep them on task and motivate them in their learning. This kind of reward is very effective, although it must be clear to children why they are being praised. It is important as you get to know children to praise their efforts as well as their achievements. They will need to have recognition for what they do, and this could take several forms, although you will need to find out the school's policy on the use of rewards, for example:

▷ verbal praise – this could be simple praise as the children are working, by saying 'well done, that is a very good drawing,' or by asking the child to go and show the teacher at a convenient moment and so gaining another adult's attention

▷ stickers, stamps and charts – there could be a school policy on how these are used, and you should be aware of this. Some schools will leave it to the class teacher to use reward systems that they find the most beneficial, whereas some may not like the free use of stickers

▷ a school recognition of a good effort, such as the child showing the headteacher, or gaining a school certificate, will offer motivation right through a child's school life.

✔ **Keys to good practice**
Supporting children during learning activities

✔ Ensure both you and the children understand what you are required to do.

✔ Use a range of questioning strategies.

✔ Make sure you listen to all the children.

✔ Reassure children who are less confident about their ideas.

✔ Give positive praise wherever possible.

✔ Adapt work where necessary.

✔ Inform the teacher of any problems which have taken place.

✔ Provide a level of assistance which allows children to achieve without helping them too much.

Equal opportunities and inclusion, including supporting children with Special Educational Needs

As a teaching assistant, you will need to be aware of the way in which children with special needs are supported in school and how the process works. Some assistants are also employed specifically to support individual children and may need training to be fully aware of that child's needs. There is a range of reasons why a child may have special needs, for example pupils with:

▷ learning needs across the curriculum

▷ specific learning difficulties

▷ sensory or physical needs

▷ emotional or behavioural needs.

The Education Act (1996) states that a child has Special Educational Needs if they have a learning difficulty which calls for special educational provision to be made for them. This may be a difficulty in learning which prevents the child from working at the same level as the majority of children the same age. The child may also have a disability which prevents or hinders them from making use of facilities available to others the same age. However, this should not mean that the child is excluded from mainstream school, and wherever possible these children should be included. (See also pages 111 and 221 for more on the Disability Discrimination Act.)

Children who speak English or Welsh as an additional language may also have special educational provision, although they should not be regarded as having a learning difficulty. This support may come from an outside agency that specialises in working with children whose first language is not English. They should not need to be put on the school's Special Educational Needs register while they are having support for their language skills. For more on supporting children who speak English or Welsh as an additional language, see Unit 3-12.

Statementing

You may encounter children who have been given a Statement of Special Educational Needs, or you may have been employed as an individual support assistant to help one of these children in the classroom. They will have been through a process to determine whether they need to have support in school, which will result in the child being given a Statement and this means they will have an individual support assistant for an agreed number of hours per week. At a classroom level, this will mean that the assistant will work with the child's class teacher, taking into account the individual child's needs. There is more about children with special needs in Units 3-13 to 3-16.

Schools need to provide a range of strategies and support while children are at different stages on the Special Needs Register, but at Stage S, or when they have a Statement, these will be specified by the Local Education Authority and written down on the child's Statement. The child's case will need to be formally reviewed annually, which means that everyone who plays a part in supporting the child in school will need to attend a review meeting. Where an assistant is specifically employed to work with a child who has a Statement, the assistant will be expected to take part in the annual review. This will involve writing a short report about the child and attending the review meeting with the Special Needs Co-ordinator, teacher, parents and other representatives. (There will be more on special needs and individual support assistants in Units 3-13 to 3-16.)

Knowledge into action

Find out about any assistants in your school who are employed specifically to work with individual children. How might their role be different from that of a classroom assistant?

Promoting equal opportunities and inclusion

At the time of writing, there is much work going into the promotion of inclusion in mainstream schools. This means that more children with special needs and disabilities are to be educated alongside their peers wherever possible. The reasons for this are as follows:

1 Human rights

▷ All children have a right to learn and play together.

▷ Children should not be discriminated against due to learning difficulties or disabilities.

▷ Inclusion is concerned with improving schools for staff as well as for pupils.

2 Equal opportunities in education

▷ Children do better in inclusive settings, both academically and socially.

▷ Children should not need to be separated to achieve adequate educational provision.

▷ Inclusive education is a more efficient use of educational resources.

3 Social opportunities

▷ Inclusion in education is one aspect of inclusion in society.

▷ Children need to be involved with all of their peers.

As a result of this, schools may be in the process of writing or reviewing their codes of practice concerning equal opportunities and inclusion. There may also be more assistants in schools supporting children with Statements. You should be familiar with your school's policies on inclusion and equal opportunities. There will be more information on inclusion in the learning environment in Unit 3-5.

Case study

Hannah is a Year 3 child with a hearing impairment who attends a mainstream school. She has two hearing aids and has a Statement of Special Educational Needs for five hours a week. As Hannah's support assistant, you receive advice from the local sensory support service who have said that she needs to build her confidence when working with others as she feels isolated by her hearing impairment.

1 How could you help Hannah and involve her with other pupils so that she can gain confidence?

2 What could other pupils do to help Hannah?

Managing problems when supporting learning activities

It may be that assistants who are supporting individuals, groups or the whole class encounter problems when supporting learning activities. These could take different forms but could relate to learning resources, the learning environment or the pupils' ability to learn.

▼ Strategies for resolving difficulties

Potential difficulties	How to resolve them
1 Learning resources	The task will usually require a certain amount of resources, for example pencils, paper, worksheets or textbooks, maths apparatus, paint-pots, science equipment and so on. If you have been asked to set up for the children you are working with, make sure that you have enough equipment and that it is accessible to the children. Also, where you have equipment which needs to be in working order, check that you know how to use it, it is functioning and that the children will be able to use it. If the teacher or another adult has set up for your task, it is still worth doing a check to ensure that you have everything you will need. In this way you will have avoided potential problems before they arise.
2 Learning environment Problems may arise if there is:	This relates to the suitability of the area where the children are working.
a insufficient space to work	If the children are working on weighing, for example, and there is no room for them all to have access to the scales, they may quickly lose their focus on the task. There may not be space around the table or work area for the number of children that you have been asked to work with. You should always ensure that you have sufficient space for people and equipment before you start.
b too much noise	The children may be working with you in a corner of the classroom but any other kind of noise will be a distraction, whether it is from other children in the room or from some kind of outside disturbance, such as grass cutting, or noise from a nearby road. It may be possible in this situation for you to investigate another area within the school which is free from this kind of noise, or inform the teacher that the noise level within the classroom is preventing the children from benefiting from the activity.
c disturbances from other children	This can often be a problem if you are working within the classroom as tasks with close adult supervision can often seem exciting to other children. They may be naturally curious to find out what the group or individual is doing, and if there is a continual problem, the teacher should be informed. A good diversion is often to say that they will all be having a turn as long as they allow others to have theirs.

Potential difficulties	How to resolve them
3 The pupils' ability to learn Here, again, there may be a variety of reasons why pupils are not able to achieve: **a pupils' behaviour**	If any children are not focused on the task due to poor behaviour, you will need to intervene straight away. If they can continue interrupting, they will do so and you will be unable to continue with the task. Always praise the good behaviour of any children who are doing what is required of them, as this sometimes makes the others try to gain your attention by behaving well. If there is a particular child who is misbehaving and disturbing others, a last resort will be to remove them from the group and work with them later.
b pupils' self-esteem	Sometimes a child with low self-esteem may not think that they are able to complete the task which has been set. Some children are quite difficult to motivate and you will need to offer reassurance and praise wherever you can to improve their self-esteem. However it is very important to remember that your role is one of a facilitator and that you are not there to complete the task for the child. Some children may just need a little gentle reassurance and coaxing to 'have a go', while others may be more difficult to work with, and require you to use your questioning skills.
c pupils' lack of concentration	There may be a few reasons for pupils finding it hard to concentrate on the task set. These could include an inability to complete the work – the teacher has made the task too difficult – or the child completes the task quickly and needs more stimulation. Some children have a very short concentration span, particularly younger ones, and the task may be taking too long to complete. If this is the case, you will need to stop the child and continue with the task later.
d pupils' range of ability	You may find that you are working with a class or group of children whose wide range of ability means that some of them are finished before others. If you are faced with a situation where one child has finished while others are still working, you may need to have something else ready for them to move on to, for example if a group of Year 2 children are working on an activity to find words ending in -ing, you could ask them to use them in sentences of their own.

? **Think about it**

You have been asked to work with a group of Year 6 children within the classroom on a task which involves the use of Newton Meters and other equipment. Although you have sufficient space to carry out the task, you quickly find that due to the interest generated, children from other groups are repeatedly disturbing your activities, as they are interested in finding out what is happening.

▶ How could you ensure that other children do not continue to disturb you?

▶ What could you say to the children with whom you are working?

Where you are faced with difficulties in supporting pupils and are unable to get them to achieve the learning outcomes which have been set, you must always make sure that the teacher is aware of the problems. This is because each child needs to be monitored with regard to their learning, and this will need to be recorded.

Case study

You are working outside with a group of children who have been asked to carry out different measuring activities using a trundle wheel. Although you are only working with six children, two of them are not behaving as they should or recording their activities.

1 What would you say to the children who are not focused on the task?

2 How could you encourage them to work with the others on what they should be doing?

3 What would you do if the children continued to behave in this way?

Element 3-3.2 Promote independent learning

Children will need to be encouraged to think and act for themselves as much as possible both during the early years and throughout their time in primary school. As an assistant, you will need to learn skills and strategies for developing these abilities in children. You will also need to be aware of different learning styles and how to adapt your support strategies to accommodate them. Remember that young children develop at very different rates – some will be able to pick things up quickly and concentrate for long periods, while others will seem 'younger' and need to have more support. As a result, the teacher will need to differentiate tasks, or give children work that is appropriate to their own ability.

For this element you will need to know and understand the following:

▶ supporting different learning styles

▶ strategies to encourage children to learn independently

▶ helping pupils to review their own learning.

Supporting different learning styles

Children need to be given opportunities to learn and discover things for themselves where possible. In this way, they will have ownership of their learning. Assistants will find that there are different ways in which children are given tasks to do within the learning framework. In order to encourage and support children with learning activities, you will need to be aware of different learning styles. Assistants will need to know the best way to support these different learning styles so that children are able to gain the most from each.

Different types of learning styles

▷ **Repetition** – the child is given a task which involves going over something which the teacher has done in class, for example the sound 'g'. The children may then be asked to complete some work which involves writing and saying 'g' several times, but is set out in such a way as to challenge the children and also to ensure that they achieve the objectives. When working on a repetitive task, children will need support which involves reminding them about what the teacher has said and provoking them to think about what they are doing, but without giving them the answers. Sometimes it is a good idea to ask the child what they have been asked to do, as it is a starting point to finding out how much they have taken in.

▷ **Instruction** – children may be set a task which involves following a series of steps. This will lead them to arriving at a set outcome, for example when they are learning to make a pop-up card or to cut and stick pictures in the right order. It could also include learning to carry out simple number operations. In this situation, assistants will find that they are leading children to a particular outcome, so the types of questions they should be asking would be, 'Why do you think we do it this way rather than another way?' or 'Do you think that this is the best way of doing this? Can you find another way?'. Questions like this will encourage children to think about what they are doing and why they are doing it in that way, which may help them to remember what they have learned.

▷ **Facilitating** – this method involves giving children the tools to carry out a task and then allowing them the freedom to devise their own outcome. An example of this may be showing them how to mix colours and then allowing them to experiment to find different shades, or giving them construction equipment and letting them discover how to use it and what they are able to do. Similar questioning styles could be used for this method as for learning by instruction, although assistants could ask children first to talk them through what they are doing and why.

▷ **Collaboration** – this method involves groups of children working together to discuss or discover ideas. In doing this, they will also learn how to work as part of a team and to listen to others' views. Some children find this easy although others will need more guidance, which is where an assistant is needed to help. An example of this could be children finding the best material to make a bag to carry potatoes, or deciding on the best way to carry out a simple maths investigation. This is one of the more challenging activities to support, as there will always be children who wish to dominate the flow of ideas and similarly children who do not mind taking a less active role. The important thing to remember is to allow everyone to give their opinion and then work out a way within the group of tackling the task.

▷ **Problem solving** – children should be given regular opportunities to solve problems and to think about different, open-ended ways of approaching tasks which may not have a set outcome. In this way they will be encouraged to think for themselves rather than relying on a particular way of working.

In a classroom, there should be a balanced mix of learning styles. However, it is important for children to have as many opportunities as possible to be responsible for their own decision-making (see below – 'Strategies to encourage children to learn independently'). This will encourage their own independence and creativity, and will also help them to gain confidence in their abilities.

▲ Allowing children to be responsible for their own decisions has some risks

Resources

These learning styles, along with the resources used, should also be agreed with the teacher before tasks are carried out. The kinds of resources you may be required to use with children will vary from books and other paper-based materials to use of the Internet and CD-ROMs. The class teacher should usually give you an indication of the resources required but you should be aware of where different curriculum areas store their resources in case you need to find them.

Strategies to encourage children to learn independently

Where you are working with children on any task, you must remember that in order to learn they should carry out the task independently as far as possible. Depending on the way that the task has been set, you should offer as much encouragement as is needed while allowing children to develop their own self-help skills.

What you can do:

▷ Give positive encouragement and praise – this will give pupils a feeling of achievement and desire to sustain their interest in learning activities. Children will be visibly boosted by praise when they are doing well.

▷ Listen carefully to pupils – children will be aware if an adult is only partially interested or paying attention to what they are saying. It is important to take notice of their contributions so that they feel that they are being valued. In this way they will feel confident in their own abilities.

▷ Motivate pupils through positive experiences which are interesting and can be made real to them. Children will particularly enjoy and benefit from having artefacts and real objects to handle when learning. For example, children learning about a religion will remember more if they have seen examples of different items which may be used.

▷ Provide a level of assistance which allows children to achieve without helping them too much. This could be simply giving them a list of things which they may need to consider when carrying out a task, or remembering not to give them help as soon as they ask for it. Try saying, ' Have you thought about another way of doing this?' or 'Are there any other things you need to remember?'

▷ Ensure that children have sufficient resources to complete the task so that they do not need to seek adult help. If you know that children are going to need particular items to carry out a task, ensure that they are accessible – or that children know where to find them within the classroom.

? *Think about it*

You have been asked to work with a group of children on individually designing and making a hat for a special occasion. What type of learning style would you use with the children? How could you encourage their independent learning without giving them too much help?

→ *Knowledge into action*

Ask the teacher if you can observe a group of children working alongside him or her. In what ways are they being encouraged to work independently?

Helping pupils to review their own learning

When children have completed a task, adults may review it with a group, or with individual children, or as a whole class. This means that they should discuss what they were asked to do and how they went about it. They may then talk about whether they think that the task went well and what they felt was successful or unsuccessful and why. This encourages the children to think about strategies and ideas they used, and also to compare their method with that of others. It is important for children to look at different ways of doing tasks so that they are aware that there may not be a right or wrong way; some children are lacking in confidence and worried about 'getting it wrong'.

→ *Knowledge into action*

Think of an example of a strategy which you have used in class to help pupils to review their learning achievements. How did this help them to plan for future learning activities?

⬛ *Case study*

Max has designed and made a lunchbox using recycled materials. He has included a handle to pick up the box. Max has found that the first handle he made was not strong enough to pick up the lunchbox, so in his review he discussed the problems that he had and how he found a better material. He then thought about and discussed with the class whether he thought any other materials may have produced even better results. Through working on different ideas and looking at other materials, Max was able to improve his design so that the lunchbox had a stronger handle.

? Think about it

You have just completed some work with a group of children on making a bag strong enough to carry potatoes. They have been given a variety of materials to look at and have discussed the different qualities of each. What types of questions could you ask the children to encourage them to think about their work? How could you reassure a child who felt unable to review what they had done?

End of unit test

1 What are the two main theories of how children learn?
2 How can you keep children motivated when they are working?
3 What are some of the factors which affect the way in which children learn?
4 How could you help a pupil who is losing concentration on a task?
5 Name the three different types of planning found in a school.
6 What are the six areas of learning in the Foundation Stage?
7 What kinds of praise can you give to children to motivate them?
8 What different types of learning styles might be found in a primary classroom?
9 What are the main principles of inclusion?
10 How can you promote independent learning in children?

References

Children Act 1989 (HMSO)

Education Act 1996 (HMSO)

Index for Inclusion (CSIE, 2000)

Curriculum Guidance for the Foundation Stage (QCA, 2000)

Review and develop your own professional practice

This unit contains two elements:

3-4.1 Review your own professional practice

3-4.2 Develop your professional practice

Element 3-4.1 Review your own professional practice

As a professional member of staff within a school, you will be expected to undergo regular staff training and courses to keep you up to date with developments in early years and primary education. You should also expect to have an annual appraisal after being in post for 12 months, or completing your probationary year. This element looks at how the appraisal or Performance Management system works within schools, and what you should expect from it. It will also explore your role and responsibilities within the school and how these fit in with the roles and responsibilities of others. For the purpose of the NVQ, you will need to collect evidence to demonstrate how you make contributions to support the teacher, the pupil, the curriculum and the school.

For this element you will need to know and understand the following:

▶ procedures and principles of self-appraisal and how to apply these to working practices

▶ school expectations and requirements about the role of a teaching assistant

▶ how to measure your own practice against the expectations of your role

▶ the main roles and responsibilities of others within the school: working with others.

Procedures and principles of self-appraisal

The appraisal system is designed to help members of staff to consider their own professional performance on a regular basis. This should ensure that they think about their career and highlight areas for development.

The main consideration is that the appraisal process is a positive and non-threatening one. Each member of staff, including headteachers, will be appraised by the person who has responsibility for managing them. In the case of the headteacher, this will usually be done by governors. With teaching staff, the process is an ongoing cycle which takes place annually. As an assistant, you may be appraised by your line manager or member of staff responsible for teaching assistants. In the case of individual support assistants, this may be done by the school's Special Needs Co-ordinator (SENCo).

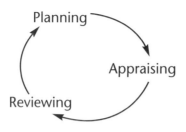

▲ The planning cycle

Assistants should find that the appraisal process is a good opportunity to discuss issues which may not otherwise be approached. It is also useful for discussing with your line manager anything you have done which you feel has been more or less successful than you had anticipated.

How the appraisal system works

The general appraisal form opposite gives some idea of how the initial discussion with your line manager might be structured. However, this is a basic outline and further ideas such as whether you would like a more formal observation of your work may be recorded. If this is the case, the focus and timing of the observation should be decided at the initial meeting. An observation may take place if you or your manager feel that you would benefit from some feedback concerning your work: for example, if you are not sure that your methods for giving children praise are as effective as you would like. You will then agree on any action to be taken and new targets for the coming year. Following the meeting, copies of the appraisal form will be given to you and to the headteacher for record keeping, but will be confidential.

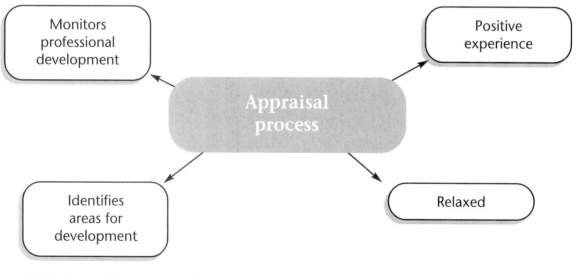

▲ Objectives of the appraisal process

✔ Check through your job description before the meeting.

✔ Be prepared by having some ideas of strengths and successes.

✔ Think about areas you may wish to develop before going to the meeting.

? *Think about it*

To help you to think about your appraisal, try completing the questions on the appraisal form below.

General self-appraisal

It would be useful if you could bring this information with you to your initial meeting, to help you to identify your needs as part of the appraisal process.

1 Do you feel that your job description is still appropriate? Do you feel that there are any changes which need to be made?

2 What targets were set at the last appraisal/when you started your job? Have you achieved your targets?

3 What are the reasons for not having achieved your targets?

4 What aspect of your job satisfies you the most?

5 What aspect of your job has not been as successful as you had anticipated?

6 Are there any areas of your work that you would like to improve?

7 What training have you received? Has it been successful?

8 What are your current training needs?

▲ The first page of an appraisal form

→ **Knowledge into action**

Find out who is responsible for carrying out appraisal for assistants within your school. Have a look at an appraisal form. How does it compare with the form above?

School expectations and requirements about the role of the teaching assistant

When starting at a new school, the duties and individual requirements of each teaching assistant's job will be outlined in their job description. It is important to keep a copy of this, as it will be useful to read it from time to time to check that it is a realistic reflection of expectations.

Assistants may take on a number of different roles depending on these criteria (see also the introduction for a description of these). Broadly speaking, their role is to encourage, guide, assist and support – both practically and on a curricular level.

? **Think about it**

What do you know about your role? Can you list some of the different expectations which are required of you?

The types of responsibilities which may be required of teaching assistants

Assistants are likely to have a number of responsibilities within the school, both in and outside the classroom. The responsibilities of a teaching assistant and individual support assistant will be slightly different, although there may be areas in which they overlap – for example helping to prepare resources in the classroom as all assistants should be prepared to give this type of help.

How the responsibilities of classroom assistants and individual support assistants may differ

Classroom assistant	Individual support assistant
Duties may include:	**Duties may include:**
Assisting teacher with classroom organisation	Developing an understanding of the specific needs of the child
Attending planning meetings	To assist the class teacher with the development of an individual programme of support
Preparing resources	
Supervising individual children or groups	To help the child to learn effectively

You will need to be aware of the many different tasks which an assistant may be asked to carry out. Although schools will usually have outlined these at interview or in a job description, you do not want to be surprised by any requests on the first day! Make sure that you are aware of the possible tasks which you may be required to do. You may require training or help if you have not done some of these before.

How would you feel about being asked to:

▷ mount and put up wall displays

▷ look after a child who has wet themselves

▷ get a computer suite ready for a class to use

▷ cook with a group of children

▷ do playground duty.

? Think about it

What types of tasks have you been asked to do in the classroom? Are any of them different to those listed above?

This list is not exhaustive and there may be a broader range of activities which an assistant may be asked to perform. In many cases, simply having another adult in the classroom will take the pressure off the class teacher when calming children or coping with practical tasks. It would be useful to have some time with the teacher on a weekly basis or access to timetable or plans so that work may be fully supported and there is some prior knowledge of the kind of work that will be required during the week. The teacher should also give more detailed guidance when the assistant is required to work with a group of children.

If there are any administrative difficulties, with details such as contracts or hours worked, they will usually be addressed by the school office in consultation with the headteacher.

It should be remembered that the role of a teaching assistant is one of support. The assistant will need to be able to take responsibility for the class on some occasions but this will always have been indicated by the class teacher. It may be difficult on occasions to 'read' a situation and the advice of the class teacher should always be sought if there is any problem or doubt as to how to proceed.

Case study

Sarah has been employed as an individual support assistant in an infant school. She has been working there for three weeks when she is asked to accompany the child she supports on a school trip. Although she is only employed to work mornings, she is expected to be on the trip for the whole day.

1 What should Sarah do if she is concerned about the hours she is expected to work?

2 Would Sarah be justified in saying that she was unable to go on the trip?

Oakhurst Junior School

Job Description

Teaching Assistant

Responsibilites

Responsible under the direction of the headteacher or another designated teacher to assist in the classroom.

Duties

Main duties will include:

▷ Assisting in classroom organisation, preparing materials and resources where appropriate.

▷ Supervising activities organised by the classroom teacher.

▷ Supervising children usually in the presence of a teacher.

▷ Providing general care and welfare.

▷ Any other duties as required commensurate with the level of responsibility of the post.

▲ An example of a job description for a teaching assistant

There may also be a 'Person Specification', which should set out personal qualities which are relevant to the particular post. It may include some of the strengths listed below.

Be a good communicator/enjoy working with others

It is vital that an assistant is able to share thoughts and ideas with others, and is comfortable doing this.

Use initiative

Assistants will need to be able to decide for themselves how to use their time if the teacher is not always available to ask. There will always be jobs which need doing in a classroom, even if this just means sharpening pencils or making sure that books are tidy and in the right place.

Respect confidentiality

It should be remembered that in a position of responsibility, it is essential to maintain confidentiality. Assistants may sometimes find that they are placed in a position where they are made aware of personal details concerning a child or family. Although background and school records are available to those within the school, it is not appropriate to discuss them with outsiders.

Be sensitive to children's needs

Whether an individual or classroom assistant, it is important to be able to judge how much support to give while still encouraging children's independence. Children need to be sure about what they have been asked to do and may need help organising their thoughts or strategies, but it is the child who must do the work and not the assistant.

Have good listening skills

A teaching assistant needs to be able to listen to others and have a sympathetic nature. This is an important quality for your interactions, both with children and other adults.

Be willing to undertake training for personal development

In any school there will always be occasions on which assistants are invited or required to undergo training and these opportunities should be used where possible. You may also find that your role changes within the school due to movement between classes or changing year groups. You will need to be flexible and willing to rise to different expectations.

Be firm but fair with the children

Children will always quickly realise if an adult is not able to set fair boundaries of behaviour. Adults should always make sure that when they start working with children they make these boundaries clear.

Enjoy working with children and have a sense of humour

Assistants will need to be able to see the funny side of working with children and it is often a very useful asset!

▲ A sense of humour is useful when working with children

How to measure you own practice against expectations of your role

As part of your NVQ, you will be expected to be able to show how you contribute to your working environment by the support you give to others. You should work closely with your line manager or supervisor, who should be able to advise you on the most effective ways of turning your experiences into evidence for your portfolio. Think carefully about your job description and how it relates to the following.

How you support the teacher within the school

This will include the type of support you give to the teacher, which may be in the form of many different tasks. It may be helpful for your class teacher to discuss with you some of the ways in which your work and roles complement one another. This could be through planning, practical tasks or support you give with often minor activities, which can build up when dealing with a class.

How you support the class or individual pupil

You will also be required to provide evidence of ways in which you support and raise pupil achievement within the school. It can be easier for individual support assistants

▲ The games you make for children can be used as evidence for your portfolio

than for teaching assistants to find this evidence. This is because they are working with one child and are focusing on individual targets and areas for that child, through working on Individual Education Plans (IEPs). They will also have the input of other professionals, as well as the class teacher, to give them ideas and support when implementing IEP targets. They will therefore be able to see how that child is developing and have more evidence of how their work has had an effect.

Teaching assistants may need to keep records of achievement of specific children with whom they work within their class in order to demonstrate that they are raising pupil achievement. When entering a new class, it is worth asking the class teacher what kinds of work you may able to use for evaluation purposes. You may also be able to photograph pieces of work the children have done with you, or any displays for which you have been responsible. If you have the opportunity to make any games which you then use with the children, it would be a good idea to photograph the children using them.

How you support the curriculum

You will need to think about ways in which you help the class to gain access to the curriculum. Consider especially the support you give during the Literacy and Numeracy hours and any additional training which you have undertaken.

▲ You can help the class to gain access to the curriculum in a variety of ways

How you support the school

This will be through your attitude to others, your reliability and sense of responsibility, the way in which you react to situations which may sometimes be unexpected, and how you encourage the children in their own development of these qualities.

? Think about it

You are an assistant working in Year 6, which is located in two mobiles away from the rest of the school. You arrive early one day to prepare the classroom and notice two children from Year 4 who are damaging some plants in the school's wildlife area.

▶ What would be your first reaction?

▶ Why shouldn't you ignore what is happening?

Ofsted has produced a useful booklet, *Teaching assistants in Primary Schools*, which evaluates the contribution made by teaching assistants, particularly with regard to the Literacy and Numeracy strategies. It is available through Ofsted at the website given at the end of this unit.

Working with others

Assistants should be aware of how their role fits into the school as a whole, in order to gain an overall view of how systems will fit together.

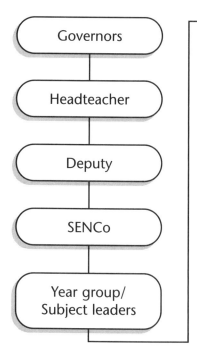

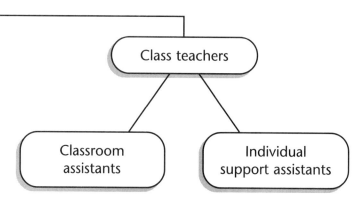

It may be that within this system, the deputy headteacher is also a year group leader, that is, responsible for all the teachers within the year. In a smaller school, with a one class entry, there will not need to be a year group leader. As will be seen later, the most important thing to remember is that the lines of communication between members of staff are kept open and that all staff are valued.

▲ Example of the management system within an infant school

The role of the school governors

Every school will have a governing body. This body is responsible, along with the headteacher, for making decisions about the school. It is made up of different groups, or committees, each of which should meet on a regular basis. These groups should then report back to the full governing body. The groups below are examples of the kinds of committees that may be found within a school governing body.

Finance Committee – this is responsible for making sure that the school's finances are managed efficiently.

Personnel Committee – this will be responsible for staffing and personnel management.

Facilities Committee – this committee has responsibility for the buildings and site management of the school.

Curriculum Committee – this will make decisions on issues involving the curriculum and whether to adopt new policies.

The governors will be representatives from the local community along with teacher and parent representatives from the school who may bring different areas of expertise. There may be a governor who has particular knowledge about legal issues. Another may be more knowledgeable in the area of finance. Together these volunteers will have a wide area of knowledge which may be useful when discussing issues relating to the school.

Find out about...

Your school's governing body.
▶ How often do they meet together?
▶ Are staff in the school aware of the role of the school governors?
▶ Is there a teacher or staff governor?

The role of the headteacher

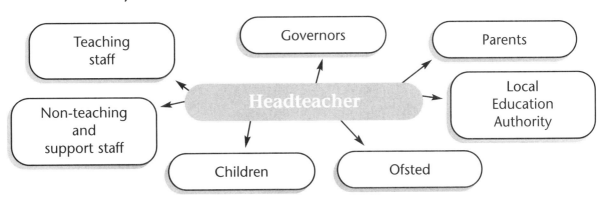

▲ The role of the headteacher is to manage all aspects of the school

The headteacher is responsible for managing the school and all those within it, as well as making sure that the curriculum is being effectively taught and managed. He or she is answerable to parents, the local authority and Ofsted for the smooth running and efficiency of the school, and whether it represents good value for money. The headteacher will be a member of all the committees in the school's governing body and will need to attend all meetings.

The role of the deputy

The deputy headteacher usually still acts in a teaching role, although in some larger schools this may not be the case. The deputy may be responsible for managing day-to-day arrangements such as organising supply staff and setting up training courses, arranging visits by student teachers and so on. The deputy needs to liaise with the headteacher on a daily basis concerning the day's priorities. The deputy works alongside the headteacher to manage the school, and can advise staff. When the headteacher is absent from the school, the deputy is responsible for its management.

Knowledge into action

What role does the deputy headteacher play in your school? If the deputy has a teaching commitment, does he or she have time out of the classroom for any managerial duties?

Year group or subject leaders

Year group or subject leaders will have responsibility for a subject or for managing a group of teachers within their year. This may be the case in both primary and secondary schools. These teachers may be members of the school's senior management team and, along with the headteacher and deputy, be involved in decisions about practical and day-to-day issues, such as:

▷ organisation of staff
▷ planning extra curricular activities
▷ fundraising events
▷ arranging the school calendar
▷ initial discussion of areas for development (School Improvement or Development Plan).

Special Educational Needs Co-ordinator (SENCo)

The SENCo is responsible for managing children with special needs throughout the school. They will need to keep up-to-date records on all these children as well as being responsible for the management of individual support assistants in the school. The SENCo will be the line of contact for any outside agencies who need to come into the school to look at individual children with special needs.

These may include the following:

▷ **Speech and Language Unit** – offers therapy and advice for children with speech and communication difficulties. Parents will usually take children for therapy. May also come into school to give advice for targets.

▷ **Behaviour Management Unit** – SENCO may refer children to this unit. They will then come into school to observe and give individual or group sessions.

▷ **Educational psychologist** – based at the local authority, the EP will come into school to assess children who are in need of extra support.

▷ **Learning Support Service** – offers advice for staff and comes into school to offer support. It may be able to provide additional help in areas such as literacy. Usually a limited number of hours per term.

▷ **English as an Additional Language Unit** – take EAL children for assessment and small group work during school hours.

▷ **Sensory Support Service** – offers advice and support for children with sensory impairment, e.g. visual or aural.

▷ **Occupational therapist/physiotherapist** – may be referred by school but usually takes place elsewhere. There may be a waiting list.

→ Knowledge into action

If you are an individual support assistant, what contact have you had with any of these agencies? How do they help the child you are supporting?

Class teachers

The class teacher is responsible for delivering the Foundation or National Curriculum to their class. In both primary and secondary schools they may also be responsible for managing a subject area. They will also advise any support staff within their class as to what they are required to do on a daily basis.

How information is passed through the school

Clear communication within any establishment is important. Within each school there will be procedures through which information reaches each member of staff. This is to ensure that everyone is aware of their responsibilities and knows what is happening in the school.

Information can be passed on through:

▷ meetings (governors, teaching staff, senior management, year groups, assistants, midday supervisors may all have their own meetings)

▷ noticeboards and newsletters

▷ informal discussions

▷ staff bulletins

▷ Parent Teacher Association.

Support staff will report to their class teacher on a daily basis and be guided by them as to their activities with children. However, classroom and support assistants may also have their own manager, or teacher who is responsible for passing on any information to them. In a larger school there may be regular meetings specifically for assistants. In a smaller school, or if there is no such meeting, it is important that there are opportunities for them to discuss their role with a named member of staff. This will ensure that assistants are aware of important issues within the school as a whole. It is also a good way of getting to chat to others who are doing the same job, and to share ideas and experiences. While classroom assistants and individual support assistants report to the class teacher on a daily basis and are guided by them as to their day-to-day activities with the children, it is usually the case that another member of staff will be their overall manager.

> ### Knowledge into action

How often do you have meetings with your line manager? What sorts of topics are discussed? Keep a record of these so that you are able to report on them if you need to.

Case study

Alex has just started as a classroom assistant at a primary school. She is told that although working with one teacher for most of the time, she is also to be 'shared' on two afternoons between two other teachers.

1 What might be the advantages and disadvantages of working between two classes?

2 What opportunities should Alex have to speak to someone about her role?

Element 3-4.2 Develop your professional practice

This element shows how you can make use of development opportunities within your employment. It will give an idea of some of the ways in which you can access specific training opportunities to benefit your own needs and those of the children you support. It will also give you examples of how you may raise your own professional development through other opportunities which arise in your normal day-to-day practice. You will also need to know how to demonstrate and present evidence that you are raising pupils' achievement within the class. Finally, you need to be aware of national and local developments and how these will affect your role within the school.

For this element you will need to know and understand the following:

▶ development opportunities and support systems which are available to assistants

▶ models of performance which apply to teaching assistants

▶ the implementation of School Development Plans and local and national plans for development which may have an impact on your role within the school.

Development opportunities and support systems

Teaching assistants may find that, following the appraisal process, there are particular targets which they need to address concerning their own professional development. In order to develop professionally, it is important for assistants to be aware of the different opportunities which are available to them. The targets which are decided upon at appraisal need to be SMART, that is, Specific, Measurable, Achievable, Realistic and Time-bound.

▷ **Specific** – you must make sure your target says exactly what is required.

▷ **Measurable** – you should ensure that you will be able to measure whether the target has been achieved.

▷ **Achievable** – the target should not be inaccessible or too difficult.

▷ **Realistic** – you should ensure that you will have access to the training or resources which may be required.

▷ **Time-bound** – there should be a limit to the time you have to achieve your target.

Example of the types of targets decided upon at appraisal

Target	Action
To develop confidence using computer. To access training and qualifications	To take at least one basic computer course during the year
To be able to take Early Literacy Strategy groups by the end of term	To undertake training in Early Literacy Strategy
To develop understanding of dyspraxia during the year	To undertake training courses with qualifications where available

The individual support assistant who was the subject of this appraisal (see table on previous page) felt that she did not have enough awareness of dyspraxia to support the child effectively. It was agreed that she should attend training courses as soon as possible in order to benefit both her and the child. She also felt that she did not have enough confidence when using the computer and that this was preventing her from helping both the child she was supporting and also other children in the class. It was agreed that she should attend further courses for this but in the meantime to use the computer in the classroom wherever possible so that she could increase her confidence. The class teacher would need to be aware of this target so that the assistant could be fully supported.

There may also be other targets which assistants feel they need to develop and which can be accessed through visiting other classes in the school or observing Literacy or Numeracy lessons. These targets should all be agreed within a set time scale so that they can be reviewed at a later date.

Finding out about courses which are available

Assistants will usually be able to find out through their school the different courses which may be available to them. You may find that the school invites people from various agencies to speak to staff about particular subject areas during staff meetings, and these may be optional for support staff. Your line manager or supervisor should be able to give you information about training and help you to decide on the best courses and meetings to attend. The SENCo may be able to give you details about specific special educational needs courses, such as those run by the Sensory Support Service, or Behaviour Management Unit. Where you are not in a school or have difficulty finding help, the Local Education Authority should publish details of courses which are run for teachers and support staff. You may also be able to contact the local borough for information about training for assistants as this is undergoing a period of national change. The borough's education department should have a member of staff responsible for training who will also be able to advise you.

Case study

Shona has been working in a pre-school attached to a primary school. She has just heard that a child with a hearing impairment is to start at the pre-school in the following term. She would like to find out more about how she may be able to help the child when he starts.

1 Where could Shona get some more information about helping hearing-impaired children?

2 Is there anything else Shona could do to prepare for the child's entry into pre-school?

Other development opportunities which may exist in school

If you are employed by the school as a teaching assistant on a permanent contract, you may find that you are able to have some say in choosing to work in an area of particular interest. For example, if you have always been in a Year 2 class but would like to find out more about the Foundation Stage and work in a Reception class, you may be able to request a change of year group through discussion with your supervisor or at appraisal. You may also find that you have always worked with the same teacher and would benefit from seeing how other teachers work. It is always worth asking about areas of interest so that your supervisor is aware of them.

On a wider ranging note, you would benefit from being part of any local cluster groups or other networks for assistants. These may be formed from a group of local schools who meet regularly to discuss early years practice or just to give each other moral support. You may be surprised at how much valuable information and support may be gained from these meetings. Your school early years manager should have information about any involvement in local groups.

Knowledge into action

What particular areas of interest do you have in the curriculum? Do you know the member of staff responsible for this curriculum area? How could you develop your interest in this area?

Keys to good practice
Areas for development

✔ Make sure you are aware of when and where courses are run for support staff.

✔ Look out for opportunities for development as they become available.

✔ Speak to your line manager or the curriculum manager about particular areas of interest.

✔ Keep up to date with national developments through reading educational publications.

✔ Join any local early years cluster groups or networks.

Models of performance which apply to teaching assistants

Assistants should be aware of models of performance which will have an impact on their training needs for professional qualifications. The National Occupational Standards for

Teaching Assistants offer guidance on the wider aspects of competent performance. They have been accredited by the Qualifications and Curriculum Authority (QCA), and are an important basis of practice. They form the basis for the NVQ and SNVQ Levels 2 and 3. Other models of performance which are accessible to assistants include local and national guidelines for codes of practice, provided by government bodies such as the DfES and Ofsted. These are often available in school or through the DfES and Ofsted websites.

Assistants should also be aware that they can access expert advice and working practices by looking at practitioners within both the school and local authority. You may need to ask your line manager if you can watch experienced assistants at work in the school, or whether you can speak to local support service staff about any particular needs which you may have.

The types of problems which may arise

You may find that while you are working towards your own professional development you come up against problems within your own school. These may, for example, be concerning other individuals with whom you work, or your own training needs. You should make sure that you address any problems as soon as possible although this can often be difficult to do.

▷ Speak to your line manager if you feel that you are not being given enough direction by the class teacher. It may be that there is a limited amount of time to discuss plans or go through work that you are going to do with the children. It is vital that you are able to communicate and will save valuable time in the long run.

▷ If there is not enough management time or advice being given to you and other assistants, you should approach a member of staff that you feel is experienced and will offer practical advice. This may be the class teacher or another person within the school who you can approach in confidence.

▷ If you feel that your training needs are not being met, or that you do not have access to training materials and information, you should discuss this with your line manager or, if this is not possible, another member of the senior management team. They will be able to advise you and give you ideas about career development.

▷ If there are any targets which have been set but which are not being addressed, again you should discuss these with your line manager.

Where there are difficulties with individual members of staff, for example your line manager is off sick long term, you may need to use your discretion and ask for advice from any member of staff in the school who you feel is approachable. Remember it is important for the school as well as your own personal development that you are properly trained and guided in your role.

Case study

You have been asked to work in a Reception class for two terms to cover another assistant's maternity leave. You feel that you should have some training on the Foundation Stage but there has been none offered. You do not like to rock the boat as you are happy in your school but feel that you need to know more about your role in order to carry out your duties effectively.

▶ What should you do?

The implementation of school development plans

School Improvement, or School Development Plans, are documents which are usually devised by the headteacher after consultation with the teaching staff. They give details of any curriculum or other areas within the school which are to be developed over the coming year. They may be broken down into sections which set out the aims and success criteria for each area of development. Support staff should be involved in areas for development as they may require training along with teaching staff. An example of this would be the introduction of new IT training within the school, or a set of new school rules. The School Development Plan may list around 8-10 areas for development over the year. There may also be a long-term Improvement Plan at the back which will give details of priorities over the next few years.

Below is an example of part of a School Development Plan in which support staff are involved.

PSHE and Citizenship	PSHE Action Plan
Aim: To improve the quality of playtime for the children	1 Raise the profile of positive playground behaviour through class 'Circle Time' and assemblies.
To improve the children's behaviour on the playground	2 Train new children as 'Playground Patrol.'
People involved: headteacher, all teaching staff, support staff, midday supervisors	3 Install new playground equipment and teach the children how to use it.
	4 Train midday supervisors and support staff and co-ordinate the introduction of playground games with the teachers.

PSHE and Citizenship	PSHE Action Plan
Targets and Success Criteria:	**5** Playground games to be taught during PE lessons and used by midday supervisors.
There will be fewer children sent to the headteacher or deputy	
Over 90% of children will enjoy playtimes	
All children will know the school's playtime rules	
Monitored by: Headteacher **Evaluated by:** PSHE Manager	

There may not be many areas for development in which support staff are specifically involved: there should, however, be school procedures in practice to ensure that they are aware of this involvement.

Any involvement which you are expected to have will have an impact on your contribution to the school's performance as a whole. It may therefore be worth considering including any involvement which you are to have as part of your own professional development targets when deciding on these at appraisal.

→ Knowledge into action

Are you aware of any involvement which support staff have in your current School Development Plan? What system does your school have in place to raise your awareness of any involvement you may have?

Local and national plans for development

As support staff, assistants will be involved with any local or national plans for development which come into effect. Recent examples of this on a national level include the introduction of the Foundation Stage in September 2000, or the Literacy and Numeracy strategies which have been implemented in all primary schools. The new Code of Practice for Special Educational Needs came into effect in January 2002 and has implications for individual support assistants in their work with SEN children. All early years settings will be expected to have a written SEN policy, and to provide the same level of support for children with special needs as schools. Support staff need to understand the implications of all curriculum changes and how they will have an effect on everyday classroom practice.

On a local level, there may not be as many changes which take place, but the Local Education Authority will advise the school, which in turn should tell you, of any changes that occur. These may involve restructuring of management within the borough or a change in documentation requirements which schools are asked to provide. If you are involved in specific requirements, you should receive guidance from your line manager or class teacher.

Within your school environment, the changes which occur are likely to be in relation to those with whom you work or working practices. If your school has a new headteacher or SENCo, or you are asked to work with a different teacher, you may find that they have a slightly different approach. You may also be able to update your own development objectives as a result of these changes, as their areas of expertise will be different.

Knowledge into action

Think about the different evidence you could present to demonstrate the work that you have done with children. How can you show that you are supporting:

a the teacher

b the pupils

c the curriculum

d the school?

End of unit test

1 Why should support staff have regular appraisal?

2 What is the role of a teaching assistant?

3 Which of the following would a teaching assistant be expected to do:

    a sharpening pencils

    b taking children to the toilet

    c doing playground duty

    d attending meetings

    e tidying the painting table?

4 What are the main committees of a school governing body? What are they responsible for?

5 Name five areas for which the headteacher is responsible.

6 What does the SENCo do within the school?

7 List some of the outside agencies who may come into school and outline their role.

8 What are the main ways in which information is passed around a school?

9 How often should an assistant expect to have an appraisal?

10 What opportunities exist for assistants to develop professionally?

11 What is a School Development Plan?

12 What types of changes may come into effect which would have an impact on your role within the school?

References

Fox, G., *A Handbook for Special Needs Assistants* (David Fulton, 1999)

National Occupational Standards L3 (CSC Consortium)

DfES, *SEN Code Of Practice*

DfES, *Performance Management in Schools* (Model Policy)

Ofsted, *Teaching Assistants in Primary Schools – An Evaluation by Ofsted 2001-2002*

Websites

www.ofsted.gov.uk

www.teachernet.gov.uk/teachingassistants

Optional units

Set A

Unit 3-5 Preparing and maintaining the learning environment

This unit looks at some of the different areas in which you will work within the school environment. It considers how you will need to familiarise yourself with different locations within the school and be able to work safely in them. You will need to know where to find equipment and learning materials for a variety of subjects as well as items in everyday use. You should also have an awareness of those members of staff responsible for maintaining stocks of materials and resources for different subjects.

Familiarisation with the learning environment

When working in a school, assistants should be aware of the different environments in which they may be expected to work. The activities within a class will not just be restricted to the classroom itself.

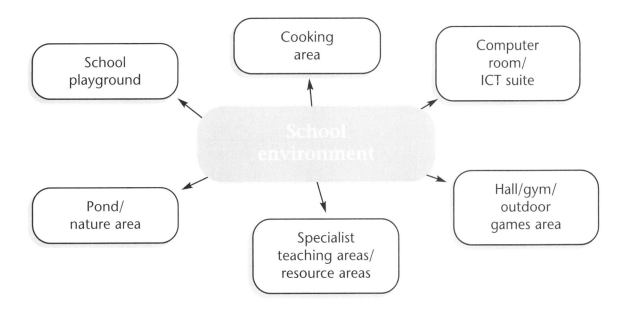

▲ The learning environment is more than just the classroom

As an assistant, you will need to be familiar with all these areas before working in them, so that you are able to plan effectively when working with children. If you are asked to work with a group or class of children and are not familiar with a particular area of the school or do not know where it is, you should always seek advice. It may not always be apparent that a particular area of the school is set aside for science activities, or where you should go to look for design and technology equipment. The school should have resource areas where members of staff will have access to equipment for each particular subject area, for example:

▷ science resources

▷ maths equipment

▷ D and T tools and equipment

▷ art resources

▷ musical instruments

▷ PE equipment

▷ geography/history resources

▷ CD-ROMs for computers

▷ RE resources

▷ personal, social and health education (PSHE) resources.

Some of these, such as PE equipment, may be immediately apparent. However, if there is a small subject area which you are not often required to teach, you may need to ask other members of staff. You should also make sure that you are familiar with how different items of equipment work before you come to use them.

⊙ *Knowledge into action*

Are you aware of where the following resource areas are in your school?

▶ Science

▶ Design and technology

▶ Art

For more information on setting out learning resources, see page 114.

The roles and responsibilities of others

All members of staff within the school will have responsibilities for maintaining the learning environment. There will, however, be certain members of staff whose responsibilities should be familiar to assistants.

▷ **Health and safety representative** – this designated member of staff has responsibility for making sure that there are systems and routines in place to maintain the safety of everyone within the school. You should be aware of the health and safety representative and the procedures for reporting any concerns to them. Health and safety will be discussed in more detail on page 116.

▷ **School keeper or caretaker** – this member of staff works alongside the safety representative to maintain a safe environment. They will also be responsible for making sure that the general environment is kept in a safe condition, for example that minor repairs are undertaken as and when they happen, or that items such as light bulbs are replaced where necessary. The school may have a maintenance book so that members of staff can report any issues as they arise. Caretakers may also help with preparing larger items for use within the learning environment, for example using a video or overhead projector.

▷ **Facilities Committee** – this part of the school's governing body is responsible for the school site and grounds. The committee will meet to discuss issues such as the repair and maintenance of the school. They will oversee contracts for people such as cleaners and gardeners who come to the school and will also make sure that health and safety guidelines are being met. Governors from this committee may include the teacher governor and will always include the headteacher.

▷ **Subject managers or co-ordinators** – these members of staff are responsible for making sure that their subject area has all the resources required. For example, the art co-ordinator will need to keep up to date on the amount of paints or pencils which are being used at any given time. They may have their own systems in place for doing this, and you will need to find out how to report shortages to them. The different subject co-ordinators will need to make sure that there are adequate resources if particular activities have been planned for a whole year group, such as working with clay.

▷ **Person responsible for maintaining stocks of materials** – this member of staff will need to be aware of the kinds of resources which are used on a daily basis and which may be quickly used up. These will be items such as paper for photocopying, sharpeners and rubbers, chalks or pens for whiteboards, exercise books, staples and so on. You should make sure that you know who this is so that you can report any shortages when you find them.

➡ **Knowledge into action**

Find out who you would report to if you found a piece of equipment was broken. What is the procedure for reporting breakages?

Considering pupils' individual needs within the learning environment

When preparing the learning environment it is important to remember that the focus of the activities is always the children. You may find that you have set up an activity to work on with a group and that materials are not accessible to all children. Assistants who support individual children with special needs will be aware that it is vital to be able to focus on the needs of everyone.

Principles of inclusive education

As has already been discussed in Unit 3-3.1, the main principle of inclusive education is that all children have the right to be educated alongside their peers in a mainstream school wherever possible. This will include children who have Special Educational Needs or a disability which means that they have been educated in another setting, or away from 'mainstream' schools. The SEN and Disability Act 2001 makes significant changes to the educational opportunities which are available to children with disabilities and those with Special Educational Needs. This means that it will be more likely for these children to be accepted into mainstream schools. There will always be some children for whom mainstream education is not possible, for example where highly specialised provision is needed, but the majority of children should not need to be separated from one another in order to be educated. The advantages of inclusive education, compared to separation, are shown below.

Separation	Inclusion
'Special' or different treatment	Equality – all children to receive the support they need to build on and achieve their potential
Learning helplessness	Learning assertiveness
Participation of some	Participation of all
Builds barriers in society	Involves all members of society

The table below shows the number of children in Special Schools in England and Wales from 1897 to 1999.

Year	Number of children
1897	4,739
1914	28,511
1929	49,487
1955	51,558*
1977	135,261*^
1999	106,000*^
*Hospital Schools not included ^Includes Severe Learning Difficulty	

(*Source:* Cole 1989, based on Chief Medical Officer, Ministry of Education, Dept of Education and Science Annual Reports (Disability Equality in Education 2001)

The current Disability Discrimination Act 1995 covers a range of services but does not include education. In September 2002, this Act will be amended to include education and cover the following:

▷ to make it unlawful for schools to discriminate against disabled pupils and prospective pupils in admissions

▷ a requirement for schools and LEAs (Local Education Authorities) to develop a plan to make schools improve access to the environment, curriculum and written information for disabled pupils

▷ a duty for schools to ensure that they do not put disabled pupils at a disadvantage.

Find out about...

Children in your school who have needed to have the learning environment adapted to help them. (You may need to ask your school SENCo.)

Look at the factors the teacher has had to consider and how they have used this information to help the child. Find out about the child's progress before and after these changes where made and evaluate how the adaptations have made a difference to the child's learning.

The implications for learning environments of inclusion is that all staff should be aware of those children who have specific needs, wherever they are in the school. For the Special Needs Co-ordinator, this may mean speaking to staff as and when children with special needs come into the school, so that children are fully supported in all learning environments.

Case study

Ramona has recently joined the Reception class. She has a hearing loss of which the class teacher and teaching assistant are both aware, and they have taken Ramona's needs into consideration during daily activities – for example, sitting her in the most beneficial place to hear effectively. However, one day the assistant is out on a course and the class teacher is off sick.

▶ What effect might this have on Ramona?

▶ How could the teacher and assistant have prepared for this eventuality so that others coming into the class can work to help Ramona?

Environmental factors

As far as possible, children should all be given equal opportunities and this should be remembered in the learning environment. All children, including those with special needs, should be considered when planning and setting out materials and resources. The environment may often need to be adapted for the needs of particular children within the class.

Factors which need to be considered include the following:

- **Light** – where there is a visually impaired child, the light may need to be adjusted or teaching areas changed if the child's eyes are light sensitive.
- **Accessibility** – a child in a wheelchair needs to have as much access to classroom facilities as other children. Furniture and resources may need to be moved to allow for this.
- **Sound** – some children may be sensitive to sounds in the learning environment, for example an autistic child may be disturbed by loud or unusual noises. It is not always possible for these kinds of noises to be avoided, but assistants need to be aware of the effect that they can have on children.

? **Think about it**

Look at and evaluate a classroom in your school and assess whether its layout takes the following into account:

▶ accessibility for all pupils
▶ maximum use of space
▶ good use of storage areas
▶ safety issues
▶ accessibility of materials.

→ **Knowledge into action**

Look at the layout of your classroom. How easy is it for children and adults to find their way around?

What adaptations do you think you would need to make for a child who was in a wheelchair?

Would the examples on page 112 be suitable?

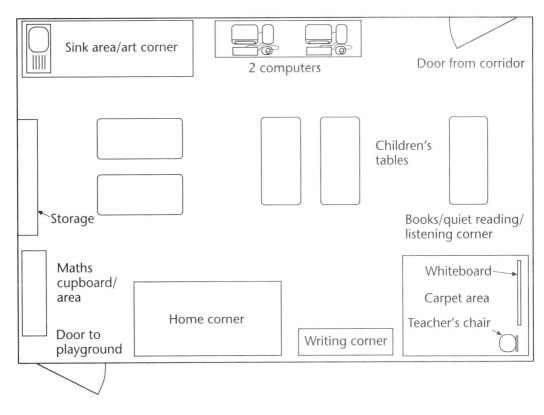

▲ Classroom layout

Understanding children's physical needs within the learning environment

In order to understand children's physical needs within the learning environment, assistants will need to have an awareness of their physical development. Stages of physical development are given in Unit 3-1 on page 4, which shows the approximate ages of different milestones. These may be divided into gross and fine motor skills.

▷ **Gross motor skills** include running, jumping, throwing a ball, using steps.
▷ **Fine motor skills** include holding a pen, pencil or paintbrush, holding a knife and fork, using a computer mouse.

Where some children develop more quickly or slowly than their peers, they will reach these milestones at different ages. The majority of children who are in their first years of schooling will develop at a similar rate. Assistants may notice that some children need more help than others within the learning environment when practising some of these skills. If some individual children have difficulties, they may have been referred through the SENCo for help and advice from outside agencies. For example, a child who has immature fine motor skills may need to be referred to an occupational therapist. Different professionals will give the school ideas and guidelines to help the child develop their skills. These may be put onto the child's IEP (Individual Education Plan) as targets.

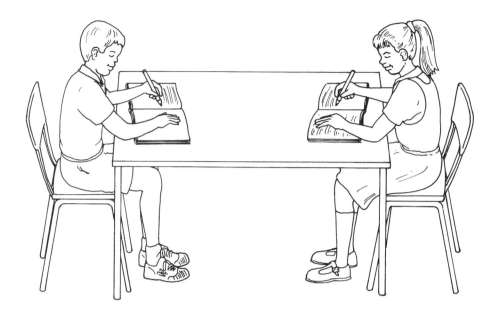

▲ Children need to be sitting properly in order to be able to write correctly

As an assistant, you will need to be aware of individual children's needs when considering how to position furniture, equipment and materials in the learning environment. For example, in order to write correctly, children need to be sitting properly at the desk with their feet touching the floor. While there will always be an 'average' size for children of a particular age, some may find the furniture too small or too big and need to have adaptations made within the classroom.

→ **Knowledge into action**

Consider the following facilities within the learning environment:

▶ access to everyday items such as pencils, rulers, scissors

▶ access to areas within the classroom such as home corner, sink, painting area.

How might you prepare these areas when managing a child with limited mobility in the classroom?

Preparing learning materials

All early years settings will have a variety of materials which will need to be prepared daily. Some of these will be easily accessible, such as putting out glue and scissors for example, but others may take longer to organise, for example where children are using different materials to make a collage. If there is more than one class in a year group, there may be several classes needing to use similar materials in the same week, and class teachers will need to ensure that there are enough resources available.

▲ It is important to have time to set out materials before use

Class teachers have responsibility for managing the room and making sure that there are sufficient general classroom resources for the children. This will include items such as maths equipment, puzzles, resources for role play and other classroom activities. Where assistants and other adults are working in other areas in the school, it should be made clear to them exactly what resources they are required to use and where to find them. It should also be clear to assistants where particular items are stored and whether they have access to storage areas and store cupboards. Teachers should also ensure that the items which are needed will be available at the time, and that there will not be other classes using the resource area. Some schools may have rotas and procedures in place for ensuring that all classes have equal access to resources and facilities.

Case study

Jackie is a teaching assistant in a primary school. She has been asked to take a group of children to the science area to do some work with toy cars and ramps. The class teacher tells Jackie where to find the ramps and cars but when she arrives they are being used by another assistant and group of children from another class.

▶ How could this situation have been avoided?

▶ What could Jackie do in this situation?

Assistants are required to prepare and set out the resources for planned activities within the classroom on a daily basis. This should have been discussed and directed by the teacher at least the day before they are needed. Assistants will also be expected to maintain the learning environment during and in between lessons. This may include jobs such as making sure there are adequate sharp pencils or keeping stocks of paper ready for use. It is important for assistants to be aware of items such as these, which are constantly in use and which may run out quickly. There will always be something to do in a classroom and when the class teacher is busy or unable to speak to assistants in between activities, the assistant should always have the initiative to keep busy!

The types of materials which may be needed within the learning environment might include:

▷ written materials: books, worksheets
▷ equipment for different curriculum areas
▷ general classroom items: pencils, paper, scissors
▷ specific items, for example buckets and spades for a 'Holidays' topic
▷ outdoor equipment for playground use
▷ large equipment such as sand and water.

Keys to good practice
Using learning materials

✔ Use the amount of materials required for the number of children.
✔ Remember safety when using tools and equipment.
✔ Keep waste of materials to a minimum.
✔ Return materials and store equipment correctly after use.
✔ Report shortages in materials to the appropriate person.

Safe use and care of learning equipment and materials

Assistants should always be aware of health and safety issues when working with young children. It is a duty of all early years workers to keep children safe, as many young children are not aware of hazards which may occur or the possible consequences. All children should be able to explore their environment in safety and security. Assistants should know who the health and safety representative is, and how to report any accidents or hazards which they discover in the learning environment. Many schools will have systems in place for reporting safety issues, but in the case of any doubt it is best to report any concerns to the health and safety representative.

First aid

Assistants should also know the location of safety equipment in school and the identity of trained first aiders. It is strongly recommended that there are first aiders in all educational establishments. They need to have completed a training course approved by the Health and Safety Executive (HSE), which is valid for three years. Assistants should also be aware of the location of first aid boxes in the school. The school's trained first aider should be responsible for ensuring adequate supply and regular restocking of the first aid box. Supplies should be date stamped when they are received as they have a five-year shelf life. If assistants find that there is not sufficient equipment, this should be reported to the health and safety officer.

There is no mandatory requirement for the contents of first aid boxes but they should include certain items, as listed below.

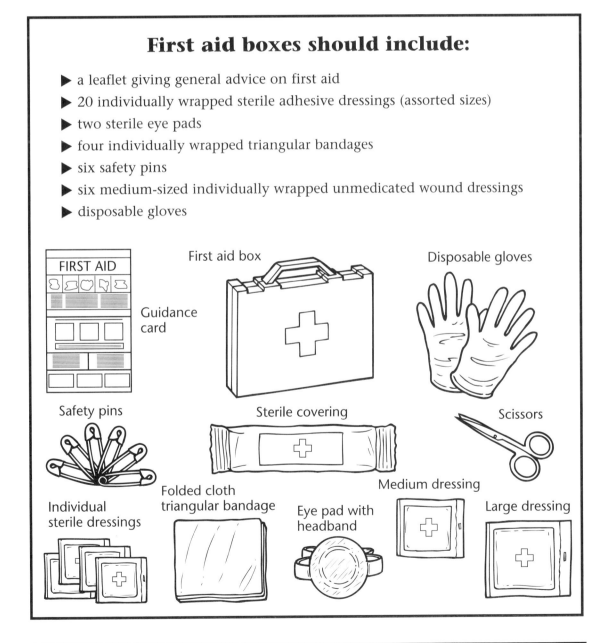

First aid boxes should include:

▶ a leaflet giving general advice on first aid
▶ 20 individually wrapped sterile adhesive dressings (assorted sizes)
▶ two sterile eye pads
▶ four individually wrapped triangular bandages
▶ six safety pins
▶ six medium-sized individually wrapped unmedicated wound dressings
▶ disposable gloves

FIRST AID

Guidance card

First aid box

Disposable gloves

Safety pins

Sterile covering

Scissors

Individual sterile dressings

Folded cloth triangular bandage

Eye pad with headband

Medium dressing

Large dressing

➡ **Knowledge into action**

▶ Find out the identity of the trained first aider in your school.

▶ Find out the location of first aid boxes.

Health and safety policy

The school will have a health and safety policy which outlines responsibilities and requirements within the school regarding health and safety. This will also set out the school's guidance within the setting when dealing with health and safety issues. There should be information available on specific requirements in areas such as cooking, PE, first aid, fire procedures and reporting accidents.

➡ **Knowledge into action**

▶ Locate a copy of your health and safety policy.

▶ Find out about procedures for reporting accidents in your school.

You will need to be vigilant and look out for situations in the learning environment which are potentially dangerous. Such situations may not always be obvious, but may be linked to a variety of factors.

▲ See how many potential dangers you can find in this classroom

Sometimes, materials and equipment which are being used within the learning environment may have related health and safety aspects to consider, for example when using electrical equipment. This should always be handled and used according to manufacturers' instructions. Assistants may require training and guidance when using some equipment, and should also be given guidelines on the disposal of any waste following their use.

It is also a good idea to draw pupils' attention to safety issues which they can control within their environment, for example pushing chairs under desks when they get up. In this way they will start to develop their own responsibility for safety.

Health and safety will be covered in more detail in Unit 3.10.

Consolidation activity

You have been asked to prepare for an activity making a Mother's Day card. You will be working with a group of children at a time and will be using a variety of materials.

▶ How would you plan for the activity to ensure that you had enough materials?

▶ What would you do with any left over materials?

End of unit test

1 Name three learning environments.

2 Who is responsible for individual subject resources within a school?

3 What are the principles of inclusive education? Name two advantages.

4 What environmental factors should assistants consider when planning the learning environment?

5 What document should assistants have access to which will give them guidelines on the school's requirements for managing equipment and materials safely within the learning environment?

6 List some of the contents of a first aid box. How often should the contents be renewed?

7 Who else in the school is responsible for establishing and maintaining learning environments? To whom would you report any damaged equipment?

References and further reading

DfES, *Guidance on First Aid for Schools: A Good Practice Guide*

DfES, *SEN Code of Practice* (2001)

Paterson, G., *First Aid for Children Fast – Emergency procedures for all parents and carers* (Dorling Kindersley in association with the British Red Cross)

Index for Inclusion (CSIE, 2000)

Training for Inclusion and Disability Equality, *Disability Equality in Education* (2001)

Websites

Disability Equality in Education: www.diseed.org.uk

CSIE: http://inclusion.uwe.ac.uk

www.dfes.gov.uk/sen

www.network81.co.uk

Unit 3-6 Contribute to maintaining pupil records

This unit will give you an understanding about the different kinds of records which you may be expected to keep when working in schools. These records may take a variety of forms and be kept in different parts of the school. You may be required to work with the class teacher to update records and need to be aware of issues such as confidentiality and legal requirements. As an assistant, you will also need to make sure that your contribution to school records is thorough and complete. Where you find any problems or issues surrounding the information you are required to maintain, you must report these straight away to the class teacher or person responsible.

The range of different records used in schools

There is a variety of different records with which assistants may come into contact when working in schools. These may be kept in different parts of the school, for example general pupil records may be in the school office, or located in the classroom. Very often, records are now kept on computer systems.

School records

All schools will keep these records, which are particularly important on a day-to-day basis. In the case of medical records, the school may also keep lists of children who have particular conditions such as asthma, and keep inhalers in school so that they are accessible in an emergency. It is vital to keep these records up to date, especially emergency telephone numbers, and schools should have systems in place to remind parents about this. If school staff are asked to administer daily medication, such as Ritalin, records need to be kept of the amount of tablets in school and the exact dosage given.

Where children are taking part in out-of-school activities, school records may need to be reviewed to ensure that staff have access to up-to-date emergency numbers. It is recommended that schools keep records of school attendance for 5 to 7 years. If children are persistently absent without parents and carers giving a written reason, these absences will be classified as unauthorised. Where children show a series of unauthorised absences, these may be noted by the educational welfare officer who should visit the school regularly.

Individual teachers' records of progress and assessment

These records are kept in the classroom and will contain the teacher's individual comments and assessments when working with children. These are necessary as they will give a breakdown of each child's progress over a period of time, and may be used

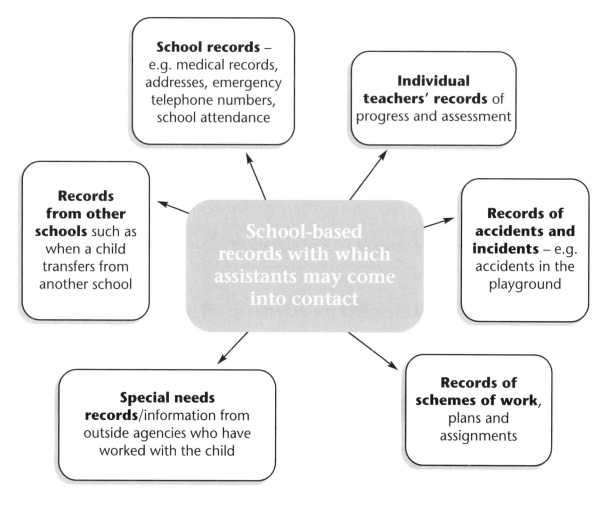

School records –
e.g. medical records,
addresses, emergency
telephone numbers,
school attendance

Individual
teachers' records of
progress and assessment

Records
from other
schools such as
when a child
transfers from
another school

School-based
records with which
assistants may come
into contact

Records of
accidents and
incidents – e.g.
accidents in the
playground

Special needs
records/information from
outside agencies who have
worked with the child

Records of
schemes of work,
plans and
assignments

▲ Different types of school records

to help with planning. They may also contain scores of any tests which the teacher undertakes with the children, such as the Baseline test when the child enters school, or end of Key Stage SATS (Standardised Assessment Tasks). They will also include copies of the child's school reports. Records of any national tests will also be collated and kept in the school's records to help to identify any areas for development.

Special needs records, information from other agencies

Children with special needs will often be the subject of a lot of paperwork. The SENCo will have their own systems for keeping this, so that information about the child is easily accessible when needed. The information which may be contained in these records will usually be reports from professionals such as speech and language therapists, who will record their findings and pass the information on to the school. Special Needs records will also contain information about what the school is doing to address an individual child's needs, and the child's Individual Education Plans (IEP's).

Records of schemes of work, plans and assignments

These records will give a breakdown of the work that is being covered with the children during the term. There may be schemes of work broken down into subject areas, and topic based activities to be carried out with the children. This will give a record of what each child in the class has learned.

Records from other schools

When children transfer from other schools, the school will forward any records which they have about the child's achievement. This will be useful for the class teacher as it will give an indication of the level which the child has reached, and the results of any tests which have been completed.

Records of accidents or incidents in school

There are times when you may be required to record details of an incident in school such as a child banging their head, or one child acting aggressively towards another. The school will usually have an accident book, as there needs to be a record kept of any incidents, particularly if a child has been injured as a result. (See Unit 3-10, page 179 for an example of an accident record form.)

An accident record

You should only be asked to access records under the direction of the teacher, or sometimes in the case of individual support assistants, the SENCo. The teacher will need to be aware of the location of the records at all times due to some of the confidential material which they contain. Assistants should be aware that records should not be removed from the school for this reason.

Knowledge into action

Find out the location of the different types of records held within your school. How often do they need to be updated?

Roles and responsibilities within the school for maintaining pupil records

The different records which are held within the school will be the responsibility of different members of staff. Usually the majority of pupil records will be held with the class teacher, but others may need to have access to them.

Members of staff who will need to maintain pupil records
Headteachers – to collect and collate school records including results of national tests and assessments
SENCos – to keep records of all children on the school's Special Needs Register
Subject managers – to keep and monitor records of achievement in their subject
Class teachers – to keep records of their children's progress
Office staff – to update and check medical and attendance records within the school

Headteachers, SENCos and subject managers will need to have a knowledge of pupils' records as it is part of their job responsibility to be able to report to others. This may include, in the case of the headteacher, reporting to governors and parents about the school's achievements. The subject managers will need to be able to report to the headteacher and staff about teaching and learning in their subject. They may also need to monitor and moderate work, as well as looking at achievements and areas for development. The SENCo will need to keep detailed records so that they have access to concerns about a specific child.

School policies for maintenance of pupil records

The school should have an Assessment, Recording and Reporting Policy, which will give information and guidelines about recording within the school. The system may be such that most of the school's records are kept on computer, so staff will need to be trained in how to use it. Assistants may have opportunities for training with other staff and this will be important if they are to help them to update records. Even if they are not expected to do this, it will be useful to see how they are used and how information is kept within the school.

Legal requirements concerning personal information

Assistants should be aware of the school's legal responsibilities when handling pupil records. This is because personal pupil information should not be used for any other purpose. According to the Data Protection Act 1998, information should:

▷ be obtained fairly
▷ only be kept for as long as is necessary
▷ be relevant to requirements
▷ not be used in any way which is not compatible to its purpose.

Schools should offer guidelines for the use of personal information and make sure that systems and documentation are secure and only restricted to appropriate staff.

They may have a policy for the storage and security of pupil records within the school and assistants should be familiar with this if they are dealing with pupil records.

The Children Act 1989 requires that children's welfare must always be put first. It outlines some of the principles which need to be taken into account when children are being considered. Its main requirements are that children should always be consulted and informed about what will happen to them, particularly in cases of family mitigation. Where their personal information is concerned, schools should ensure that this is only accessible to the adults who need this information.

The Statementing Process is the way in which schools send information to the local authority to decide whether a child qualifies for extra support in school. This information will be detailed and confidential, and assistants who work with children with special needs will need to be aware of issues surrounding confidentiality.

Find out about...

Guidelines for data protection within your school.

Name some of the ways in which your school protects information.

Your role in helping to maintain records

Assistants will not have overall responsibility for maintaining records, but they may be asked to help teachers to keep them up to date and in order. Records which are medical or relating to special needs should be updated as and when changes occur since it is vital that the school has up-to-date information. Those assistants who support children with a Statement may be required to help with records for that child, although it is more likely that this will be done by the SENCo. Records which relate to the curriculum will be updated at least once a term or as planning takes place, and assistants should be aware of these but will not usually need to help with them. Most records should be updated on a regular basis since they are working documents. For this reason, it is important to be aware of the school procedures for this. Records relating to assessment are the most likely to be completed by assistants and this may consist of a number of tasks, including filing and transferring information. If a child has recently transferred from another school, information about them will need to be put onto the new school's records.

Knowledge into action

Find out what kinds of records you may be asked to contribute to in school.

Confidentiality

All staff who work in schools will need to be aware of issues concerning confidentiality. They will be building up the trust of parents, children and other staff with whom they work. It is important for assistants to ensure that any information which they are given is not passed onto other people. This is because the trust which has taken time to build up can be quickly damaged by a few careless words. There is also a legal requirement for schools to keep records of children and staff confidential.

Case study

Simone is working as an assistant at an infant school for Saad, who is autistic. She has just found out from Saad's teacher that he has scored very highly in an assessment which has just been carried out in school. Simone tells another assistant and the news somehow reaches one of the parents.

1 Why should Simone have kept this information to herself?

2 What should she have done if she was unsure about repeating the information?

3 What damage will she have done to the school's relationship with the parent?

Guidelines for keeping information secure

▷ Computer systems should not be left unattended when personal information is accessible.

▷ Passwords should keep information secure.

▷ Passwords should not be displayed in office or classroom areas.

▷ Disks and files should be locked away when not in use.

▷ Review and dispose of any unwanted personal data.

Find out about...

Does your school have a confidentiality policy?

Keys to good practice
Maintaining pupil records

✔ Ensure you understand what you are asked to do.

✔ Make sure records are kept up to date and accurate.

✔ Ensure records are relevant.

✔ Maintain confidentiality.

✔ Report any problems or breaches of confidence to the appropriate person.

Problems when recording and storing information

When you are asked to update pupils' records, you may find that you come across problems. There may be a variety of reasons for this:

▷ **Instructions are unclear** – the class teacher may not have fully explained the system, or what you have been asked to do may not make sense to you. Make sure that you clarify any queries as soon as they arise.

▷ **Record keeping system is difficult to access** – you may find that the system (either electronic or paper based) is complicated and you need more help to complete the task. If you have not had sufficient training, you must not be afraid to say so.

▷ **Information is not complete** – you may not have enough information to complete the task. Always point out any gaps in the records to the class teacher.

▷ **Information is not from a reliable or valid source** – you may be unsure about the information which you are dealing with, for example information which has been given verbally.

▷ **Record keeping system is not secure** – you may be concerned if you find that the system you are being asked to use is not secure. It could be that for example it is not accessed by passwords, or information can be seen by other adults who come into the school. You should speak to the class teacher or to your line manager if you feel that the system is not secure.

▷ **Information which you find may indicate potential problems** – if the school has been sent information about a child who has just started

Whenever you come across something which you feel is a potential problem, it is important that you report it straight away to the teacher so that it can be resolved.

? Think about it

Why is it important for records to be clear and accessible for those who need to use them? Have you come across any examples of unclear record keeping in your school?

Consolidation activity

You have just started to work as an assistant in a Reception class and have been given all the forms which the children's parents have been asked to fill in regarding their child. These include:

▷ medical forms and declaration

▷ family circumstances, siblings, religion, language spoken at home

▷ home–school agreement

▷ information from pre-school or nursery

▷ special needs information

▷ emergency telephone numbers.

You are asked to go through and check the forms and file them in the children's record folders. There are a number of records that are incomplete as parents have not returned all the information needed.

▶ What would you do when filing the information?

▶ How would you go about finding the information which was needed?

End of unit test

1 What types of records exist in schools?

2 Where might different records be kept?

3 Which staff might be responsible for different types of records?

4 Why might assistants need to access different records?

5 Outline four requirements of the Data Protection Act.

6 Why is confidentiality important?

7 What sorts of problems might assistants face when maintaining pupil records?

Websites

Data Protection Act 1998: www.legislation.hmso.gov.uk/acts/acts1998/19980029.htm

Children Act 1989: http://www.doh.gov.uk/busguide/childhtm/cpt6/htm

Unit 3-7 Observe and report on pupil performance

This unit looks at how assessment and observation of pupils takes place in schools. You will need to be aware of methods of observation and how the process may affect children. You will also need to know the purpose of any observations you undertake so that you can pass on the required information to the class teacher. There are different methods of observation and ways of organising children, so this unit gives a breakdown of situations in which you may find yourself when carrying out observations. Assistants should also make sure that when they are observing pupils their presence is not a distraction to the children, and that they are acting in a supporting role to both pupils and teachers. Finally, you will need to be able to record your observations so that you are able to report back to the teacher.

Why children need to be observed in school

When working as an assistant, you may be asked to undertake observations of pupils working in a variety of different situations. This is because the class teacher will need to build up a profile of each child. Assistants will need to be able to observe children and report back to the teacher on what they have seen. Before undertaking observations you should be given some guidance as to what the teacher is looking for and how it should be approached. As you become more experienced, you may need less support when observing children.

The types of learning you may be asked to observe will include the following skills:

▷ **social and emotional skills** – working and playing co-operatively with others
▷ **physical skills development** – using gross and fine motor skills
▷ **intellectual and cognitive development** – how children apply concepts and knowledge
▷ **language and communication skills** – how children communicate with others.

Social and emotional skills

Assistants may be asked to observe children who are playing or socialising with their peers. This may be for a variety of reasons, for example children who are experiencing social difficulties and find it hard to make and retain friends, or those who have behaviour problems. When observing play situations you may be asked to ensure that the child is unaware that you are watching, as this could have an influence on how they behave. Clearly in this situation you will need to observe the pupil's interaction with others and whether they are proactive in seeking out other children with whom to socialise. Those children who often spend playtimes on their own, or are not confident when socialising with others may need support in school to help them to develop these skills.

Physical skills and development

Assistants may be asked to observe children in situations where they are demonstrating their physical skills. One of the situations which you may be asked to observe is recording children's progress during PE lessons. This is because it is difficult to observe individual children when teaching a class. In this situation, the best way to record information about children's progress is by exception. For example, if the lesson is a gymnastics class and the objective is to learn about balance, the recording may be about a child or group of children who are finding the skill difficult. Sometimes a particular child may display difficulties with gross motor skills, which needs to be recorded as evidence so that the school can seek help for the child. Assistants may also be required to observe children who have difficulties with fine motor skills, such as using scissors or pencil control. These areas of development may be immature when children first come into school, and teachers will need to be aware of those children who need extra support.

There are also occasions in the classroom or other areas in the school where assistants may be asked to record how children with disabilities are organising themselves within the learning environment. This may be a child who has sensory loss, such as a visual impairment, or a child with cerebral palsy who relies on a wheelchair for mobility. These children will need careful monitoring at all times and if assistants see a particular problem they should report it straight away to the class teacher.

? Think about it

Have you worked with children in school who need extra help with developing fine or gross motor skills?

▶ What kind of support have they been given?

▶ Have you been asked to observe any children who have problems with motor skills?

Intellectual and cognitive development

Assistants will often be asked to work with groups and individuals to complete tasks. They may also be asked to sit back from a group and observe how they interact with each other when completing a task. It should be clear whether you are expected to join in with the task or whether your role is purely to observe the children. Teachers should give clear instructions as to why you are observing the child or children and exactly what you need to record.

You may need to look at how the child or children is approaching the task. For example, if undertaking a maths activity such as the number of ways you can make ten – is the child methodical? You may be looking at whether the child has understood a new concept or one which should be familiar to them. It is also useful to observe whether the child approaches the task with confidence or will wait for assistance from other children or adults.

Find out about...

The Individual Education Plan or IEP targets for a child in your class.

How does the class teacher plan to take account of these targets and made sure that the child is given the opportunity to work on them?

Language and communication skills

Language and communication skills are an important part of how children learn. Those who experience difficulties when communicating with others may need to be observed both in the classroom and in other environments, such as the playground or dining hall. Assistants should have a clear idea of what they are expected to observe and whether they should intervene. The school may have been given advice and targets from a speech and language therapist about how to maximise the child's speech development, so that the school and therapist can work together.

Where children have communication difficulties, such as autism, assistants may be asked to observe and monitor their behaviour and interaction with other children. Agencies such as those who support social and communication difficulties may be available to offer help and advice when working with these children. The school may also have been given advice and targets from a speech and language therapist about

▲ It is important to be aware of individual children's targets

how to maximise the child's speech development, so that the school and therapist can work together. Assistants should always be aware of individual children's targets, particularly if they are supporting children with special needs. These will be set out on the child's Individual Education Plan or IEP. If you are an individual support assistant and have not seen the targets of the child you are supporting, it is important to have these from the class teacher.

Behaviour to be expected at various stages of development

As already seen in Unit 3-1 page 6, children will display a range of behaviours at different stages in their development. When working with a particular age or stage of child, assistants will quickly start to learn the kinds of behaviours which are 'normal' for that age. Children who display abnormal behaviours for their age will usually be showing a type of behaviour as shown in the diagram below.

Where children are not on task for reasons of behaviour, assistants will need to intervene, particularly if the group or individual is working away from the class teacher. You will need to determine what is the cause of the behaviour so that you can encourage the child to return to the task. It is important to have clarified the boundaries of behaviour and how to deal with any problems with the class teacher. This is because if the behaviour continues, you will need to have agreed strategies for how to proceed (see Unit 3-1 on page 13 about the management of pupil behaviour). It is important for adults to be firm and for children to know what is expected of them. Your school should also have a behaviour policy which you can refer to if you are unsure of the kinds of sanctions which you should apply.

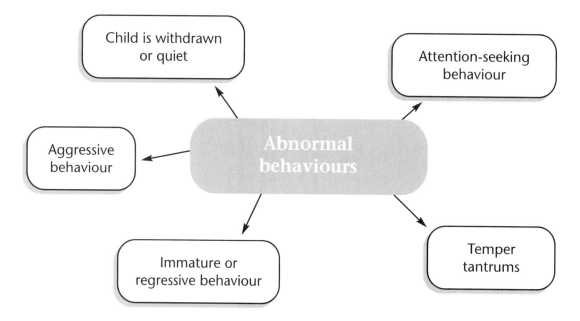

▲ There are different types of abnormal behaviour

▲ You must keep the objectives of the observation in mind

Your role when observing pupil performance

Although you will have been given guidance by the school and class teacher when carrying out pupil observation on exactly what is required, there will be other factors which you need to consider. It is important that you always keep the lesson objectives and required observation in mind, so that you can redirect the children to what they are doing if they start to go off task. You must also be aware of how you can maximise the pupils' interest and focus on the task, through questioning and directing their work.

Other factors to remember when carrying out observations

It is important to be aware of recording information which is relevant to the observation you have been asked to carry out (see page 136 on how to record information). This is the case unless you notice something which you feel needs to be reported to the class teacher. This could include one of the following:

▷ child is distracted/showing disruptive behaviour which is preventing them or others in the group from completing the task

▷ child is showing uncharacteristic behaviour – for example, is unusually quiet during the session

▷ child is playing up to being observed – the observation may not be a realistic interpretation of the child's abilities

▷ environmental factors and interruptions – these could be caused by physical factors, such as noise levels, and will prevent the task being carried out successfully.

If a child is disruptive or does not participate in the activity owing to others' disturbance, this information should be recorded as part of the observation because it will have an effect on whether the children are fulfilling the required learning objectives of the lesson.

You may be aware of potential causes of disruption and should always speak to the class teacher if you anticipate any problems before starting the observation. It is also important to be aware of and to try to maintain the normal rules and routines of the school or classroom before undertaking any observations. This is so that the children will not be working in an artificial situation. If you set out the activity in a different environment, the children may find this too much of a distraction to focus on the activity.

Other potential sources of disruption include:

▷ children's behaviour
▷ task too difficult/too easy for children
▷ physical factors – noise or light levels
▷ interruptions by other children in the class
▷ insufficient space, materials or equipment to carry out the task
▷ faulty equipment.

Case study

You are observing a group of six Year 2 children who are trying to find out the best material to use for insulation. You have been asked to observe the group to see how they work together and only intervene if necessary. They have been carrying out the investigation without support but one of the boys has started to display disruptive behaviour which is preventing the others from staying on task.

1 What would you do to prevent the child from disturbing the activity further?

2 Following your intervention, what would you do if the disruptive behaviour continued?

3 What effect might this have on your observation of the session?

Influences on pupils when being observed

Assistants may also need to encourage pupils who find it difficult to demonstrate the extent of their knowledge or skills when being observed. It is important therefore to know the children with whom you are working before undertaking the observation. Some children will be able to work on the task without being distracted by the observer, while others may play up to the adult to seek attention. Assistants may also need to put the child or children at ease so that they are more likely to work constructively with one another. You may need to encourage some children to participate so that you are given a clearer idea of their understanding.

Groups of children will need to be chosen carefully so that there are not combinations who may disturb or influence the reactions of one another. This may be due to a number of reasons.

Cultural factors: in schools where there is a high percentage of mixed cultures, there may also be problems of language and understanding where children speak English as an additional language. Some bilingual assistants are employed by schools in areas where there is a high number of children who speak English as a second language. Assistants should be aware that there are currently developments to raise the achievements of ethnic minority children in schools, as many of these children are under-achieving. This also includes children from traveller families, who may not spend more than a few weeks at a time in school. Your school may have a strategy in place for helping these children to achieve their full potential, and local authorities may soon be offering staff training, so that all staff can help to raise attainment.

Social factors: some children may not be able to work with those who they feel are more able or more confident than themselves. This will have an influence on the observation as they will be less likely to put their ideas forward. If children have confidence in themselves, they will gain more from what they are doing.

Gender-based factors: i.e. children who are not comfortable with, or find it difficult working with children of the opposite sex. This may be because there is a group of children who are more confident, or because they have preconceived assumptions – for example, that boys are better at science or girls are better at art. This may make them less likely to volunteer information when working in a group.

Children who are being observed individually may be working on their own or as part of a group. Those who are working on their own may not react to the observation in the same way, mainly because they will not be interacting with others to complete the task. When you are observing an individual, you may find that you need to ask the child questions about what they are doing so that you have more understanding of their approach to the task. Questioning strategies will need to be consistent with the objectives of the task and the child's age and understanding (see questioning pupils on page 28).

How to record when undertaking pupil observations

Schools may have different guidelines when approaching observations and, as we have seen, there may be a number of reasons for asking assistants to observe children. The principal points to remember are as follows.

Make sure you understand exactly what you need to observe. You must only record information which is relevant to the observation, although see page 133 for awareness of other factors. One way of doing this is to record at set intervals, or only to write down relevant observations.

Use any methods of recording which are consistent with what you have been asked to do. For example, when observing children for a specific assessment, the school may have an observation form which will give guidelines for required information. You may be asked to make notes of your own, or simply use a checklist to make sure the child has achieved a set of criteria.

Below are examples of a blank observation form and also one that has been filled in, together with comments on the observations made.

Hazelwood Primary School
Pupil Observation Form

Name of pupil(s) .... Class: ....

Date: .... Lesson: ....

Teacher .... Assistant: ....

Lesson objectives:

Group/class activity:

Focus of observation:

▲ An example of an observation form

St Peter's Primary School

Pupil Observation Form

Name of pupil(s) ..Keith Crewe...   **Class:** ....2JM..................................

Date: ..22 February 2002..............   **Lesson:** ....Mathematics.............

Teacher ...Sara Shorter................   **Assistant:**..........Jackie Brown.........

Lesson objectives:

To understand place value through using Dienes rods.

Group/class activity:

Completing worksheet to demonstrate understanding of place value.

Focus of observation:

How much child relies on others in the group, and how much he works on his own.

Easily distracted, several times disturbing others and off task. Able to work well for 5 minutes initially. Gradually drifted off task and distracted others in the group. Not able to stay focused. Worked with Anthony on questions 5 and 6, and discussed his answers to 3 and 4. Used Dienes to help him with tens and ones but was unable to use 100's. Clear idea of the fact that ten ones make ten, a ten and two ones make twelve, and so on as he demonstrated this several times and enjoyed building up the squares.

Further comments:

Keith was not able to work independently for a sustained period. If working on his own he may have been able to do this. He could not stay focused on his work or leave other children alone during the observation period.

Did child meet learning objectives?

Difficult to say as he did not complete enough of the work on his own.

What pupil should know by the end of the lesson.

This shows what the pupil or the group they are in is expected to do.

This gives clear indication of what the observer is expected to record. The observer has written more than is required here but this information may still be useful to the teacher under 'further comments'.

The comment about if he had worked on his own is subjective and therefore should not have been included.

This commentary does not give an indication of how much time was spent doing the activity, so does not demonstrate how long the child worked during the session.

? *Think about it*

What sort of observations have you been asked to carry out in school? Have you been encouraged to report back formally to the teacher with written evidence, or verbally?

Keep your recording as simple as possible. You will need to report your findings to the class teacher and it is important that you are able to remember what you observed, so you will need to record clearly and legibly. You may need to summarise the information you have gathered, or simply explain to the teacher what you have observed. Whatever you report will need to have evidence to support it, so you should be careful to back up your findings.

Remember to keep your written observations confidential. If you need to use them for any reason apart from classroom records, for example for training purposes, you should always change the names of any children you have observed.

If you are carrying out an observation which requires you to record information in any other way, for example using a video or still camera, you should always ask permission beforehand from those concerned. This is so that they are aware of what you are doing and why.

Remember that all observations are subjective. You should report what you see but do not need to give an opinion about it. Pupil observations are to give the teacher an idea about the child's progress or how the pupil copes in particular situations. Do not be tempted to give any more information than is needed.

✓ Keys to good practice
Observing pupils

✔ Record clearly.

✔ Keep information relevant.

✔ Remember confidentiality.

✔ Follow school guidelines.

Case study

You have been asked to carry out an observation during an outdoor games lesson on Joseph, who has been demonstrating 'clumsy' behaviour and giving his teacher cause for concern. He has shown some physical behaviours which the class teacher feels are not in the normal spectrum.

1 How would you go about recording your observations?

2 How would you know whether his physical behaviour was age appropriate?

Consolidation activity

Carry out an observation to record how a child or group of children work through a new maths concept during the Numeracy session. You will need to observe and record how they work in all three sections of the lesson, and note whether they have achieved the intended learning outcomes. You may like to use the suggested form on page 136.

End of unit test

1 Why might children be observed in school?

2 What types of skills will assistants be asked to observe?

3 What sort of 'abnormal' behaviour might you see in a classroom?

4 What should you do before starting an observation in order to minimise disruption?

5 Why might a child from another culture find it difficult to participate in a group activity?

6 What should you remember when recording observations?

References

Teaching Assistant's File (DfES)

Managing Support for the Attainment of Pupils from Minority Ethnic Groups (Ofsted 2001) or on the website www.ofsted.gov.uk

Unit 3-8 Contribute to the planning and evaluation of learning activities

This unit looks at the way in which assistants work with the class teacher to plan and evaluate learning activities. It is important for assistants to be able to work collaboratively with others and to judge the effectiveness of the learning activities with which they are involved. This unit looks at the way in which you plan, manage and evaluate teaching activities through the support of national, local and school-based documentation. You will need to be aware of the types of documents which are available and should know where to find them in your school. You will also need to manage any difficulties as they arise and be able to report back constructively to the teacher about them.

Your role and that of others in planning, implementing and evaluating learning activities

Planning activities

In your role as a teaching assistant, you may be asked to help with the planning of learning activities in the learning environment. Although the class teacher will have completed long-term plans for the class, you may be asked to work with the teacher to discuss and plan activities for the week so that you are aware in advance of what you are required to do. You will need to work with the class teacher to ensure that the work you are covering fits in with activities and topics which have been planned for the term.

Example of part of a weekly Literacy Hour plan for Year 2

Big Book – *Six Dinner Sid*

CT = Class teacher, TA = Teaching assistant, I = Independent

Group D are the more able, Group A are the less able.

		Group A	**Group B**	**Group C**	**Group D**
Monday	Discuss cover and first 4 pages of text Close look at capital letters. Plen: Look at Group C's work	Guided Reading/ Starspell (computer)	Playing a word game/listening corner	Worksheet on capitals	Worksheet on capitals (2 groups)
		CT	TA	I	I

		Group A	Group B	Group C	Group D
Tuesday	Continue to read next 4 pages of text; focus on story and descriptive vocab. Plen: Look at Group A's work	Worksheet on descriptive vocab, e.g. Sid was a .... cat.	Guided Reading/ Starspell	Word games/ listening corner	Work on story structure
		I	CT	TA	I
Wednesday	Finish reading book. Plen: Group D	Word games/ listening corner	Descriptive vocab sheet	Guided reading/ Starspell	Comprehension on *Six Dinner Sid*
		Parent helper	I	TA	CT
Thursday	Ask children what they can remember about the story. Discuss key issues in the book: what happened to Sid? Shared writing session using story as a base. Plen: Some of group B to read their stories so far	All groups – writing after shared writing session.			
		CT to work where needed. TA to sit with group A			
Friday	Remind children about shared writing. Those who need to complete to continue.	Wordsearch on pets	Wordsearch on pets	Comprehension on *Six Dinner Sid*	Word games

Your class teacher's weekly plan should show which individuals or groups of children are to work on tasks at a particular time, and give an indication of whether they are to be supported by an adult.

Consider and discuss in groups those occasions where you have been able to plan with the class teacher, and compare with times where you have not been given the opportunity.

What are the main differences that you notice?

Principles underlying effective communication, planning and collaboration

Schools should have positive opportunities for teaching assistants to share information about the school and about pupils. It is important to make these times available, as many teaching assistants work part time, or work in one class with one pupil. Assistants need to have opportunities to share ideas and experiences with others so that they do not feel isolated. These could include:

▷ regular meetings for teaching assistants

▷ sharing information about the school

▷ assistants working together to support classes or individuals

▷ notice-boards and year group meetings.

These meetings and opportunities for discussion do not need to be long, but are an important part of an assistant's role. They are part of a communication process which should take place within the school for passing information between all staff. If these kinds of opportunities are not given to staff for communicating with one another, they will find it much more difficult to work with one another and use time effectively.

When meeting with the teacher, the main areas for discussion should be the planning and evaluation of learning activities. Your role and the role of the teacher should be one of a partnership, where there are clear roles and responsibilities for working together to support the pupils. You may also be involved in planning a series of activities to be carried out over several sessions. This could be with the same group, if the children need to work on a particular idea, or with different children on a similar, perhaps differentiated, task. As you become more experienced, or if you are working with a child who has special needs, you may add some of your own ideas during the sessions so that the child or children builds on work done each time.

Ideally, assistants should be given this opportunity to input some of their own ideas into class activities when they are at the planning stage. This is because they may have their own areas of expertise, or ideas which may help the teacher to formulate activities for children. This is especially true for assistants who support individual children with special needs, as there will be some activities in which these children need more structured tasks. You should also be aware of your own areas of weakness:

if you know that you will find it difficult to take a group of children for an art activity on printing, for example, because you have not done this for a long time, then say so. You should feel comfortable with what you are doing because it is important to be confident when carrying out the activity. If you anticipate any other difficulties in carrying out the plan which the teacher has not foreseen, you should also point these out.

Case study

Ryan is a 7-year-old child in Year 3 who has Asperger's Syndrome. He is supported for two hours each morning and one hour each afternoon by Bhumika, his individual support assistant. Ryan's teacher always plans for the week on a Friday lunchtime with his assistant so that she is able to give her input and ideas for Ryan's learning activities. One day a supply teacher is in the classroom and asks Bhumika to take Ryan's group for some number work on place value. Bhumika has not been given any advance warning about this and when she sees the task is not sure about some aspects of what the group has been asked to do.

1 What would you do in Bhumika's situation?

2 What would you do if you were unable to speak to the teacher about the task as they were busy with another group?

Think about it

What opportunities have you been given in the school setting for planning activities alongside the class teacher? How often are you involved with planning? If you have not been involved, find out whether this would be possible.

Keys to good practice
Planning learning activities

✔ Ensure you understand the learning outcomes.

✔ Contribute your own ideas to planning sessions.

✔ Include any of your own strengths.

✔ Make sure you have time for what you need to do.

✔ Be aware of relevant policies and guidelines.

Implementing activities

When working with individuals, groups and the whole class, teaching assistants need to ensure that they are aware of the learning objectives of the lesson. The class teacher should always include the learning objectives in their planning, and should also tell the children what they are. This is so that they will be able to direct all children towards the correct outcome. For example, if a Year 2 child is working on a design and technology activity using Lego, they will have been asked to make a specific type of model which fits in with the class topic. Assistants should be aware of what individuals and groups of children are working towards so that they can act in a fully supporting role. There may sometimes be problems of time, for example if the assistant comes in to school just as the teacher is starting the day's activities. It is often helpful to have either a copy of the short-term planning, or a notebook containing the assistant's tasks for the day along with the children's learning objectives. Assistants will also then be able to judge how success can be measured when they are evaluating learning activities.

Making use of allocated time

Assistants will need to make sure that they are fully aware of the constraints of time when implementing learning activities. There are many parts of the school day during which time is restricted, and this needs to be considered, especially if there is a large group of children to work with on an individual basis. If the work seems unrealistically long for the length of time allocated, you should not try to complete it all and rush the children to finish. This will make them feel that their work is less valued. Although time is limited in school, assistants should wherever possible try not to communicate

---

Lesson plan for Geography (Year 6) Date ....

Learning objective: For children to be familiar with and understand the water cycle.

Introduction: Find out what the children know about the water cycle. Class discussion to see how much children can remember about water from previous learning.

Main part of lesson: Children to work in groups: Group 1 with teacher, using the Internet and reference books to see what they can find out. Group 2 to work with teaching assistant using artwork and models to explain what happens. Groups 3 and 4 to explain the water cycle in their own words and draw diagrams.

Conclusion: Children to discuss with one another what they have found out and to give examples.

▲ Example of an individual lesson plan for Year 6

this to pupils when they are working on a task. If there is an unavoidable limit on time, you should give the pupil or pupils an opportunity to return to it later the same day if possible.

Case study

You are working with Omar, a Year 5 child, on some history towards planning a project on everyday life in Tudor times. He has been given some ideas and has started a rough outline of what he needs to cover, but he needs to finish his plan before the end of the day as it has to be handed in.

1 How could you help Omar without making him feel he needs to rush?

2 What could you do if the plan was not completed by the end of the lesson?

Individual targets

Children should also now all have their own individual termly or half termly learning targets for English and maths, and should be aware of what these are. This is to help children to be more focused on their own development and to involve them in their own achievements. When in Reception, the targets may be simple ones for the whole class, such as learning to count to 10 and back again. By Year 1, children's targets will be more aimed at their own specific needs, and this will continue throughout primary school, with the children becoming more involved in the kinds of targets they are aiming towards. Targets may be written in children's books or on the classroom wall, but it is important that they are aware of them.

Knowledge into action

Find out about targets within your class or year group. How often are they revised? How does the class teacher assess whether the children have or have not achieved these targets?

Lesson evaluation

Following the lesson, or even while it is taking place, there will need to be some form of evaluation to determine whether the learning objectives have been met and how much the children understand. It may be clear during the activity which children do not understand the concept and those who are able to explain it.

Where children are working independently, their work may be all that is needed to check that they understand what they have been asked to do. Where the work has been practical or verbal, particularly with younger children, assistants will need to record the names of those children who have found it difficult to complete or understand. If assistants find that some of the children with whom they are working are clearly finding the work difficult, the class teacher should always be told. If any problems arise during the course of the activity, which mean that it cannot be carried out properly, this should also be pointed out to the teacher, for example a distraction which carries on over a period of time. Assistants also need to know exactly how success for each activity is to be measured, for example whether each pupil in the group has fully understood a new concept. When recording or annotating plans, you should be clear about the amount of information which is needed. You also need to be careful about how you report back when the information is verbal. If you have had a difficult session with a group or an individual, make sure you give all the information about the session to the teacher so that they are able to make a balanced judgement.

Think about it

You are working on an activity with individuals in a Reception class to evaluate their mouse skills on the computer. Some of the children have clearly had experience at this while others find it difficult. One of the children is very confident, and while you are working with other children insists on coming over to see how they are getting on and to try to intervene and show them what to do.

▶ How could you prevent this from disturbing what you are doing?

▶ What would you say to the teacher either during or at the end of the session?

▶ Can you think of any other strategies that might work if the child persisted in disturbing you?

▶ What might you say in your evaluation?

Keys to good practice
Lesson evaluation

✔ Be clear about what and how you need to report.

✔ Report any distractions or disturbances.

✔ Report strengths and weaknesses constructively.

✔ Be aware of outside influences on the lesson.

Possible problems when planning, implementing and evaluating learning activities

Assistants may find that they come up against a variety of problems when planning, implementing and evaluating learning activities. As already pointed out, it is important to point out any anticipated difficulties at the planning stage. Where you encounter problems carrying out tasks, you must act immediately so that pupils do not become distracted from what they are doing.

Possible causes of difficulty when carrying out tasks include:

▷ insufficient space in area

▷ insufficient subject knowledge

▷ too many/too few children for task

▷ bad combination of personalities in group

▷ insufficient time to carry out task

▷ poor or insufficient materials

▷ work too easy/too difficult

▷ differences of opinion when working with others.

When evaluating, the main problem may be a lack of time for reporting back to the teacher. However, there may be occasions where there are differences of opinion or ways of reporting which could cause friction between the teacher and assistant. Be careful that you report things to the teacher in a way that is not confrontational.

? Think about it

Look at these two conversations:

Teacher: How did the red group get on with their work on number bonds to 10?
Assistant: Most of them understood the concept, but Jake and Ellie found it very hard – I don't think they should be in that group, they don't ever manage well with numbers over 6. I think you should put them in another group.

Teacher: How did the red group get on with their number bonds to 10?
Assistant: They were all fine except Jake and Ellie, who always seem to trip up on the higher numbers to 10. Maybe we should plan to do some extra work with them on their own to help them to reinforce the higher numbers.

▶ Which is the better way of reporting back to the teacher?

▶ Why do you think the teacher might prefer the second example?

How children learn and the implications for planning and evaluating learning activities

When looking at the planning and evaluation of children's work, all staff should remember the variety of needs which exist within each classroom. Some children will learn and develop at a different rate, and this will have an effect on how their work is approached. School staff need to be able to cater for a variety of abilities while all the time challenging and motivating pupils to do their best. Unit 3-3 looks in detail at the different ways in which children learn, and gives some ideas about how this will affect planning and differentiation within the classroom.

There will be a spread of attainment which children at any age will be expected to achieve, but it is important to take into account those children who fall outside this expected level. This will usually be those children who the school has put on the Special Needs register, and teachers should plan differentiated work for them in line with their Individual Education Plan (IEP) targets (see also Units 3-13 to 3-16 on special needs, and Unit 3-3.1 on equal opportunities and inclusion). Those children who are more able should also have opportunities to extend their knowledge. Teachers will usually cater for this by planning similar activities for them with extension work. At the very early stages, the greatest differences will be evident in Literacy and Numeracy.

Lesson objective: to reinforce children's knowledge of coin values and give practical experience of using coins. Also reinforce counting in multiples.

Introduction and mental starter:

Behind a screen or board, drop coins of different values into a jar. Children to mentally count up the values. Using 2p, 5p, 10p coins.

Teacher to give brief introduction on different coin values. Using large card coins, demonstrate how we can make the same amount using different coins. Ask children to participate in making up coin values.

Main focus:

▶ *More able group* (8 children) to work on target board and find different ways of reaching values using coins. Extension activity – to make their own target board, ensuring that they use numbers which can be reached using coin values.

▶ *Middle two groups* (12 children) to complete worksheet on shopping. Buy different items with shown values using a variety of coins.

▶ *Less able group* (6 children) to carry out money game with parent helper. Using 2p and 1p coins, build up picture after rolling money dice. If they understand this, build in 5p.

▶ *Special needs group* (4 children) to work with ISA on coin recognition and representation.

Plenary: Ask some of the children to report back on their work. See if the group can apply their knowledge of coin values to make up totals on the board: e.g. 10p, 50p.

▲ Example of a Year 2 differentiated Numeracy lesson on money

As can be seen from the lesson on page 149, the teacher has planned for varying abilities while carrying the same theme through the lesson. When evaluating, you will need to look at whether the children you were working with were able to meet the learning objective through their task. If the majority of children achieved the objectives but one or two found certain aspects difficult, it would be appropriate to record by exception, i.e. 'This group were all able to complete the task and had a good understanding but George and Bayram could not understand the representation of 2p and 5p coins'. Similarly, if a child completes the task quickly and is more able than the rest of the group, this should also be recorded.

School, local and national policies and their implication for how you work with pupils

Your school should have a number of curriculum policies which will outline their aims and objectives for different curriculum areas. This will influence the way in which staff teach, both because of the content of what they teach and in how their time is organised. They will be updated in line with the school's School Development Plan which gives priorities for development each year. You should be aware of where to find policies for different subjects, as they should be accessible to all staff. You should also know the layout of your school's policies and how they affect the planning of various activities within the classroom.

Curriculum policies

The school's curriculum policies will also be influenced by local and national guidelines such as the QCA (Qualifications and Curriculum Authority) curriculum documents or exemplars which are published for each subject. These give suggestions for schemes of work to be used in each subject and at each Key Stage. Schools may adopt the QCA documents as part of their long-term planning, but this is not obligatory, and schools may use them as reference documents for schemes of work. They may be found on the QCA website: www.qca.org.uk/.

→ Knowledge into action

Ask your class teacher to show you a policy for one of the subject areas. Does your school use the QCA schemes of work as a basis for its planning?

Curriculum policies will also be valuable documents as they will outline aims and objectives for each subject and give information about how staff can guide pupils.

Some of the headings within a curriculum policy may be:

▷ Aims and objectives
▷ Delivery
▷ Assessment
▷ Policy links.

The staff guidelines may include:

▷ planning advice
▷ teaching and learning
▷ progression
▷ differentiation
▷ assessment, recording and reporting
▷ resources
▷ health and safety
▷ equal opportunities
▷ quality assurance

Knowledge into action

Find a copy of your school's science policy. Does it include staff guidelines for planning?

The Foundation Curriculum is separate from Key Stages 1 and 2 and should be supported by an Early Years Policy, as well as the DfES Curriculum Guidance for the Foundation Stage. This will guide early years teachers through the six Early Learning Goals and is designed to help with planning, assessing and teaching.

National documentation to support the curriculum will be sent to schools and local authorities by the DfES and given to staff by the headteacher. They may also be given to curriculum managers at local meetings to pass onto staff at the school's staff meetings.

End of unit test

1 What might an assistant need to do when helping to plan learning activities?

2 What are the main opportunities for assistants to share information in school?

3 Why is it good practice for assistants to plan alongside the class teacher?

4 Why is it sometimes difficult to implement?

5 What kinds of problems might assistants experience when evaluating learning activities?

6 Why do schools need to have curriculum policies?

References

National Numeracy Strategy (DfES)

National Numeracy Strategy – Guidance to Support Pupils with Specific Needs in the Daily Mathematics Lesson (DfES, 2001)

Curriculum Guidance for the Foundation Stage (QCA, 2000)

Websites

www.qca.org.uk/

Set B

Unit 3-9 Contribute to the planning and evaluation of learning activities

In this unit you will learn how to promote the social and emotional development of the children with whom you come into contact. You will need to know how to help pupils to form positive relationships with others. Pupils will need to learn respect for and rights of others and the importance of acceptable behaviour. They will start to develop skills of self-reliance and self-esteem as they grow in independence, and also begin to recognise and deal with their own emotions.

How to support pupils in developing relationships with others

In your role as a teaching assistant, you will need to know how to help pupils to develop relationships with others in the school. There are several different groups of people that children will need to be able to relate to and form relationships with while they are at school.

Their peers

This can be the easiest group for many children to form relationships in, but for some it can be difficult. Where children have a special need which affects their ability to communicate with others, if they speak English or Welsh as a second language, or if they have different home circumstances from others in the school, they may need to have support to help them to develop in this area. Strategies which may be useful for children with these types of difficulties can include the following:

▷ Small groups to develop the types of skills which these pupils need, for example learning the 'norms' of conversation: taking turns and responding to what the other person is saying.

▷ Adult intervention to help the child to mix with others, for example playing board and outdoor games with one or two other children. These types of activities will help the child to gain confidence when socialising.

▷ Small group activities to develop awareness of how people interact with others.

> **Teaching tip**: It's OK for adults to join in too. You can 'model' good social skills for children when playing games with them.

▲ Children may need support to develop their social skills

Pupils from different backgrounds and cultures

Children will need to be able to mix with pupils who are from different backgrounds. The school should have its own policies relating to equal opportunities and multiculturalism, which should outline the ways in which children's awareness is developed. Some children at the school may feel isolated or uncomfortable if they are from a different culture from the majority of pupils. They may be the only one who has to wear a particular item of clothing, for example, and may find that this makes them feel self-conscious. Staff should ensure that they surround children with positive images of those from all backgrounds and cultures.

➔ Knowledge into action

Find out about your school's policy for multiculturalism. How does the school teach and encourage children to find out about other cultures? What kinds of images of other cultures are available or have been brought to children's attention through assemblies, visits and so on?

Younger and older pupils

Children in a primary school should also be encouraged to mix with those from a different year group than their own. This may be done through extra curricular activities, or groups of children of different ages supporting one another and carrying out projects or investigations together. This is helpful for children as it encourages them to develop their social skills and learn to respect one another. If they are helping younger pupils, it will be a valuable experience in showing them how to help others.

Knowledge into action

Find out if you can take a small group of children to do some work with those of another age group in the school. Ask the older children if they can help the younger ones with investigative tasks, such as science or maths activities.

With adults

Children will need to be able to relate to different adults with whom they come into contact in school, for example parent helpers, teachers and teaching assistants, midday supervisors and others. It is important that adults are seen as good role models for all children. This means that children should also see adults forming positive relationships within the school and working effectively together.

Think about it

How often do children in your school see adults working co-operatively together?

Other circumstances affecting social development

There may be other issues which make it difficult for children to form relationships with others, and if children are having difficulties this may need to be investigated by school staff in order to help the child.

Home circumstances or upbringing

A child who has had a traumatic home background, or comes from a different environment from other children, may feel different from other children. A child who lives in bed and breakfast accommodation, or a traveller child might be very aware of the fact that they live in different circumstances from others.

Physical and emotional health

Children who have physical or emotional problems may feel isolated and 'different', which in turn may affect their social skills. If you are an assistant supporting a child with a physical disability or emotional difficulties, you may need to help them to mix with other children using some of the strategies shown above.

In order to help children to develop their social relationships, you will need to be aware of the different stages of social development which can be expected of the pupils with whom you are working.

Stages of social development

Reception: children will enter school and start to have an awareness of how they fit in to the group as a whole. They will start to develop friendships with others. They will learn about what is expected of them in school and respond well to praise and encouragement – for example, 'I wonder who can sit as nicely as Saad'.

Years 1 and 2: pupils may start to become more confident in school and test barriers of behaviour and co-operation. When there is any disruption to routines, or excitement such as at Christmas, they may find it hard to maintain levels of co-operation. They will have established friendships with others and be aware of acceptable levels of behaviour.

Years 3 and 4: children will become more self aware and may be critical of themselves and their own efforts. They may be influenced by others and how others see them. Their friends become more important to them although they may start to have disagreements, which can be traumatic.

Years 5 and 6: children at the end of the Primary phase will be more mature in their attitudes and staff should be able to give them more responsibilities.

Effects on children's behaviour

Where children have difficulties in their social development, this will sometimes result in behaviour problems. These types of conflicts may be minor, in which case children should be encouraged to try to resolve them amicably without involving others. The school may have a set of rules to help children to think about working and playing co-operatively with one another and you may need to remind them of these (see Unit 3-1 page 14). However, children may resort to more serious kinds of anti-social behaviour, including racist or sexist remarks, that will call for adult intervention. The school may have policies that relate to behaviour management and child protection for pupils when dealing with a range of abusive or anti-social behaviours (see also Unit 3-1). There may also be a scale of sanctions or strategies that are applied by staff when dealing with these behaviours. As a teaching assistant, you should know how to respond in such situations, particularly if they pose a threat to your own safety or the safety of others. However, if you have problems dealing with a situation you should always call on another member of staff.

You are on junior playground duty with one other adult when you notice that a group of Year 4 boys have started to taunt two new Year 3 children who have recently started at the school. You can hear them shouting racist remarks and following the children around the playground.

▶ What would you do in this situation?

▶ How would you deal with the problem if the situation became more difficult and the older boys refused to stop?

How to contribute to pupils' development of self-reliance and self-esteem

From an early age, pupils will need to start to develop their independence. In school, the development of their self-esteem and self-help skills will be encouraged from Reception, where the Early Learning Goals support pupils in thinking about how they will make their own decisions. As they progress further up the school, pupils will be expected to be able to have a range of self-help skills, which they will need to apply to their own learning. One of the most important roles you will have as an assistant is that of listening to children so that you can encourage them in their need to communicate their own ideas.

▲ Assistants can help by having positive relationships with children

Development of self-esteem in children

Children will begin to develop their self-esteem through the love and care given to them by their parents. If children grow up in a secure and stable home environment with love and affection, they will develop a positive self-image and feel valued. It is important for children that the love given to them by their parents and family is unconditional, and is not dependent on their looks or abilities. In the document *Curriculum Guidance for the Foundation Stage*, one of the aims of the curriculum is to 'provide opportunities for all children to succeed in an atmosphere of care and feeling valued'. The National Curriculum for Key Stages 1 and 2 promotes the development of self-help skills such as problem solving, decision-making and independent learning skills. As they grow older, children still need continued love and support to retain a positive self-image and to help their self-development. In school surroundings, we can help children to feel secure and valued by giving them routines and responsibilities, and by ensuring that staff are consistent. This will help them to feel confident in applying the skills they have learnt.

(See also Unit 3-15 page 218 – strategies to promote self-esteem in children, and Unit 3-1 page 6 for stages of social development.)

Developing and promoting children's self-help skills

Self-help skills emerge as children start to develop their own independence and choices when working. These include opportunities to learn skills in:

▷ independent learning – finding out and learning things for themselves through their work

▷ decision-making – thinking about the next step and being responsible for their actions

▷ problem solving – being able to think things through using their learning skills

▷ self expression – being able to express what they feel

▷ exercising choice – making their own choices about what they are going to do

▷ general life skills – being able to help themselves and others.

As a teaching assistant, children will ask you for your help with tasks that they may be able to do unassisted. For example, very young children may need help with putting on coats or getting changed for PE, as their co-ordination is still developing but as they get older they can do these things by themselves. You may need to break tasks down into smaller and more manageable steps, or talk children through them. As they become older, children may need help with organising themselves and planning their work, but you should be able to encourage them to be independent wherever possible. Your expectations should always be for children to succeed at what they are doing, and they should be encouraged and praised as much as possible. In this way, they will continue to attempt to be independent. For example, sometimes you might start something off for a child to encourage them to continue it.

How often are you asked by children for help with activities that they can do with a little encouragement? Do you always try to make the children carry out these activities for themselves?

You should make sure that you do not make stereotypical assumptions about pupils' self-reliance for any reason such as gender, disability or cultural background. You may not be aware that you are doing it, but by mentioning these issues, pupils' self-esteem and motivation can be easily damaged. You should also make sure that if you hear any children making comments about others in negative terms, you speak to them straight away.

Case study

Reece in Year 2 has completed a maths assignment very quickly with the group working on your table. One of the other boys on the table is now telling everyone that the boys will have finished before the girls as they are better at numbers.

1 What would you say to the boy who has made this comment?

2 Why should you make sure that you say something to him?

▲ Children must develop a good self-image in order to fulfil their potential

Levels of self-reliance and self-esteeem

Children who are developing normally will show levels of independence and self-reliance at about the stages defined in the tables of social and emotional development (see pages 6 and 163). It is important for adults to help children to build up their self-image and self-esteem through giving them tasks that are achievable for their age and stage of development. Children's self-image will be largely based on adults' reactions to what they do, which will in turn help them to gain a positive view of themselves. It is vital that children develop a good self-image as this will give them greater confidence in their abilities and enable them to fulfil their potential.

? Think about it

Jemma is in Year 6 and has to complete a history project on the Victorians. She has planned what she is going to do and been to the library and used the Internet to collect information. It is the first big project Jemma has been asked to complete and she is finding it difficult to organise. She asks you if she can show you what she has done one lunchtime.

▶ How could you encourage Jemma with her work?

▶ What would you do if Jemma asked for your help in organising her project?

Encouraging and supporting children in decision-making

As children become more mature, they will be given tasks which require them to make their own decisions and choices. They will need to be given guidance as to how they can think the process through to help them to do this.

The types of strategies you may like to use with children could include:

▷ asking them about the different factors which will affect their decision

▷ getting them to think about what will happen if they make a particular decision

▷ thinking about how to test whether this is the right decision

▷ making sure that you listen to their ideas and the reasons for making their choices.

Case study

A group of Year 4 children have been asked to think about the best material to use to make a picture frame. They have been given the choice of wood, plastic or any another material they can bring to school. The group are thinking about the advantages of each.

1 How would you question and support the children in their decision?

2 What kind of support would you give children who are finding it difficult to make a decision?

Giving positive praise and recognition to children

When children are in a learning environment, they will need to be given positive praise and encouragement to build up their self-esteem and to make them feel valued. When this happens, a child will be more likely to attempt to gain the same adult reaction by trying hard next time. If a child does not have any encouragement, and staff do not notice when they put in more effort, they will be less likely to do it again (see also Unit 3-1).

Your school may have policies and procedures for the recognition of achievements by pupils. These will be designed to encourage children to try hard with work and behaviour both inside and outside school. Schools will vary in the rewards that are given, but these may include:

▷ house points

▷ certificates

▷ awards for achievement in games or PE

▷ merits

▷ sent to headteacher/deputy/year group leader for verbal praise

▷ stars, stickers and stamps

▷ written encouragement of children's work

▷ special assemblies which recognise children's achievements

▷ giving children responsibilities.

Hurst Primary School

Certificate of Achievement

Awarded to: Lucy Burnham   3SB

for

20 good pieces of work

Signed... C. Roberts ...(headteacher)   Date... 30 October 2002

▲ A school certificate of achievement

? *Think about it*

What sorts of rewards and encouragement are given to children at different stages in your school?

The types of rewards and recognition that are given to children may depend on their age. Children who are in a Reception class may respond well to verbal praise or a smiley face sticker, whereas a Year 6 child may be given house points for working hard. Schools may also give responsibilities to children, to show that they are valued and respected as part of the organisation. This may vary from giving children a chance to be a 'helper' for the day, to being captain of the school netball or football team. You may also find that families have different ideas about what their children will achieve, due to family or cultural expectations. Some families might expect their children to be given responsibilities, as previous siblings have done well, while others may have high expectations of boys rather than girls. Some parents will have low expectations of their children and will not believe that they can do well.

? *Think about it*

Have you had experience of parents or families whose expectations for their children have been unrealistic? How have their expectations been different?

Keys to good practice
Encouraging children to be self-reliant and independent

✔ Praise children's achievements and their efforts.
✔ Do not talk negatively about children.
✔ Support children with choices and decision-making.
✔ Always give children tasks which they are able to do.

Contribute to pupils' ability to recognise and deal with emotions

When you are working with pupils as a teaching assistant, you will get to know them and learn how they are likely to deal with their emotions. Some children find this more difficult than others, and will have outbursts and behaviour problems if they feel that they are being treated unfairly. Others may keep their emotions hidden so that you are unable to tell if there is a problem. Emotional development is very closely linked with social development, as children are learning to become more confident in themselves. They will need to be able to show how both positive and negative emotions affect them. You must be aware which children in the class are likely to find the expression of emotions difficult. It is important for children to learn how to recognise and deal with their emotions so that they will grow up with more control over them.

(Stages of social development are to be found in this unit on page 156.)

Stages of emotional development

Children aged 4–6: Children entering school in reception will still be emotionally immature. They may have strong emotions as they become more independent and there will often be quarrels with other children. They may become easily upset by another child saying something which can seem like a short-lived comment to adults – for example, 'he's not my friend'. Some children may still have tantrums if they do not get their own way. These can sometimes be forgotten just as quickly as they have started if children are distracted or taken away from the situation.

Children aged 6–8: Children are starting to feel confident and have a sense of their own identity. They will start to feel proud of their achievements and abilities. They may be more self-aware and critical and become annoyed with themselves if they are not happy with their work. They should be able to recognise their emotions and adults may be able to explain to them why they are feeling like this and how they can deal with these emotions.

Children aged 8–11: Children may be more influenced by others and how they are perceived. They may be part of a group of children and these friendships will be very important to them. They may start to compare themselves with other pupils and can feel insecure and need reassurance.

School policies and practices for children with emotional and behavioural needs

Your school may have a range of strategies in place for supporting children who have emotional or behavioural difficulties. As discussed in Unit 3-1, the strategies you may need to use with these children should be those which are used by the whole school. It is important that children are aware of the consequences of their actions and why these sanctions are necessary.

School policies which relate to **children's emotional development** may include:

▷ behaviour policy – this will give staff strategies and guidelines when managing behaviour in school

▷ PSHE policy – this will give details of the way in which staff carry out the National Curriculum with regard to personal, social and health education

▷ inclusion and equal opportunities policies – these policies will promote the school's ethos and procedures in these two areas

▷ anti-bullying policy – since September 1999, schools have been legally required to implement anti-bullying policies

▷ child protection policy – this will have an effect on the way staff are alert at all times for signs of abuse or neglect in children. It will give you an indication of the key points which you need to observe and the person you need to go to in order to report any concerns

▷ schools are also now required to have a clear anti-racism policy.

You will need to know the range of strategies the school uses to diffuse and manage children's emotions.

In your class, you may find that the class teacher uses various strategies for managing negative emotions. Circle time is often used in classrooms although it is not always appropriate for very young children, as they need to sit for a long time to wait for their turn.

Staff will need to know how to recognise the types of activities which will encourage the expression of feelings and emotions. As an assistant, you should be able to support children and encourage them to express and discuss how they are feeling. You will need to be:

▷ **observant** – make sure you are always looking out for pupils. The class teacher may not be aware of a child who has been particularly quiet – but this could be a sign that there is a problem. There may also be a child who is behaving in a different way from usual, for example, is short tempered or seeking attention.

▷ **approachable** – if children feel comfortable with you and relaxed, they are more likely to come to you if they have a problem or are upset. They may also want to tell you about something good that has happened which is making them feel positive. You will need to try to develop good relationships with all children over time, through being interested and listening to what they have to say.

Teaching tip: Make sure you don't appear to favour only one child.

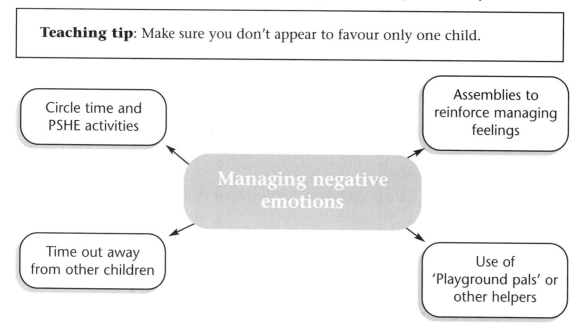

▲ There are different strategies for helping children to manage negative emotions

▷ **aware of confidentiality issues** – you must be aware that any information about a child is confidential and you should not discuss any issues outside the school environment. The school will also have policies and procedures for ensuring confidentiality, by making sure that computer passwords and files on children are only seen by those who are authorised to read them. Alternatively, a child with an emotional problem may approach you, or you may feel that they need to discuss something which is upsetting them with an adult. In this situation you will need to tell the child before they confide in you that you cannot guarantee that you will not tell another adult, for example, if a child is being harmed in any way.

▷ **possible causes of children's negative outbursts and reactions** – there is a variety of reasons that children may have negative outbursts or react in an uncharacteristic way. It is important that staff are aware of the different factors that can have an effect on children's behaviour.

Possible reasons for negative reactions by children
Bullying – the child may have been bullied intermittently for periods since they have been in school. They may be reluctant to tell staff as they are unsure of the response.
Inability to cope with academic work – the child may be finding that they cannot manage their work and need to have extra support, or be diagnosed as having special educational needs. This may be difficult for the child to manage emotionally.
Divorce or separation in family – the child may be angry with either parent, or be unable to express their emotions. They may also blame themselves for what has happened.
New baby – this may cause a child to feel insecure and need more attention. If this is not given at home, the child may try to gain attention in school.
Death or illness in family – this will upset the child and could cause outbursts or regressive behaviour, such as withdrawing or thumb-sucking.
Changing class or school – this may cause pupils to feel insecure and unsure about where they fit in with other children.
Substance abuse – children may seem to be detached and show signs of neglect or tiredness.
Sexual abuse – this may cause mood swings and changes in behaviour. The child may behave differently with other children or adults.
Physical abuse – children who are being physically abused may be nervous or jumpy around adults. They may find it difficult to trust adults and could be quiet or withdrawn and lack self-esteem.
Verbal abuse – children who are verbally abused may be very quiet and may also have low self-esteem.
Change in carer – this will have a disruptive influence on the child's home life and could affect their self-esteem as they may feel rejected. Children may become detached from others because of a fear of this happening again.
Moving house – this may be difficult if children need to start at a new school and form new relationships. Even moving home within the same area can be hard for some children.

Any of these factors may make it difficult for a child to manage their behaviour and emotions in school. Assistants will need to voice any concerns they have about particular children to others within the school.

Problems when dealing with children who have emotional difficulties

You may find that pupils are the victims of cultural or gender stereotypes, and are not freely able to talk about their feelings as they are not encouraged to at home. Some parents may not feel that boys, for example, should be able to discuss how they feel but should 'put a brave face on it.' This may limit the child's emotional development and make it difficult for them to bring their feelings into the open. If this is the case, you will need to be understanding and reassure them that it is acceptable to talk about feelings and emotions rather than keep them hidden.

When pupils are not able to express how they feel, there may be problems later and behavioural problems could arise, especially if pupils become frustrated by their inability to discuss their feelings.

Keys to good practice
Managing pupils' emotions

✔ Form good relationships with pupils.

✔ Look for any signs of distress/unusual behaviour.

✔ Always remain calm and reassure pupils.

✔ Be aware of confidentiality issues.

End of unit test

1 What different groups of people should children be encouraged to form positive relationships with in school?

2 What are the criteria that can affect the way in which a child relates to others?

3 What types of school policies can assist when helping children to develop positive relationships?

4 Why is it important for children to have a stable and secure home environment?

5 Name some of the different self-help skills we may need to help children with in school.

6 What kinds of factors will have an impact on a child's self-esteem?

7 Why might some families have higher or lower expectations of their children than the school?

8 What types of school policies will relate to children's emotional development?

9 How can you encourage children to come and discuss their emotions if they need to?

10 What kinds of signs may a child display who is suffering from emotional difficulties?

References

Curriculum guidance for the Foundation Stage (QCA, 2000)

National Curriculum document (QCA, 1999)

How to stop bullying: Kidscape, Training Guide

Websites

www.dfes.gov.uk/bullying

www.bullying.co.uk

www.childline.org.uk

www.kidscape.org.uk

Contribute to the maintenance of a safe and secure learning environment

In your role as a teaching assistant you will need to be aware of health and safety issues, both within the school and grounds and while visiting other places on school trips. Health and safety is a responsibility of all staff in the school, and you will need to know types of risks which may occur and to whom you need to report any safety issues.

If you are called upon to take action in the case of an emergency, you will need to know the level of assistance you should start to take, and the types of action you should not. As any other responsible adult who is first on the scene, teaching assistants should always assess the situation and act accordingly. If they are trained in first aid, they should do what they can to remove any immediate danger to the casualty but wait for the first aider or emergency services to arrive.

School policies and procedures for health and safety and your responsibilities within the school

When you first start at a new school, you should have access to or be informed about the school's policy for health and safety. The Health and Safety at Work Act (1974) was designed to protect everyone at work through procedures for preventing accidents. The types of precautions all those in the workplace are expected to observe are as described below.

Report any hazards

You will need to be alert to any hazards which are likely to cause injury to yourself and others in the school. The school is required to carry out an annual risk assessment to determine which areas and activities of the school are most likely to be hazardous, the likelihood of this occurring, and those who are at risk. Children and staff need to be vigilant and report any hazards which they notice immediately to the appropriate person. This may be the school's health and safety agent, the headteacher or another member of staff. You should be aware of the designated person to whom you should report health and safety matters.

(See pages 170 and 173 for the types of hazards which may occur.)

Follow the school's safety policy

The school's safety policy should give information to all staff about procedures which the school has in place for ensuring that the school is as safe as possible. All new staff joining the school should be given induction training in safety procedures and what to do in case of emergencies. Safety should be a regular topic at staff and assistants' meetings.

Make sure that their actions do not harm themselves or others

Staff also need to ensure that any actions which they take are not likely to harm or cause a danger to others in the school. This will include tidying up and putting things away after use. It also includes taking no action if they discover a potential danger: this would go against the employee's responsibilities according to the Health and Safety at Work Act.

Use any safety equipment provided

Staff will need to ensure that safety equipment which is provided for use when carrying out activities is always used. This will include safe use of tools which are used for subjects such as design and technology, or gloves when handling materials in science activities. There should be guidelines in the school's policy for the safe use and storage of equipment.

All staff working within a school have a responsibility to ensure that children are cared for and safe. The Children Act (1989) also requires that we protect children as far as we can when they are in our care. This includes preventing any risks which may occur.

The types of health, safety and security risks which may occur

(You will also need to read Unit 3-5 page 116 – Safe use and care of learning equipment and materials.)

Hazards which may be found in schools

The table below shows some of the hazards which may be found in schools and the action to take for them.

Internal hazards

Type of hazard (indoors)	What to do
Dangerous items left within children's reach (scissors, cleaning equipment and materials, kettles, hot drinks)	Remove or put away
Trailing electrical wires/overloaded plugs	Tidy if possible, or report
Untidy areas (things which can be tripped over)	Tidy if possible, or report
Fire doors obstructed	Always keep clear

Schools should carry out regular checks to ensure that these types of risks are kept to a minimum and that staff are aware why they need to be vigilant and what to look for.

There are also other materials and equipment used in schools which may present a risk if not used and stored correctly. Different stages or subject areas may use equipment and materials which are potentially hazardous to children or adults, although health and safety issues are relevant through all subject areas and all parts of the school:

▷ **Foundation Stage** – sand, water, play equipment. Young children will need to be taught to handle equipment safely and to consider how their actions can harm others.

▷ **PE** – apparatus use, movement and storage. In PE lessons, children will need to learn how to use equipment carefully and safely. Equipment should be regularly checked.

▷ **Design and technology** – tools or equipment. As these tools may not be used often, staff will need to talk to children each time about using them carefully.

▷ **Science** – living things, pond areas, use of equipment. Children should be taught always to wash their hands after touching animals, and to use any equipment safely.

▷ **Food technology** – cooking areas should be regularly checked and care should be taken with cookers. Cleaning substances should be stored out of reach of small children.

▷ **ICT** – Computers are in use all the time in schools and should be regularly checked. Office staff will probably be the only people using them for long periods and they should be aware of the importance of taking breaks.

▷ **Other electrical items** – equipment used in school will all need to have an annual safety check. If staff bring their own electrical appliances into school, these should always be checked before use, using a portable appliance tester, to prevent a risk to others.

Find out...

The person in your school who is responsible for checking electrical equipment. Where is this recorded?

Storing and moving equipment

All items should be stored or moved carefully, and only by those who are authorised to do so. Adults should not attempt to move items which are heavy or difficult to move. Items which may form a potential hazard should be locked away until they are needed. Storing items safely is important as people will often need to find them quickly and they will need to be able to see where they are and be able to reach them. Staff should ensure that storage areas are kept tidy and materials are not piled up to form a further danger.

▲ Materials should always be stored safely

Accidental breakages or spillages

When breakages and spillages do occur, they will need to be cleaned up as soon as possible to prevent any danger to others. If you are in a situation where an accident has occurred and you are not aware of where to find cleaning equipment, you should not leave the area unattended but send for another member of staff.

Disposal of waste

If you have been carrying out any activities, for example in science, where you need to dispose of waste materials, you should do so in such a way that will not cause harm to others. The school should offer guidance on the disposal of these types of materials. If you are in any doubt you should contact your school's health and safety agent.

Ensuring others are aware of where you are

You should ensure that the class teacher knows where you are at all times. This is so that in case of emergency, such as fire or a bomb scare, they will be able to find you. Different schools may have different procedures for doing this, so the class teacher should inform you of what to do if you are out of the classroom. It is particularly important if you are taking children away from the classroom for any reason.

There may be other hazards which are found outside, for example in playgrounds and pond areas. These will include dangers such as poisonous plants, areas which have not been fenced in, and risk of drowning. If you are taking children on a school trip, a member of staff should always visit first to check, among other things, for potential dangers.

External hazards

Type of hazard (outdoor/during school trips)	What to do
Playground areas – broken /faulty equipment – using equipment inappropriately, e.g. skipping ropes, bats and balls	Remove and label or report immediately Warn children or remove
Poisonous plants	Fence off area/warn older children
Litter bins	Keep children away from unsafe bins
Danger from animals	Ensure children always wash their hands after contact. Keep children away from animal faeces
Pond area	Ensure any cuts on hands are covered before getting wet (risk of leptospirosis – Weil's disease)

Visiting swimming pools

For visits to swimming pools, there are set minimum standards in safety. The headteacher is responsible for ensuring that all teaching staff involved have had sufficient training and information to allow them to carry out the sessions safely. There should always be an adult present who is competent in carrying out a rescue and artificial resuscitation. Other helpers will all need to be aware of emergency procedures.

Case study

You have been asked to accompany the Year 5 swimming class to their weekly lesson. Although you are aware of emergency procedures, and another teacher will be going to teach the class, the teacher who usually accompanies the group and supervises is off sick and you are unsure whether any other adult in the group is qualified in safety issues.

What should you do in this situation?

Visits to farms

When visiting farms, staff will need to be aware of school guidelines on these visits. The Health and Safety Executive has produced an information sheet – 'Avoiding ill health at open farms – advice to teachers' (AIS23 Supplement). This recommends that schools should ensure that children:

▷ wash their hands thoroughly after contact with animals

▷ cover cuts and grazes on hands with waterproof dressings

▷ eat only in designated areas

▷ stay in areas which are for visitors and keep gates closed

▷ wear appropriate footwear.

Disability Discrimination Act

With the introduction of the Disability Discrimination Act into schools from September 2002, staff will need to be increasingly aware of any increase in potential hazards when taking children on school visits. Children should not be excluded from any school visit because of their disability.

Knowledge into action

Investigate an area of your school (indoor or outdoor) for safety. Can you find any potential hazards? What are the school's procedures for reporting these?

School security

Schools need to ensure that they take measures to protect all adults and pupils while they are on school premises. This includes making sure that all those who are in school have been signed in and identified. Schools may have different methods for doing this, for example visitors may be issued with badges. If staff notice any unidentified people in the school, they should be challenged immediately. If you are on playground duty and notice anything suspicious, you should also send for help. Schools may also have secure entry and exit points which may make it more difficult for individuals to enter the premises.

Keys to good practice
Minimising risks in the learning environment

✔ Be vigilant.

✔ Use and store equipment safely.

✔ Report anything which is unsafe.

✔ Challenge unidentified persons.

Minimising risks arising from emergencies

What to do in an emergency

There are different types of emergencies and conditions which can occur in school. You may find that you are first on the scene in an emergency and need to take action. If you are the only adult in the vicinity, you will need to make sure you follow the correct procedures until help arrives. It is vital to send for help as soon as possible. This should be the ambulance if necessary and the school's qualified first aider.

Warning! If not trained in first aid, and if at all unsure about what to do, you should only take action to avert any further danger to the casualty and others.

Different emergencies and what you should do
Injuries – check the injury. For minor injuries such as a bump on the head or a graze, you should apply cold water. If the injury is more serious, you may need to take the victim to the qualified first aider in school. All injuries to the head should be recorded.
Epileptic seizure – do not try to move or restrain the patient. If possible, put something soft beneath their head to prevent them from hurting themselves. Clear a space around them.
Burns and scalds – cool the affected area immediately using cold water. Do not remove any clothes which are stuck to the burn.
Electrocution – cut off the source of electricity by removing the plug. If there is no way to do this, stand on dry insulating material, such as newspaper or a wooden box, and push the victim away from the source using something wooden such as a chair. Do not touch the victim until the electricity has been switched off. After this, place the victim in the recovery position (see pages 176–7).
Choking or difficulty with breathing – if a child, encourage them to cough to dislodge the blockage. Bend the casualty over with the head lower than the chest and slap between the shoulder blades five times using the heel of the hand.
Poisoning – find out what the child has taken or swallowed if possible. Stay with the child and watch for signs of unconsciousness. Take the suspected poison to hospital with you.
Cardiac arrest – if the patient is conscious, place in a half sitting position and support with pillows and cushions. Place another pillow under the knees. Do not give the patient food or water. If the patient becomes unconscious, place in the recovery position (see pages 176–7).
Substance abuse – if you can, find out what has happened so that you can inform medical staff. If the person is unconscious, place in the recovery position (see pages 176–7). Do not try to induce vomiting.

Falls – potential and actual fractures: all cases should be treated as actual fractures. Do not attempt to move the casualty. You will need a qualified first aider to come to the scene. Support a fractured leg by tying it to the other leg, using a wide material such as a scarf or tie. If the knee is broken, you must not try to force it straight. If you suspect a fractured arm, support in a sling and secure to the chest. If the arm will not bend, secure by strapping it to the body.

Faints or loss of consciousness – treat those who feel faint by sitting down and putting their head between their knees. If they do faint, lie them on their back and raise their legs to increase blood flow to the brain. Loosen clothing at the neck and keep the patient quiet after regaining consciousness.

Severe bleeding – it is important to reduce the flow of blood as soon as possible. You should summon the first aider and call for help. Lie the casualty down and remove clothing around the wound if possible. Press down hard on it with any absorbent clean material, or squeeze the sides together if there is no foreign body in the wound. If possible, raise the wound to above the level of the heart. This will slow the flow of blood. Maintain the pressure for up to ten minutes and then place an absorbent material over the wound and bandage firmly. Do not remove the bandage. If there is a foreign body in the skin, do not remove it but bandage around if possible without putting pressure on the object. If you remove the object, it will cause the victim to lose more blood.

Shock – lie the victim down and treat whatever may be causing the shock. Loosen clothing at the neck to assist breathing. Raise the legs if possible and keep warm. Do not give the victim anything to eat or drink in case they need an anaesthetic, but moisten lips if necessary.

Putting a casualty into the recovery position

If you are dealing with an unconscious person, you will need to place them in the recovery position. This will prevent any blood, vomit or saliva from blocking the windpipe. You should always do this unless you suspect that the victim has a fracture of the spine or neck.

1 Kneel beside the victim and turn their head towards you, lifting it back to open the airway.

2 Place their nearest arm straight down their side and the other arm across their chest. Place the far ankle over the near ankle.

3 While holding the head with one hand, hold the victim at the hip by their clothing and turn onto their front by pulling towards you, supporting them with your knees.

4 Lift the chin forward to keep the airway open.

5 Bend the arm and leg nearest to you, and pull out the other arm from under the body, palm up.

Put 2 fingers under the child's chin and 1 hand on the forehead.

Gently tilt the head back. Straighten limbs. Bend the arm nearest to you so it is at right angles to the body.

Bring the other arm across the child's chest. Place the hand against the child's cheek - with palm outwards. Pull up the child's far leg, just above the knee, using your other hand.

Pull on the far leg and roll the child towards you, still pressing the hand against the cheek - until the child is lying on their side.

Make sure the child's head is well back - to keep airway open and stop them from breathing in vomit or choking on their tongue.

To stop the child rolling too far, use your knees as support. Bend the upper leg so that it is at a right angle from the body.

Make sure the upper arm is supporting the head.

▲ Putting a casualty into the recovery position

If you are treating a casualty, you should be aware of the dangers of contamination from blood and other body fluids. Always wear protective gloves if you can when treating an open wound or if you have contact with other body fluids. Many infections such as HIV and hepatitis can be passed on through contact with these fluids.

You should always stay with the casualty and give as much support as you can, both by giving as much care as you are able and by your physical presence. If you feel that you are not able to deal with the situation, you should always do what you can and reassure the patient as much as possible while sending for help. Where a child has been injured badly, their parents or carers should be notified immediately. They will need to know exactly what is happening – if the child is being taken to hospital they will need to know where.

Religious and cultural restrictions on the actions which you may be able to take

When dealing with an emergency, you should be aware that some religions or cultures may not agree with some treatments – for example, some Muslims may only wash under running water. If you are in any doubts as to what action you can take, always speak to parents first if at all possible.

Knowledge into action

Have you ever needed to deal with an emergency at your school? What kind of treatment were you able to give?

Treating others

If others are in the vicinity at the time of the accident, they may need to have support after the initial danger has passed. This could be due to emotional distress or shock, which can have a serious effect. If you have been involved with treating the victim but another person has now taken over, you should offer what support you can to others in the area. This may include giving them privacy and making the area safe.

Completing accident forms

By law, the school will have procedures for recording and reporting accidents. All accidents, whether they are serious or minor, must be recorded. There may be a school accident book and a local authority accident form. The type of information required will be:

▷ the name of the casualty (child or adult)

▷ what happened

▷ the date and time of the accident

▷ the cause of the accident

▷ the treatment given.

If there has been an accident you should send for the designated first aider straight away, but in the meantime:

▷ remain calm

▷ check there is no further danger to the victim or others.

You should always stay with the casualty and give as much support as you can, both by giving as much care as you are able and by your physical presence.

Your school may give you the opportunity to go on a recognised first aid course to gain a certificate or qualification in first aid. If you are able to attend, these courses are worthwhile and could be beneficial both for yourself and for others.

Other emergencies

All workplaces must carry out regular fire practices so that staff are aware of procedures. In a school, this ensures that children also know what to do. These procedures will also apply to bomb scares and any other need for building evacuation. If you discover a fire, you should sound the nearest alarm and ensure everyone leaves the building as quickly and calmly as possible. It is important to remain calm and to check that all children

Sunnymead Primary School
Accident report form

Name of casualty . . . .

Exact location of incident . . . .

Date of incident . . . .

What was the injured person doing? . . . .

How did the accident happen? . . . .

What injuries occurred? . . . .

Treatment given . . . .

Medical aid sought . . . .

Name of person dealing with incident . . . .

Name of witness . . . .

If casualty was a child, what time were parents informed? . . . .

Was hospital attended? . . . .

Was the accident investigated? . . . . By whom? . . . .

Signed . . . . Position . . . .

and adults have been accounted for. Remember to include any parent helpers or other adults who are in school by checking the school signing-in book.

→ *Knowledge into action*

Are regular fire practices carried out in your school? Are there clear guidelines for evacuation and assembly points?

Fire extinguishers

There are different types of fire extinguishers, and if you need to use one you should make sure that you read the instructions carefully. These will be printed on the outside of the extinguisher.

Water – for wood, paper and textiles

Foam – for wood, paper, textiles, petrol, oil, fats, paints, etc.

Powder – for wood, paper, textiles, petrol, oils, fats, paints, electrical hazards, vehicle protection

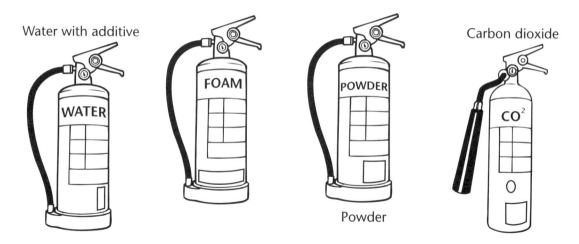

Water with additive

WATER

FOAM

POWDER

Powder

Carbon dioxide

CO^2

▲ Different fire extinguishers must be used for different types of fire

Carbon dioxide – for petrol, oils, fats, paints, electrical hazards

Fire blanket – for smothering a fire (usually kept in a kitchen) and putting around someone whose clothes are on fire.

End of unit test

1 What are your responsibilities under the Health and Safety at Work Act?

2 Name three hazards which may be found in a classroom.

3 Of what should you be aware when bringing an electrical appliance into school for use?

4 What types of areas may be hazardous outside the school building?

5 What should you do in the event of a burn?

6 When should you put a patient in the recovery position?

7 How can you help others once expert help has arrived to treat the casualty?

8 Why must you be careful with different types of fire extinguisher?

9 What sort of information is recorded on an accident form?

10 Why do you need to be careful when handling body fluids?

References

What to Do in an Emergency (Readers Digest Association, 1988)

Tassoni, P., *Certificate in Child Care and Education* (Heinemann, 2002)

Websites

www.teachernet.gov.uk/visits (good practice guide to health and safety of pupils on educational visits)

Unit 3-11 Contribute to the health and well-being of pupils

This unit deals with the care and support given to children while they are adjusting to a new setting. Assistants will need to show that they support the teacher in the strategies which are used to help and reassure pupils. They will also need to be able to deal with any particular difficulties which the child is experiencing in settling in. Where pupils have any medical needs, assistants will need to know the school policies for the storage and administration of medicines and how to care for pupils with signs of ill-health. (For details of what to do in an emergency, see Unit 3-10 page 175.)

How to support pupils in adjusting to a new setting

If you are helping pupils to adjust to a new setting, this may be for a variety of reasons:

▷ the children have just started school in Reception

▷ pupil(s) are joining an existing class

▷ the class is transferring at the start of a new academic year

▷ pupil(s) are re-joining the class after a period of extended absence.

Assistants will need to be able to help pupils in each of these situations to become used to the new setting through a range of strategies. Some children may not need to have much adult intervention to help them to settle in, while others may find it more difficult.

Pupils starting school in Reception

The year group leader, if there is one, class teacher and assistants will all need to discuss the strategies which they will use with the new group of children. The school may have set guidelines and procedures that are to be used with all children. These may be routine and include:

▷ coming to the school before the start date to meet the class teacher and look at their new classroom

▷ staggering the children's entry so that they start at 5- or 10-minute intervals on the first day

▷ staying for part of the day and building up to include lunchtimes and then afternoons

▷ having separate playtimes for the first week or two

▷ being shown around the school so that they are aware of different areas and when they are likely to use them (office, hall/dining hall, playground, etc.).

As the children become settled in school, they will gradually learn the rules and routines which they will be expected to follow. This process will take place over time as the children become used to being in a school environment.

→ **Knowledge into action**

Are you aware of procedures which teachers in the Reception classes in your school follow for settling in new children? Do they have any that are different from those listed above?

Pupil(s) joining an existing class

When pupils join an already established class, they may find it quite difficult to come into a class where the majority of children already know rules and routines. Assistants and teachers will need to work together to help them to adjust and feel part of the class. The strategies that could be used in this situation would include:

▷ encouraging other children to make new arrivals feel welcome through interacting with them and showing them around

▷ showing them around the classroom and class routines

▷ giving them information about the school which you feel would be useful for them to know – playtimes, lunchtimes, location of key areas, school rules

▷ being approachable and available if the child needs help in any way.

→ **Knowledge into action**

Have you been in a class which has been joined by a new pupil? Think about the kinds of strategies you have used to help them to settle in.

Class transferring at the start of a new academic year

If you support an individual child, you may be in a position where you are moving with all the children into a different class. This may make the process easier for them, since they will have an adult they recognise who will know them. However, children will become more used to changing class each year as they progress up the school, and most will be excited to be moving up into the next year group. If you are a teaching assistant working within a class, you can help the children to settle in by:

▷ emphasising the importance of moving into the next year group

▷ showing them the layout of the classroom

▷ encouraging them to join in with class activities

▷ discussing with them any rules or responsibilities which are specific to the year group, e.g. 'Now you are in Year 6, you are allowed to go in first at lunchtime', 'Years 3 and 4 are in charge of changing the words on the overhead projector in assembly'

▷ being approachable and available for any questions the children may have.

Have there been any cases in your school where children have found it difficult to settle into a new class? What have been the reasons for this? How has the problem been resolved?

Pupil(s) rejoining the class after a period of extended absence

Sometimes pupils may leave the class for a period, for example if they are travellers, or if they have special needs and have required help within another setting for a time. They may find it difficult to adjust to a new environment or be self-conscious about returning and their reasons for being away from the school. You can help them to settle back into the class by:

▷ being available for them to talk through any concerns

▷ support their integration with other children

▷ helping them with any specific problems.

Case study

Paul is from a travelling family and often misses school for extended periods. He is not unhappy about returning to the school environment but often finds it difficult to settle and focus on his work. How would you encourage Paul to become used to the school and become involved with other children?

Factors which may affect a pupil's ability to adjust to a new setting

Sometimes pupils may find it difficult to settle due to external factors. These may include:

▷ the home background of the child – the child may have a disruptive or traumatic home life

▷ the care history – the pupil may not like change if there have been changes in carer at home

▷ if the child speaks English or Welsh as an additional language (see Unit 3-12)

▷ any special educational needs which the child has – this may affect the child's understanding of what is happening.

You will need to be able to support children in all these situations through discussions with teachers, parents and helpers. These children may need more reassurance and help and sometimes display challenging behaviour (see also Unit 3-1 for strategies for managing this).

It is vital that the class teacher is aware of any problems or difficulties that a child has in adjusting or settling in. If you notice or find out about any issues, or if a parent or other member of staff tells you about a child's home circumstances and you do not think the teacher is aware, you must talk to the teacher about it immediately.

School policies and practices relating to medical issues

The school may have a number of policies relating to the medical care of pupils while they are in the setting. These may follow guidelines set out by the Local Education Authority, which should be available to all schools. You should know where to go to ask about them and to find out about your responsibilities.

When the child first enters school, parents will be asked to provide health details which may include whether their child has any allergies, medication and so on (see below).

St Marks Primary School

Declaration of Health Form

Child's surname . . . . Date of birth . . . .

First names . . . .

Address . . . .

. . . .

Telephone number (home) . . . .

Parent/carer's work/mobile telephone numbers:

Mother . . . . Father . . . .

Name and address of GP . . . .

. . . . Telephone no . . . .

Health Details

Does your child have:

Asthma YES/NO   Eczema YES/NO   Epilepsy YES/NO   Diabetes YES/NO

Any allergies . . . .

Details of medication . . . .

Is there any other information you feel we should know about your child?

. . . .

. . . .

▲ Parents complete a form like this when their child first starts school

These types of records will be kept in the child's file, although if there is any medication which needs to be administered in school, or medical treatment for conditions such as asthma or allergies, these should be kept in a central area such as the school office and treated as confidential. There may be a member of staff who is responsible for administering medication, although this is a voluntary role and should not be expected of staff. If there is not a member of staff who is prepared to administer medicines, parents should be informed in writing and told that an ambulance will be called immediately in the event of an emergency.

Find out...

Is there a volunteer in your school who administers medication to children and how often are they called upon to do it. What training have they had?

Common medical conditions

Medical conditions which may require medication to be administered in schools may include the following:

▷ **Asthma** – children needing inhalers due to a respiratory condition should have access to these quickly in case of emergency.

▷ **Diabetes** – if hypoglycaemia occurs, the child will need to take oral glucose, for example food, glucose tablets or glucose gel.

▷ **Epilepsy** – children who are on medication for epilepsy are seldom required to take it during school hours, as it is usually taken twice a day. However, if medication is required three times a day, volunteers in the staff may be asked to administer it.

▷ **Anaphylactic shock** – some children have severe allergic reactions to certain substances such as nuts or milk and can suffer anaphylactic shock. The only way in which this can be treated in school is through the administration of adrenalin via an Epipen or Anapen. For this to be administered, staff will need to have had specific training.

▷ **Attention Deficit Hyperactivity Disorder (ADHD)** – school-aged children are being increasingly diagnosed with this disorder and the most common form of medication which is used to treat these children is Ritalin.

Schools may also be asked to administer antibiotics and may have a policy as to whether or not they do this. If antibiotics are prescribed to be taken three times a day, it is not necessary to administer them during school time, but children who need four doses may need to have one at lunchtime. It is likely that the school will have a policy as to whether or not they will administer medication which has not been prescribed by a doctor. They should also keep a record of medication given. Medication that is to be administered in school should always be correctly labelled and locked in a safe place until required.

Administration of medicines record sheet

Name of pupil . . . .

Date	Time	Name of medication	Dose given	Any reactions	Signature

▲ Where medication is given, it should be recorded

Keys to good practice
Administering medicines in school

✔ Gain parental consent to administer medication.

✔ Keep a record of medication given.

✔ Store all medication in a safe place and keep labelled.

✔ Keep any urgent medication close to the child.

✔ Keep a list of children who have medication in school.

✔ Make sure medicines are not out of date.

Access to routine and emergency medical care

In school there must be at least one qualified first-aider who is trained to administer immediate help to casualties with common injuries or illnesses while in school (see also Unit 3-10 page 175). They will be trained to deal with routine medical incidents such as bumps on the head and cuts and grazes. You should be aware of who these people are so that you can send for them in an emergency along with the emergency services. Where children have needed medical treatment or have hurt themselves, the school may decide to telephone the parents to tell them what has happened. Any injuries to the head should also be recorded. Staff will need to be aware of the school's confidentiality requirements when recording and reporting health problems.

The school may have to decide whether to phone a parent if the child is ill or has been hurt. If the child is very ill, distressed or badly injured, the parent will need to be informed immediately by telephone (see Unit 3-10 page 177 for informing parents in cases of emergency). You will need to give reassurance and support to children who are ill or suffering from a condition which is distressing to them. The support or advice which you give them will be dependent on the age and stage of development of the child.

Case study

Michael is in Reception and has conjunctivitis. The school policy states that he should be sent home as the condition is highly contagious. Michael has become very distressed about his eyes and says that they itch and hurt. He is worried because he has come out of his classroom and the school has called his mother.

1 What would you say to Michael to reassure him?

2 How would the treatment and advice be different with an older child?

School policies relating to health and hygiene issues

The school should have policies relating to the way in which health issues are managed. These will include routines and procedures for everyday health and hygiene, such as washing hands before lunch and after using the toilet. All staff should be aware of how children need to be reminded about health issues and how these will affect themselves and others. The school should have a policy for PSHE (personal, social and health education) which will include information about the way in which children are taught about health. This may be through cross-curricular activities or taught on its own. Pupils will need to learn about healthy lifestyles and may have visits from people who work in the community such as the school nurse, ambulance service and road safety officer.

If you need to answer any questions from pupils about health and hygiene, you should make sure that you are following school policy.

Case study

Amira is a classroom assistant in a Year 1 class. The children have been incubating eggs as part of their topic on living things. Once they have hatched, Amira has been allowing the children to handle the chicks when they are a few days old. However, Amira forgets to remind the children to wash their hands after handling the chicks.

1 Do you think that this is important?

2 What might be the repercussions?

You may notice that pupils have different attitudes from home towards health and hygiene issues. Some families may bring their children up in more clean and hygienic environments than others and this may be reflected in the child's clothing or personal hygiene. Different factors may affect a child's personal hygiene habits:

▷ Age – very young children may not yet have established routines for cleanliness and hygiene.

- Gender – boys and girls may have different attitudes towards keeping clean.
- Cultural/ethnic background – this may affect the importance of cleanliness, particularly if the child has a religion which requires them to be extremely clean.
- Specific medical conditions – children may need particular help, for example if they are catheterised.

These factors may also affect the actions you can take when attending to a child's signs of ill-health. For example, if a child already has a medical condition and is on medication, you will need to inform any others who come to attend to them.

You will also need to adhere to health and safety regulations and guidelines when you are attending to children's health. Guidance on health and safety regulations will be given in the school's health and safety and child protection policies and through information provided by the local authority. The main points to remember are as follows.

- If children need to be changed or undressed, following wetting or soiling themselves, they should do this themselves if possible and in private. If staff need to change children for any reason, they should not do it on their own but should have another member of staff present.
- Where a child's necessary medication needs to be administered other than orally, for example through a suppository, staff should again always be accompanied by another member of staff.
- Ask for assistance in any situation in which you feel uncomfortable about administering medication or health care unaccompanied by another adult.
- Always report any possible signs of abuse which you may notice when administering medical or health care (see also Unit 3-1 page 11).

Signs and symptoms of some common illnesses

All staff should be aware of the types of illnesses that may occur in children. They should also be alert to physical signs that may show children are incubating an illness. This can vary between illnesses, from 1 day to 3 weeks in some cases. General signs that children are 'off colour' may include:

- pale skin
- flushed cheeks
- different behaviour (quiet, clingy, irritable)
- rings around the eyes.

The Department of Health has issued a useful poster to schools which could be displayed in the first aid area as a quick reference: 'Guidance on infection control in schools and nurseries'. This clearly sets out some common illnesses and their characteristics. Some of these are listed below, although this list is not exhaustive.

Common illnesses and their characteristics

Illness and symptoms	Recommended time to keep off school/ treatment	Comments
Chickenpox – patches of red spots with white centres (itchy).	For five days from onset of rash. Treat with calomine lotion to relieve itching.	Not necessary to keep at home until scars heal.
German measles (rubella) – pink rash on head, trunk and limbs. Slight fever, sore throat.	For five days from onset of rash. Treat by resting.	Child is most infectious before diagnosis is made. Keep away from pregnant women.
Impetigo – small red pimples on the skin which break down and weep.	Until lesions are crusted and healed. Treat with antibiotic cream or medicine.	Antibiotic treatment may speed up healing. Wash hands well after touching the child's skin.
Ringworm – contagious fungal infection of the skin, shows as circular flaky patches.	None. Treat with anti-fungal ointment, may require antibiotics.	Needs treatment by GP
Diarrhoea and vomiting	Until diarrhoea and vomiting has settled and for 24 hours after. No specific diagnosis or treatment, although keep giving clear fluids (no milk).	
Conjunctivitis – inflammation or irritation of the membranes lining the eyelids.	None (although schools may have different policies on this). Wash with warm water on cotton wool swab. GP may prescribe cream.	
Measles – fever, runny eyes, sore throat and cough. Red rash, often starting from the head and spreading downwards.	Rest, plenty of fluids, paracetamol for fever.	Now more likely with some parents refusing MMR inoculation.
Meningitis – fever, headache, stiff neck and blotchy skin. Dislike of light. Symptoms may develop very quickly.	Urgent medical attention, antibiotics.	Can have severe complications and be fatal.
Tonsillitis – inflammation of tonsils by infection. Very sore throat, fever, earache, enlarged red tonsils which may have white spots.	Treat with antibiotics, rest.	Can also cause ear infections.

Staff will need to be alert to signs and symptoms of these types of illnesses, and notice changes in children's behaviour which may indicate that they are unwell. Children often develop symptoms more quickly than adults, as they may have less resistance to infection.

Maintaining your own health and safety when dealing with pupils who have health problems

You must remember to think about your own safety when you are dealing with pupils who have health and medical problems. You should make sure that you are aware of the kinds of situations which are potentially hazardous when dealing with first aid situations. Remember good personal hygiene at all times, and that the risk of transmission of infection is minimal if staff adopt sensible precautions:

▷ Cuts to the hands should be covered by a waterproof dressing to minimise risk of infection.

▷ Always wear disposable gloves when dealing with blood and body fluids.

▷ Wash your hands after removing the gloves and prior to eating or drinking.

▷ Any spillages of blood or body fluids must be reported to the caretaker immediately.

Other medical professionals who come into school or ask for information about children may include the school nurse, or visitors from medical establishments who come to discuss children who have special needs. If children have any medical condition which you feel needs to be discussed with another professional, you should speak to the class teacher or SENCo.

Sometimes, the child may be in a class where there are cases of head lice, ringworm and other conditions which are contagious. The school will usually write to inform parents if there is more than one or two cases. When keeping children off school, parents should be aware of the school's normal policies for different illnesses. For example, if a child has had sickness or diarrhoea, the school may say they must have been better for 24 hours before coming back.

Contacting parents

The school may have to decide whether to phone a parent if the child is ill or has been hurt. If the child is very ill, distressed or badly injured, the parent will need to be informed immediately by telephone (see Unit 3-10 page 177 for informing parents in cases of emergency).

Many schools have a standard letter for head lice.

Holy Cross Infant School

Dear Parent

We have been informed by a parent that one of the children in your child's class has had to be treated for head lice. We feel it is important to inform you so that you will be extra vigilant and take the simple steps needed to combat the problem.

In a normal school environment, where children work and play closely together, head lice find it easy to transfer from head to head. Remember, head lice prefer clean hair, so the possibility of infection is quite high. Your child has as much chance of being infected as any other.

Fortunately head lice are easy to treat and you should follow the attached guidelines from the health authority to do this.

As a preventative, the only form of treatment is to comb your child's hair thoroughly every day, and if your child has long hair, to keep it tied back.

Yours sincerely,

J A Sampson
Headteacher

▲ A standard letter informing parents of a head lice outbreak

End of unit test

1 In what circumstances might you need to help pupils adjust to a new setting?
2 What sorts of strategies could you use to help pupils to settle in?
3 What factors would make it more difficult for a child to settle?
4 What types of policies may relate to medical issues?
5 Who should administer medicines in school?
6 When would staff need to report or record any medical treatment?
7 Why might pupils have different factors which influence their attitude to personal hygiene?
8 In what kinds of situations would you require another adult to be present?
9 Name five common illnesses which may be prevalent in schools.
10 What would a school do if there was no member of staff prepared to administer medication?

References

Stanway, P., *Mothercare Guide to Child Health* (Conran Octopus, 1992)

Websites

Information on infectious diseases: www.phls.co.uk

Health information for teachers: www.wiredforhealth.co.uk

Department of Health: www.doh.gov.uk

Useful addresses

National Asthma Campaign, Providence House, Providence Place, London, N1 ONT (020 7226 2260)

Department of Health, Richmond House, 79 Whitehall, London SW1A 2NS (020 7210 4850)

Diabetes UK, 10 Parkway, London NW1 7AA (020 7424 1000)

Epilepsy Action, New Anstey House, Gate Way Drive, Yeadon, Leeds, LS19 7XY (0808 800 5050)

Provide support for bilingual and multilingual pupils

This unit looks at the way in which pupils develop their language skills. Children from bilingual and multilingual backgrounds will need more support in the classroom when developing these skills. Assistants will need to be aware of the way in which all children process language and the importance for bilingual and multilingual pupils of retaining their identity through valuing and promoting their home language. In this unit, you will identify strategies for promoting children's development in speaking and listening, reading and writing in the target language, which may be English or Welsh. You will need to build on the pupils' experience when developing their skills in the target language and encourage them to develop as independent learners.

Processes and stages of language acquisition and how to promote language development

In order to build up a picture of how we learn language, it is important to consider the two different stages which linguists consider all children pass through. These are known as the **pre-linguistic stage** and the **linguistic stage**:

▷ The pre-linguistic stage is during the first 12 months, when babies begin to learn basic communication skills. During this time they will be starting to attract the attention of adults and repeat back to them the different sounds they hear. This will be true of any language, and although very young babies will make the same sounds all over the world, by the age of around 12 months children will only be repeating back the sounds which they have heard around them.

▷ The linguistic stage is when babies start to use the words that they are hearing and begin to learn how to make sentences. Children will develop this stage gradually over the next few years so that by the age of around 5 they will be fluent in their home language. Children who are learning more than one language may learn to speak slightly more slowly as they absorb two different systems. This should not, however, affect their overall language development.

The table on page 194 shows the stages of language development in children. Adults will need to support children through all of these stages in order to encourage and promote their language development. At each different stage, the role of the adult may be different. For example, a baby will need positive recognition of their attempts to communicate through eye contact and speech. A 5- or 6-year-old may need adults to help them to extend their vocabulary through the use of open-ended questions, or 'what if?' strategies. Where children's language progresses more slowly through these stages, there may be other factors involved, such as:

▷ learning more than one language

▷ a communication difficulty such as autism

▷ a speech difficulty such as a stutter

▷ lack of stimulation from others

▷ a hearing impairment.

Stages of language development in children

Age	Stage of development
0-6 months	Babies will try to communicate through crying, starting to smile and babbling. They will start to establish eye-contact with adults.
6-18 months	Babies start to speak their first words. They will start to use gestures to indicate what they mean. At this stage, they will be able to recognise and respond to pictures of familiar objects.
18 months-3 years	Children will start to develop their vocabulary rapidly. They will start to make up their own sentences. At this stage, children will enjoy simple and repetitive rhymes and stories.
3-8 years	Children will start to use more and more vocabulary and the structure of their language may become more complex. As children develop their language skills, they will be able to use language in a variety of situations.

Theories of language acquisition

There have been several theories put forward about how children learn or acquire language. In the early part of the twentieth century there were a number of theories with the same broad idea. This was that children acquire language by learning a word together with the thing it means or stands for. Through interacting with adults they will begin to develop sounds which have meaning and which will gain a positive response. This is called the **associationist theory**.

Noam Chomsky, an American linguist working in the 1960s, claimed that we are all born with an innate knowledge of the system of language, or a 'Language Acquisition Device'. In this way, whatever language we need to learn and the accompanying grammar will be decoded by the child. This theory helps to explains how children will often apply grammatical rules which they have heard, sometimes wrongly, because they have not yet learned exceptions to these rules. An example of this might be 'I bringed my drink'.

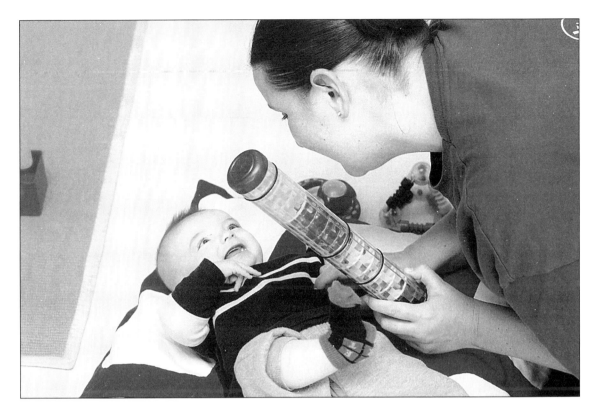

▲ Babies love to communicate from a very young age

John Macnamara, working in the 1970s, proposed that children are able to learn language because they have an ability to make sense of situations. This means that they will understand the intention of a situation and respond accordingly. For example, if a child sees that an adult is beckoning towards them and holding out their hand, they will know that the adult's intention is for the child to come towards them. This will be the case even if the child does not understand the words that the adult is saying.

Although there have been many theories about how children develop language, there are still no definite answers about how language development takes place. Adults who work in educational settings will need to be aware of ways in which we can help all children to develop their language skills and build on their present knowledge.

Further research has shown that children who are bilingual or multilingual must be able to relate their home language to individuals when they are first learning language. For example, if a child speaks Arabic with their parents, it is important for the child to speak only Arabic with them and not to switch languages when first learning to talk. This is because for the child it is important to develop a distinction between languages which is easier for them if they relate to different people.

Opportunities for developing language

Children from all backgrounds, whether they are learning one or more languages, need to be given opportunities to develop their language skills in a variety of different ways. The list below shows the types of opportunities we must give to bilingual or multilingual children in school. All of these areas need to be considered when the school has even one bilingual child.

Keys to good practice
Opportunities for developing language

✔ Creating a secure and happy environment where the children feel valued and part of the class and school

✔ Raising cultural awareness in school

✔ Reinforcement of language learning using resources such as dual language texts

✔ The reinforcement of language learning by giving children immediate verbal and non-verbal feedback and praise

✔ Making sure that children are given time to think about questions before they respond

✔ Creating more opportunities for speaking and listening. These could include opportunities such as paired conversations with other children.

Backgrounds of pupils with more than one language and how this can affect their learning and the development of the target language

Where children have come from a different background, culture or language to others in the class, entering school may be a challenging experience for them. They may find it difficult due to lack of confidence or self-esteem, and staff will need to be aware of their needs. Sometimes bilingual assistants will be employed, especially where there are a large number of children who speak English as a second language. Usually the school will have systems in place when children enter school so that they are aware of those children who speak English or Welsh as a second language. Parents will have been asked to fill in forms before the child enters school, which will include this information.

Staff must be aware of the different backgrounds of individual children as they come into school, as these will all influence their learning and the development of the target language. It can be very difficult to assess the needs of bilingual pupils, and staff will need to find out whatever they can about the child when they first enter school in order to support them fully. The different backgrounds of children will influence their behaviour in school and the way in which their language skills develop.

Educational backgrounds

When children enter school at the age of 4, there will be some information about their background from the forms which parents and carers are required to fill in. There may also be records from the child's pre-school or nursery which will give some indication of their progress to date in the target language. If your school is the first contact the child has had with the target language, the school will need to devise some educational targets for them to work on so that they can begin to develop their language skills (e.g. see below).

It is important to gain as much information as possible about the child's previous school if they have transferred. The school will be required to send records of assessment and attainment but these may take some time to come through, and the class teacher may need to telephone the previous school, particularly if there is an area of concern. Where children have come from very different educational backgrounds to others in the class, they may take more time to settle into school, for example if they have come from an area where there are many bilingual children to one where there are very few, or from an area where learning styles are different.

There may also have been other agencies such as speech therapists involved with the child's development, and records from these professionals will be useful in finding out about the child.

Language Targets – Spring Term 2002
Jamilla Khan – Year 1

Targets:

1 To familiarise Jamilla with the school and routines, and start to learn school vocabulary.

2 To learn initial sounds and begin to use core words from National Literacy Strategy.

Support:

Assistant to work with Jamilla daily on learning initial sounds and core words, through use of phonic scheme. Work with other children to include games such as sound lotto.

Review:

End of Spring term 2002

▲ Example of individual targets to develop language skills

Home backgrounds

These may be varied and will have the greatest influence on the child. Children whose home backgrounds have been traumatic, such as refugees, may have had wide and varied educational experiences. It would be helpful to obtain as much information as possible about the child's background and if possible seek the help of an interpreter so that the school can discuss this directly with the parents.

The experiences that the child has had may also affect their behaviour, for example being non-responsive. It may be difficult to obtain information from home and this can cause problems, for example with issues such as sickness notes or forms being completed and returned to school. Children who come from backgrounds with a different culture or religion from the majority of others in the school may feel isolated and it is important for them that the school values cultural diversity. Staff will also need to be aware of religious issues which can affect children's learning, for example children may be fasting during Ramadan. Issues of health and physical development may have been discussed with other professionals, and these checks should be included in the child's records.

Language backgrounds

Children who come into school with English or Welsh as a second language, or those who are multilingual, may find settling into school difficult due to the development of their language skills in the target language, or to a combination of factors. If staff know that the child has never been exposed to the target language before, this knowledge can help them to devise their educational plan. However, children who come into school at 4 will need a different level of support from those who come into school at 10. The school will need to ensure that each child has an education plan which takes individual learning needs into account.

➡ Knowledge into action

Devise an education plan for a Year 3 child who has come into school speaking English as a second language. How would it differ from a plan for a Year 1 child?

It is very important for all children that staff in school are aware of their home language and culture. This is because children's self-esteem will be affected by their perception of how others see them and in their confidence when using language. If their parents do not speak English, this may be child's first experience of having to communicate with others in a language other than their own. It is important for the child to be able to communicate in school and, although children will usually pick up language reasonably quickly, this can be a difficult time for them. If you notice that any children are finding it hard to make friends, it is important to discuss this with the class teacher. You may also be able to help them to socialise with others if you are on duty in the playground through the introduction of playground games.

Saraya has recently started at your school aged 7 and does not speak any English. She is a quiet child and you have noticed that she spends playtimes and lunchtimes on her own. What sort of strategies could you use to encourage her to socialise and suggest to others, such as midday supervisors?

Strategies for supporting bilingual and multilingual pupils in the classroom and helping them to access the curriculum

School strategies

When supporting bilingual and multilingual pupils, all staff will need to think about how they can promote the development of the target language while valuing the child's home language and culture. This is particularly important if the child is an isolated learner in the target language. The school should therefore have its own policies and practices for how children with English as an additional language are supported. The different types of strategies which the school has in place may therefore include:

▷ school policies to promote positive images and role models

▷ school policies and practices on inclusion, equal opportunities and multiculturalism

▷ identification of bilingual/multilingual children – for example, photos in staff room so that all staff are aware (if there is only a small group)

▷ providing opportunities for pupils to develop their language skills

▷ finding opportunities to talk with parents of bilingual children

▷ celebrating cultural diversity.

? Think about it

What policies does your school have which may be relevant to children from bilingual or multilingual backgrounds? How are these made available to parents?

These policies will have been directed by local and national guidelines for schools. Schools must have policies which encourage and promote equal opportunities for all children.

Outside support

Children who are bilingual or multilingual may have support from a local EAL (English as an additional language) teacher. They may also have an EMAG (Ethnic Minority Achievement Grant*) teacher or assistants who will come into school to help raise standards. These teachers will be able to offer advice and support to both teachers and parents, as well as putting them in touch with other professionals who may be able to help. They will carry out assessments on children and may also have centralised resources, such as dual language books, which may be useful to borrow, particularly if schools only have one or two EAL children. When children's progress needs to be discussed with parents who do not speak English, they may also be able to offer help when finding interpreters. If your school does not have this kind of support but it is needed, it is worth contacting the local authority through the school's representative to find out whether it is available for your school.

Assistants may find that it is often the SENCo (Special Educational Needs Co-ordinator) who is responsible for monitoring and working with children who speak English as an additional language. These children do not necessarily have special needs, and may not be on the special needs register or have Individual Action Plans. Occasionally, they will also have specific learning needs which will need to be assessed, but this will be in addition to their language needs.

* This grant was set up in April 1999 to assist schools in their work to address under achievement for all under-achieving ethnic groups, including those learning English as an additional language.

Find out...

Who is responsible in your school for children with EAL? What contact does the school have with the local EAL support team?

Strategies for classroom teaching and learning for EAL pupils

Assistants will need to work together with teachers and EAL tutors when supporting children in classrooms to enable them to develop their language skills effectively. Planning and development should be clear so that each child is encouraged to respond and to further their own knowledge of language. It is necessary to have specific strategies in place so that all staff have clear ideas about how these children may be supported. It is also important for staff to consider the abilities and needs of individual children and to get to know them, as they may have particular strengths in different curriculum areas.

Find out about...

A bilingual child in your school. Are they supported by the EAL service? What kind of input is given through the school? Over time, look at the kinds of strategies which are used to support and develop the child's use of language. Comment on the effectiveness of these strategies.

When developing the language skills of bilingual and multilingual children, these three areas should be considered:

▷ speaking and listening
▷ reading
▷ writing.

Speaking and listening skills

These skills must clearly be developed in EAL children, and assistants may find that they are working with individuals or small groups to facilitate this. In very young children the approach may be different from junior school children, but the strategies should be the same, and should apply across the curriculum:

▷ **Finding opportunities to talk** – children will need to be given as much opportunity as possible to talk and discuss ideas with others. At a very young age this would include opportunities such as role play, whereas older children may enjoy discussions.

▷ **Using physical cues and gestures** – for example thumbs up, thumbs down. This will enable the child to make sense of the situation more quickly.

▷ **Songs and rhymes** – children will develop concepts of pattern and rhyme in language through learning nursery rhymes and songs. They are also an enjoyable way of developing the children's language skills as well as being part of a group. We may also be able to introduce rhymes and songs in other languages for all the children to learn and so develop their cultural awareness.

▷ **Using games** – these opportunities are useful as they will help children to socialise with others as well as practise their language skills.

▷ **Using practical examples** – these can be used to help children when they are being given instructions, for example showing a model when the children are going to do group work.

▷ **Discussing with a partner first** – this may help when EAL children have to tell their ideas to the class, to help them to gain confidence. They should work with a variety of children who will provide good language models.

▲ Games can help children with their social and language skills

▷ **Use vocabulary which is appropriate** – staff will need to think about the language that they use with bilingual and multilingual children, to ensure that it is appropriate to the child's age and level of understanding. If the teacher is talking to the class and has used language which is difficult to understand, assistants may need to clarify what has been said for them.

▷ **Using purposeful listening** – if children have come into school with very limited experience of the target language, assistants may be asked to work with them on specific areas of language. For example, the teacher may be focusing on positional words to ensure that the child understands words such as *behind*, *above*, *below*, *next to* and so on. You may work with pictures or other resources to help the child to develop their understanding of these words.

▷ **Explain the purpose of the activity** – children should be aware of why they are undertaking a particular activity and what they are going to learn from it.

Reading and writing skills

Children who are learning to speak English or Welsh as an additional language will need to have opportunities to read and listen to books in the target language. This is so that they can associate their developing verbal and written skills with the printed page. Bilingual children will also benefit from working with the rest of the class during the

Literacy Hour. They will be able to share texts with the whole class and with groups of children, although teachers may need to use additional strategies so that they maximise learning opportunities. These should be clear to teaching assistants so that they can support the children through reinforcing the skills which are being taught.

Such strategies may include:

▷ using repetitive texts

▷ revising previous weeks' work to build confidence

▷ using pictures more in order to point out individual words

▷ making sure they pace the lesson to enable bilingual children to have time to read the text

▷ grouping EAL children according to their actual ability rather than their understanding or knowledge of English

▷ praise and encouragement wherever possible

▷ use of computer programs to help with reading.

Children who are learning to speak English or Welsh may need to decipher the meaning of some words with adult support when they are learning to read. They may need more support during Guided Reading sessions but should benefit from these as they will be able to model good practice from other children. As with all children, they will need to experience a wide variety of texts, both fiction and non-fiction, in order to maximise their vocabulary. It may be that the child is able to read and understand more than has been expected: in this case staff should always continue to extend their vocabulary by discussing the text further.

After consultation with the class teacher, assistants may find that they need to adapt and modify learning resources which the child or children are using. This will help them to access the curriculum more fully. Assistants may also need to explain and reinforce vocabulary which is used in the classroom, for example during a topic. Often, the types of resources which benefit bilingual children will also be useful for other children in the class or group.

Problems which may occur when providing support for bilingual pupils

There may be short- or long-term problems which occur when supporting bilingual pupils. If the group or individual which is being supported for a particular activity is finding it too challenging, assistants may need to modify or change plans to accommodate this, as it will not always be possible to speak to the teacher immediately. However, it is important that the teacher is informed as soon as possible in order to inform future planning. Some pupils may take a long time to become confident in a second language, and it will be apparent that they understand much more than they are able to say. This is not unusual, and staff must not push children into talking before they are ready. The most important thing to do is to encourage and praise children wherever possible, repeating back to them so that they develop a positive view of themselves.

Where pupils have a specific learning difficulty, this can take longer to detect if they are bilingual. This is because staff may feel that they are finding school more difficult owing to their development of the target language. If assistants who are supporting groups of children find that a particular child is not able to manage the tasks set and is not progressing, they should always speak to the class teacher.

Other problems could include inadequate or unsuitable resources, and disruptions within the learning environment, as outlined on pages 75–76.

as outlined on pages 75–76.

> ## ✓ Keys to good practice
> ## Teaching bilingual and multilingual pupils
>
> ✔ Group with children of similar ability.
>
> ✔ Use strategies which develop self-esteem and confidence.
>
> ✔ Provide visual and physical supports to help understanding.
>
> ✔ Model language using other children.

End of unit test

1 What are the stages of language development?

2 When will babies start to speak their first words?

3 What do adults need to do to encourage language development in babies and young children?

4 What theories exist about how language develops in young children?

5 Name two opportunities for developing language skills in children.

6 Which of these issues are important when looking at children's backgrounds:

  a health records

  b home environment

  c language background?

7 What types of strategies may the school have in place for supporting bilingual and multilingual pupils?

8 True or false?

  a The school should educate bilingual pupils separately.

  b Bilingual and multilingual children need to be given opportunities to show off their first language to the rest of the class.

  c Children who are learning to speak more than one language may take longer to develop language skills.

References

Browne, A., *Developing Language and Literacy, 3–8* (Paul Chapman Publishing, 2001)

Donaldson, M., *Children's Minds* (HarperCollins, 1986)

National Literacy Strategy: Supporting Pupils Learning English as an Additional Language (DfES, 2000)

Managing Support for the Attainment of Pupils from Minority Ethnic Groups (Ofsted, 2001)

Lindon, J., *Working with Young Children* (Hodder and Stoughton Educational, 1997)

Macphee, J., 'Bilingual learners' in *Child Education,* June 2002

Tassoni, P., *Certificate in Child Care and Education* (Heinemann, 2002)

Websites

www.becta.org.uk/inclusion/inclusion_lang/community/index.html

QCA scheme: *A Language in common: Assessing English as an Additional Language.* This booklet outlines issues relating to EAL assessment and guidance on profiling and monitoring EAL pupils.

www.naldic.org.uk (National Association for Language Development in the Curriculum). A professional organisation which aims to raise the achievement of EAL learners.

3-13, 3-14, 3-15 and 3-16

Support children with special needs during learning activities

There has been a great deal of development in this area in recent years following the introduction of inclusive education and the new SEN Code of Practice. Many more children with special needs are now being educated in mainstream schools, and as a result there will be more assistants employed to support children with Statements of Educational Needs. (Also see Unit 3-3.1: Provide support for learning activities.) They will be asked not only to support children with learning difficulties and enable them to access the curriculum, but also to help them to develop relationships with others. Other children in the class will also need to learn to respond appropriately to children with difficulties, encouraging them to take turns.

For these units you will need to know and understand:

▶ supporting pupils with communication and interaction difficulties (Unit 3-13)

▶ supporting pupils with cognition and learning difficulties (Unit 3-14)

▶ supporting pupils with behavioural, emotional and social development needs (Unit 3-15)

▶ providing support for pupils with sensory and/or physical impairment (Unit 3-16).

Unit 3-13 Support pupils with communication and interaction difficulties

Normal patterns of communication

Where children are developing normally, their language and communication skills will follow a pattern of development. (See Unit 3-12 for stages of language development.) This will mean that they gradually learn and start to reproduce a series of sounds and gestures to help them to communicate with others. Children who have difficulties with communication may develop these skills more slowly than other children, or find it difficult to order their language. They may need to learn alternative methods of communication, or need to have specific learning programmes to help them to develop certain areas of their language.

Characteristics of communication disorders

Assistants may be required to support children in school with a number of communication difficulties. These may include problems concerned with:

- ▷ speech and language
- ▷ sensory impairment such as deafness or blindness
- ▷ specific learning difficulties such as dyslexia and dyspraxia
- ▷ autistic spectrum disorder
- ▷ moderate, severe or profound learning difficulties.

Speech and language delay and disorders

These may be varied and range from problems such as a stutter, to more complicated disorders where children have difficulties in processing their language. Some children may require frequent speech and language therapy input to help them develop their communication skills.

Sensory impairment

Children with a permanent sensory or physical impairment, such as deafness or deaf/blindness, are at a disadvantage when communicating, and they may not have the benefit of additional cues such as body language. They may need to have access to alternative means of communication such as sign systems, Braille or specialist equipment (see also Unit 3-16).

Specific learning difficulties

These may not be obvious straight away when a child enters school, and it can take a while for them to become apparent. Children with these kinds of difficulties may have slower language processing skills or have difficulty following instructions. They may also have a limited understanding of non-verbal communication, and find concentrating or organisational skills difficult. As a result, their communication skills will be poorer than those of other children.

Autistic spectrum disorder

Autistic children have a developmental disability which affects the way in which they relate to others. This may vary in its severity so that some autistic children will just seem distracted, while others will display quite disruptive behaviour such as frequent interruptions. They will find it difficult to empathise with other children and to play imaginatively, and may react inappropriately in some social situations. Autistic children will need varying degrees of support in these areas.

Moderate, severe or profound learning difficulties

These children have a more general learning difficulty which will affect many areas, including their communication with others. Assistants will need to respond to the pupils' level of language to encourage them to interact with others, while drawing on advice and support from other professionals.

Quite often, children will have communication difficulties in more than one of these areas; for example, there may be an autistic child who also has input from the speech and language unit. In all of these cases, pupils will need varying degrees of support to enable them to interact constructively with others.

Case study

Michael is an 8-year-old who has Asperger's Syndrome, a form of autism. He finds it difficult to relate to others and regularly plays alone in the playground. In the classroom, Michael particularly enjoys working on the computer and often asks the teacher if he can use it.

1 How could you encourage Michael to develop his social and communication skills with others?

2 What difficulties might you have and how could you resolve them?

School policy for supporting pupils with communication and interaction difficulties

Although the school may not have a policy specifically written for these pupils, the procedures and guidelines for working with them should be incorporated into the school's special needs and inclusion policies. Assistants will need to be familiar with these as they will outline the school's commitment to supporting all children. Children who have communication and interaction difficulties may have a range of problems and staff should have access to specialist support from outside agencies (see box below).

Specialists support from outside agencies

▶ **Speech and Language Unit** – will give support to children with a range of difficulties, from minor speech impairment to more complex language disorders.

▶ **Sensory Support Service** – deals with difficulties such as permanent sensory or physical impairment, including deafness and blindness.

▶ **Complex Communications Service** – will diagnose and advise on disorders such as those in the autistic spectrum.

Assistants should work alongside the class teacher and also the school's Special Educational Needs Co-ordinator (SENCo). They should work together to set up educational targets for the child's Individual Education Plan (IEP). When other agencies come into school to advise and help, support assistants should be given the opportunity to discuss children with whom they work as they are often the adult in school who spends the most time with the child.

Factors which may affect communication

The way in which we relate to others plays a crucial role in the development of our self-esteem. As we develop, we learn to interact with others and in doing this we develop self expression and find our own identity. Children who have communication difficulties may find social interactions difficult to the point of trying to avoid them. Other children and adults may find them difficult to understand or be unable to relate to them easily. Children may have come from another setting and take a while to gain confidence in a new environment. Assistants who support these children will need to be able to promote communication between them and others, while encouraging them to be as autonomous as possible.

You can do this by:

▷ ensuring that you have accurate and up-to-date information about the child's language and communication skills and are working alongside the class teacher to develop these

▷ actively encouraging the child to participate in learning activities and have an awareness of the planned learning objectives

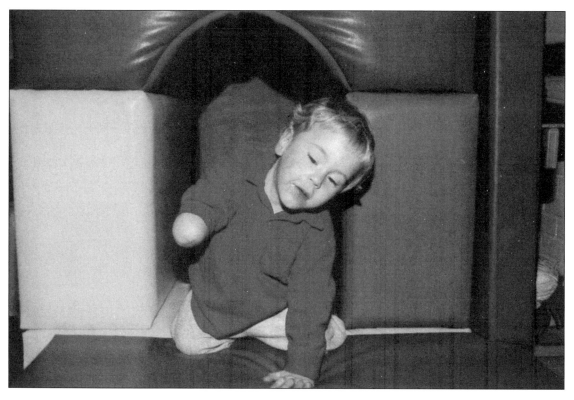

▲ Children may need to have the environment adapted so that they are more comfortable and able to interact with others

- ▷ reinforcing spoken language wherever possible – this will need to be done through the most appropriate method of communication for the child, for example using Makaton
- ▷ encouraging the child to respond to the contributions and ideas of others
- ▷ where necessary, adapting the layout of the room or using any equipment which is needed to enable the child to participate more fully in the learning activities, for example a visually impaired child may be very sensitive to sunlight or glare from shiny surfaces such as whiteboards.

Other strategies for supporting children in school

Assistants will need to ensure that the child who is being supported is given opportunities to develop their independence and self-esteem when communicating with others. They will need to experience a sense of achievement when interacting and may need assistance to encourage this, particularly when they first start school.

Where pupils need additional communication methods, assistants should be offered some training so that they are able to support the children more fully. There may be additional equipment needed to enable them to communicate, some of which may be technical. Assistants may also need to adapt some of the more general vocabulary used by the teacher so that pupils are included in all class activities. Where non-verbal communication is used, pupils should to be encouraged to show other children in the class the methods which they use. This will help others to understand how they communicate, and also develop their confidence and self-esteem.

Unit 3-14 Support pupils with cognition and learning difficulties

For effective learning to take place, children will need to have developed a range of cognitive skills in order to process and store information. When children have cognitive difficulties, there will be an impact on the development of these skills. Children will therefore need help in the following areas:

- ▷ **Language, memory and reasoning skills** – children who have cognitive and learning difficulties will take longer to develop language skills. This will in turn affect their learning, as they will be less able to store and process information.
- ▷ **Sequencing and organisational skills** – children may need help and support when organising themselves, as they may find it difficult to follow sequences of ideas.

▷ **Understanding of number** – the abstract concepts of arithmetic may be difficult for these children to grasp, and they will need practical help with number.

▷ **Problem solving and concept development** – understanding new ideas may take some time for these children, and they may need individual input from assistants.

▷ **Improving gross and fine motor competencies** – these physical aspects of the children's development may be affected, and they may need regular practice or therapy.

Assistants who work with children with cognition and learning difficulties will need to help them to develop learning strategies and begin to take responsibility for their own learning. Assistants will need to agree areas and levels of support with the class teacher following advice from outside agencies and specialists. Children who demonstrate features of cognitive and learning difficulties may have some of the following special needs:

▷ moderate, severe or profound learning difficulties

▷ specific learning difficulties (e.g. dyslexia, dyspraxia, specific language impairment)

▷ autistic spectrum disorder.

Moderate, severe or profound learning difficulties

Pupils who have these difficulties are said to have a global learning difficulty which means that all aspects of their learning can be affected. They may need help not only in the classroom but in all areas of school, and should have individual learning programmes.

Specific learning difficulties

Children with specific learning difficulties such as dyslexia and dyspraxia may have problems with abstract ideas. They will find it difficult to organise themselves in the classroom and will need to have input in the particular areas.

Autistic spectrum disorder

Children who have been diagnosed as having autistic spectrum disorder may need support in learning activities as they find it difficult to think in an abstract way. They may also rely on routines and set patterns and find it very difficult if these are changed for any reason. Autistic children may become obsessive about routine and react strongly to loud noises, which may mean that they can also disturb other children.

School policy and procedures for pupils with cognition and learning difficulties

Following the introduction of the new Special Educational Needs Code of Practice in January 2002, schools have been required to offer places for all pupils who have a Statement if their school is specified. This means that mainstream schools are likely to have a higher number of children with special needs (see also Unit 3-3.1 on inclusion). Teachers must plan for all children so that they achieve at their own level within the guidelines of the National Curriculum. Children whose difficulty or disability hinders them from achieving at National Curriculum levels will be assessed using the P Targets. These have been drawn up so that children who have not reached level 1 can be assessed using a scale which shows their rate of progress, rather than just assessing them at W (Working towards).

School curriculum policies should give teachers guidance on planning and inclusion, and they may also have advice and help when planning educational targets from specialist teachers and agencies, such as the local Sensory Support Service. Children with special needs will need to have Individual Education Plans so that they have manageable targets to work on within a set time limit (see Unit 3-19 page 258 for an example of an IEP). Children will be working on the same topics and concepts as other pupils, and assistants will need to monitor the children's progress and report back to the class teacher (see also Unit 3-8 for more detailed curriculum planning).

 Find out about...

Find a copy of the P Targets in your school. Are they accessible to all staff?

Helping pupils to develop effective learning strategies

Assistants will need to be able to help children to sequence and structure their learning so that they begin to develop independence skills. For example, an autistic child will need to be aware of the routines and timetables of the classroom and will benefit from a visual timetable to show what is going to happen. It may be helpful to give the child the responsibility for changing the timetable daily along with another child. This will also help to develop social and communication skills (see page 214).

The timetable may or may not need to have the actual time of day but will give the child an idea of what to expect. It will also be helpful if there is a change in routine, for example a visitor to the school. The timetable may also benefit other children in the class.

Children with cognitive and learning difficulties may benefit from 'chaining' activities to help them with their organisational skills. This involves encouraging the child to

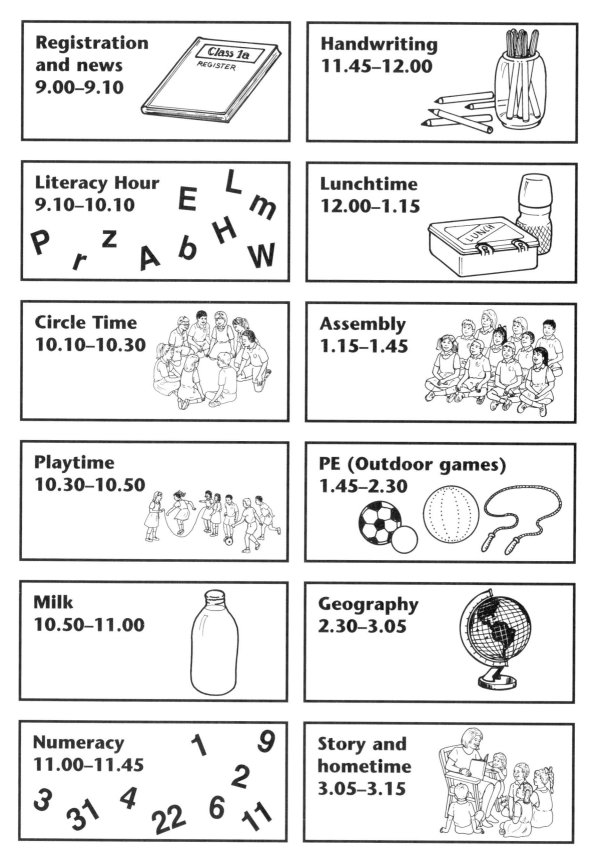

▲ Example of a visual timetable for a Year 2 child

think about the next step when working through a series of actions. For example, if the child needs to organise themselves to start an activity, the assistant will need to talk the child through what the next step might be and encourage them to think ahead. This will help the child to start to develop these types of skills independently.

Case study

Sara is a Year 3 child who has dyspraxia and finds it difficult to organise herself within the classroom. The teacher has asked the class to get out their history books and write the date at the top of the page. Sara has gone to her tray to find her history book but seems unsure what to do next.

1 How could you help Sara to organise herself?

2 Are there any other ways in which you could help Sara without staying beside her?

Assistants will need to support pupils with cognition and learning difficulties so that they act in an enabling role, rather than encouraging the child to become dependent on their support. This is known as **active learning**, and means that staff should provide opportunities for the pupil to develop skills such as decision-making, problem solving, and exercising choice. It is also important to think about the other children in the class or group and how they can work together. Assistants will need to give positive reinforcement and praise to encourage all children when working with them on projects, to give them a feeling of achievement and to sustain their interest.

Think about it

How could you support a Year 5 pupil with moderate learning difficulties during the Literacy Hour? What sort of approaches do you think you would need to undertake in this situation?

Problems when supporting pupils with cognition and learning difficulties

Assistants may find that they experience problems when supporting pupils with these difficulties. These may be related to the learning environment – for example, if you are trying to work with an autistic child and there are loud noises disturbing you from outside. You may also have problems with the resources you are using – although see pages 75-76. You should also be aware if the child you are supporting is on any medication, as this may affect their behaviour.

The pupil may have difficulty with the task that has been set, and you may not always be able to speak to the class teacher. You will need to be able to adapt to unexpected changes in activities, and be able to modify what you have been asked to do. If you know the child well, and are aware of other areas which have been targeted in the IEP, you may need to change the focus of the activity to another which will benefit the child. Where possible, however, you should always try to aim towards the intended learning outcomes of the activity.

✔ Keys to good practice
Supporting pupils with learning difficulties

✔ Ensure you have up-to-date information about the pupils' needs.

✔ Check that you have details about the planned learning objectives.

✔ Liaise with the teacher and modify work where necessary.

✔ Monitor pupils' responses to learning activities.

Unit 3-15 Support pupils with behavioural, emotional and social development needs

This unit explores the reasons for antisocial behaviour in school and how assistants can manage pupils' behaviour in the learning environment. You will also need to read Unit 3-1 Contribute to the management of pupil behaviour, and Unit 3-9 Promote pupil's social and emotional development. Children with these difficulties will need to learn to develop their self-help and self-control skills, and assistants must be able to encourage and foster these, as well as helping them to develop relationships with others.

In addition to a policy on inclusion (see page 72), the school should also have a behaviour management policy (see also Unit 3-1, page 15). Assistants should be aware of this since it will give the school's guidelines for managing children's behaviour. You will also need to know the types of strategies and sanctions which the school uses when there are problems with behaviour, and should agree these with the teacher. Pupils should be aware that these are to be consistently applied at all times, as they may attempt to play staff off against each other if they find that this is possible. Where there are pupils in school with particular behaviour, emotional or social difficulties, all staff should be aware of these children and their needs.

Levels of co-operation to be expected of pupils at different ages

When working with primary school children, you will need to be familiar with the levels of behaviour and social development to expect of them at different ages and stages. (See table in Unit 3-9 page 156.)

Children's backgrounds and the impact of their experiences on their self-esteem

Children who have emotional and behaviour problems may have had traumatic experiences during their lives, or be experiencing a difficult time at the present. They will often feel different or less valued, and may have low self-esteem as a result. In order for children to learn, their self-esteem will need to be developed, as their negative opinions of themselves will damage their ability to learn. Their behaviour is often a way of seeking attention, and even though this may be negative as a result, to these children some attention is better than none at all. Such children need to start to feel valued again and gain positive experiences from their time in school. It is important for staff to find out as much as they can about a child's background to enable them to work with parents and help the child in school (see also Unit 3-1 page 7). Staff must also be careful not to have stereotypical assumptions.

Case study

Aaron is a Year 4 child who has always had minor behavioural problems in school, but this behaviour has recently become more disruptive. You are working with Aaron alongside a group of other children when he says that he is not going to continue with the task and refuses to carry on.

1 Why might Aaron have recently become more disruptive in school?

2 What could you do to encourage Aaron to re-engage in the task?

Children who have experienced negative emotional experiences in their early years may find it difficult to form relationships with adults or their peers. They will need to have good role models in school to encourage them to develop their social and behaviour skills. Staff should always model the behaviour they would like to see in school and show respect and consideration towards others. Where you see good behaviour, it is important for this to be recognised, either verbally or through a reward system.

You will need to be able to recognise the kinds of behaviour patterns which may indicate forms of abuse such as child abuse or substance abuse, or bullying (see Unit 3-1 page 10). If you are at all concerned about any aspect of a child's behaviour you should always report these to the class teacher.

Strategies to promote self-esteem

Assistants will need to be aware of ways in which they can develop self-esteem in children and encourage them to be more self-reliant. Many schools now use strategies such as **circle time**, which gives a good forum for group discussions and decision-making, and allows children to discuss their feelings in a non-threatening way.

Schools also need to develop other ways of promoting self-esteem in children. Some of these may include the following:

▷ Giving responsibility to children to enable them to gain attention and approval without seeking negative means. This is an ideal opportunity to give the child a chance to do well while giving adults a chance to praise good behaviour. It may be necessary for the child to partner another to start with, to ensure that they are able to manage the responsibility. Ensure that you are aware of any differences in family or cultural expectations which may have an influence on the use of responsibility.

▷ Use strategies which reward and recognise pupils' efforts in school. These will need to be in line with the school's strategies and guidelines. Some schools may issue stickers and certificates for good behaviour and effort, while others may prefer to reward the class as a whole.

▷ Always listen to children and give them your attention when speaking to them. If an adult is clearly showing that their thoughts are elsewhere, and they are not

▲ Group activities can promote children's self-esteem

interested in what is being said, this will damage the child's confidence and self-esteem.

▷ Encourage pupils to think about their behaviour and take responsibility for their actions. Circle time will give the group an opportunity to discuss issues such as class rules, and to show how the whole class how they are all responsible for maintaining a good working environment.

▷ Group pupils carefully, as the other children with whom they work can have an effect on pupils and how they work. If they are with a group of children with whom they have had negative experiences, this can prevent effective learning and damage their self-esteem.

▷ Adults will need to show that they notice positive as well as negative effort and behaviour. If a child is trying hard to achieve their individual targets and this effort goes unnoticed, it will make it less likely for the child to continue to work at it. There are different ways in which adults can show approval, apart from verbally, to boost a child's self-esteem.

? Think about it

A child in your class has been diagnosed as having Attention Deficit Disorder, which means that it is very difficult for her to sit still and concentrate for any length of time. You notice that she is sitting over on the other side of the classroom and has been working hard at her task for some time. She looks up and catches your eye.

▶ How could you show your approval at what she is doing without talking?

▶ What else could you do to follow this up later?

Establishing relationships with others

Pupils who have emotional and behavioural difficulties will sometimes need encouragement to help them develop relationships with others. This does not only mean other children within the class, but all other individuals such as parents, carers and teachers. It may be difficult for pupils, and sometimes adults, to develop these social skills and assistants may have to help them to establish contact and relationships. You can do this by:

▷ ensuring that pupils are encouraged to interact positively with others

▷ giving pupils opportunities to work co-operatively with others in groups and pairs

▷ showing that pupils are able to work with others by giving them tasks which are appropriate to their age and ability.

Managing conflict and anti-social behaviour

You may find that you have to deal with situations of conflict when managing challenging behaviour. This may involve aggression or abuse in the form of racist or sexist remarks. If you have not been in these sorts of situations before, you will need to be prepared for them and ensure you protect your own safety and that of others. You may also need to rebuild damaged relationships between the two parties following areas of conflict, which may involve negotiations and discussions with both sides.

The situations you may find yourself in may escalate due to the needs of the pupils with whom you are working. They may find it more difficult to control their feelings than other children, or sometimes display aggressive behaviour. If they are on medication, this can also affect the way they behave.

Ways in which to manage conflict
Talking to pupils – where there has been a disagreement or argument between pupils, the first way to calm the situation should always be through listening to both sides to try to establish the cause of the problem.
Negotiating – this is a way of teaching pupils to talk to one another and try to resolve the disagreement sensibly, through talking about their responsibilities towards one another and reminding them of school policies.
Positive handling – it is better to manage conflict in a non-aggressive way and try to discuss the issue rather than to become angry with pupils. In this way, children will be more likely to put forward their own views and problems.
Time out – this may be a last resort and will be to remove one or both sides from the situation to calm down.

If you are in a situation where you feel that it is necessary to use physical restraint, this should only be used in circumstances where children are likely to cause harm to others or yourself. You should always seek help as soon as possible in this situation, by sending another child if necessary. If you are on your own with the child, try to move to another area if possible where there is another adult who can act as a witness.

 Find out about...

Your school's policy for child protection and the use of physical restraint.

Unit 3-16 Support pupils with sensory and/or physical impairment

The Disability Act 2001 amends the Disability Discrimination Act 1995 and strengthens access to mainstream school education for all children.

> From September 2002 all schools must:
>
> ▶ 'not treat disabled pupils less favourably, without justification, for a reason which relates to their disability
>
> ▶ make reasonable steps to ensure that disabled pupils are not placed at a substantial disadvantage compared to other pupils who are not disabled
>
> ▶ plan strategically for and make progress in improving the physical environment of schools for disabled children, increasing disabled pupils' participation in the curriculum and improving the ways in which written information which is provided to pupils who are not disabled is also provided to disabled pupils.
>
> From *Inclusive schooling – Children with Special Educational Needs: Nov 2001*

Assistants who support pupils with sensory and/or physical impairment will therefore need to be prepared to manage a range of special needs for children with hearing, visual and physical impairment. You will be expected to enable these children to participate in learning activities alongside other children as far as possible, and be prepared to implement structured learning programmes alongside the class teacher.

The school should now have a policy for inclusive education, (see also Unit 3-3.1 page 9 and Unit 3-5 page 110) and assistants should be aware of their role in relation to this. Your responsibilities will include:

▷ making sure that you have up-to-date information about the nature and level of the child's needs

▷ ensuring that you have detailed information from the class teacher about the planned learning tasks and objectives

▷ adapt the learning environment and materials where necessary to enable pupils to participate in the planned tasks

▷ assist and encourage pupils and give positive reinforcement.

Apart from the class teacher, there will be others both within and outside the school who will contribute to the support of pupils with sensory or physical impairment. You may also have access to written information and reports from these people:

▷ **The school's SENCo**, or Special Needs Co-ordinator, will be available to support the class teacher and support assistant in the development of Individual Education Plans.

▷ **Specialist teachers** – these professionals may be available from the local Sensory Support Service to offer advice and equipment and to visit the child from time to time.

▷ **Physiotherapists/occupational therapists** – may be able to visit the school, or children may have to go on a waiting list before they are able to see them. They will develop individual programmes for children to use at home, with advice for activities they can work on in school.

▷ **Other professionals** – these may be inside or outside the school, but may have experience of dealing with children who have physical or sensory impairment.

You will also need to provide these people with information about the pupil's progress and participation in learning activities, whether these are cognitive, creative or physical.

The impact of a primary disability on pupils' learning and social, emotional and physical development

There may be differences between the children's classmates in several areas of their development. Pupils with these impairments may be less able to concentrate than their peers. They may find that they tire easily, or become frustrated if they are unable to complete tasks as quickly or as well as they would hope to. It is important that assistants are able to reassure them and give them encouragement to sustain their interest and enthusiasm. This can be done by praising them for their efforts, and by giving them levels of assistance which are consistent with their abilities. If too much help is given, children will not experience a sense of achievement and independence, but if too little is given, they will become frustrated and lose interest. Assistants should be able to encourage the children to use their other sensory and physical functions to help them to achieve.

Case study

Hayley is a Year 1 child who has a hearing impairment, and the teacher and assistant need to use a microphone so that she can hear them. Hayley has an individual support assistant for 10 hours a week. She has lots of friends in the class, but the children sometimes have difficulty understanding her. She is working on a group data handling activity to find out what time children in the class go to bed. You feel that she may need some help as she will not be able to hear all the children's responses, but are not sure whether you should intervene.

1 What would you do in this situation?

2 How could Hayley develop another way of asking the question?

If pupils take medication, this may also have an effect on their abilities and behaviour. Children may seem to be less able to concentrate or find it difficult to sustain their physical effort. If it is clear that it is difficult for a child to carry on, you should always stop the activity and carry on if appropriate at another time.

Selecting and using appropriate materials and equipment

Assistants will need to select and use the correct kinds of equipment when working with pupils with sensory and/or physical impairment. You will need to know the kinds of equipment which are appropriate to use to help the child with whom you are working. You may be given some advice and equipment from outside agencies, such as Brailling machines and auditory aids. The school may also be visited by professionals such as the local institute for the blind, who may give advice on equipment which could be used in school. They may also advise on how the school could assist pupils, such as making certain areas more visible by painting them – for example, the edge of the playground, or the edge of steps.

Pupils may be accustomed to using some equipment and so may also be able to show assistants how to use it: this would be another way of developing their self-esteem. Ideally, they will become used to managing some of their own equipment, for example if they need a sloping desk they may be able to go and get it independently.

Pupils who have **visual impairment** will need to sit as close as possible to the class teacher. They will be affected by lighting and should not be facing bright and direct sunlight, or be in an area which is too dark. If teachers use whiteboards, these may be difficult to see as the light will glare, and staff may be advised to use paper to avoid this. Where Brailling machines are used, other children in the class should also be introduced to the machine so that they are aware why it is being used. Children who use Braille may also be able to teach simple messages to other pupils in the class.

Pupils who have **auditory impairment** should also sit close to the class teacher to enable them to lip-read if necessary. They may require the use of specialist equipment such as hearing aids and microphones to help them, and be sensitive to acoustics within rooms such as dining areas. If they use sign language or Makaton, they may also teach some of the signs to others. The impact of showing and teaching other children will be to make the child feel less isolated within the classroom.

Pupils who have a **physical impairment** may need to sit away from the teacher so that they are able to access any larger equipment. They may also need to use computers and other specialist equipment to enable them to complete learning tasks.

If pupils are less independent due to physical impairment, assistants may need to help with physical management such as lifting.

You may need to lift a child in a wheelchair. In this case you will need to make sure that the brakes are applied before you start, and that the child is sitting well back in the chair (1). Ensure that the wheelchair does not have detatchable parts such as arm rests which will come off if you attempt to use them as you carry the chair. Support the chair from each side and carry as shown (2). Never carry a wheelchair by the wheels.

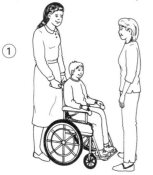

When lifting a child from a wheelchair, the bearers will need to bend at the knees and grasp each others wrists as shown, beneath the child's legs (3) using the four-handed seat. The child will then need to put an arm around each of the bearer's shoulders (4). The bearers should then stand up together.

▲ Safe lifting methods

End of unit test

1 What types of communication difficulties might children have?

2 What outside agencies might be involved with children who have communication difficulties?

3 Why should children who use non-verbal communication systems show others how to use them?

4 What skills do children need in order to develop effective learning?

5 What is 'active learning'?

6 Why is good self-esteem important in children?

7 How might schools develop self-esteem in children?

8 How can you encourage the formation of positive relationships between children with social and emotional problems and others?

9 Name three ways in which you could manage conflict.

10 When should you use physical restraint?

11 What is inclusive education?

References

Collins, M., 'How to deal with Autistic Children' in *Five to Seven* (Vol. 8, Dec. 2001)

McNamara, S. and Moreton, G., *Teaching Special Needs* (David Fulton, 1993)

Mosely, J, *Quality Circle Time* (LDA, 1996)

Planning, Teaching and Assessing the Curriculum for Pupils with Learning Difficulties (QCA) General guidance plus individual guides for each National Curriculum subject.

Websites

www.nas.org.uk (National Autistic Society)

http://inclusion.ngfl.gov.uk/

www.dfes.gov.uk/sen

www.nasen.org.uk (National Association for Special Educational Needs)

Set C

Unit 3-17 Support the use of information and communication technology in the classroom

Information and communication technology (ICT) plays a major role in the school curriculum, as it can be a part of all subject areas. There is now a statutory requirement for the application of ICT in the core subjects (English, maths and science) at Key Stage 1, and in all subjects except PE at Key Stage 2. In the Foundation Stage, children will begin to use ICT equipment in the classroom and learn appropriate vocabulary. This means that assistants will need to be able to support children when using a range of ICT equipment in school. This unit is about ensuring that such equipment is available and ready to use when required and that you know how to support teachers and pupils when preparing and using equipment safely.

The types of ICT equipment you will need to use in the classroom

When working as an assistant in a primary classroom, you will be expected to know how to prepare and use different ICT equipment. This may range from setting up computers in classrooms and computer suites to knowing how to operate recording equipment. You should make sure that you are familiar with the different equipment you will need to use. These may include the following:

▷ **Classroom computers and related equipment such as printers.** There are many different computers and printers available, and you will need to know how to operate those which you are expected to use. Computers should usually be kept in classrooms, although some schools also have computer suites or rooms.

▷ **Recording and playback equipment.** Most classrooms will have access to tape recorders, CDs and videos, and you will need to know where these can be found, how to find extension leads, and keys to unlock storage cupboards if necessary.

▷ **Overhead projectors and screens.** These will almost certainly be stored away until needed, as it is unlikely that they will be permanently kept in classrooms. You will have to find out where they are kept so that you can get them out for use in the learning environment.

▷ **Roamers, pixies and other directional equipment.** These will also be stored away until they need to be used. You will require some training before using them, as you will need to be clear exactly what you are doing when working with the children. They may also have batteries which will sometimes need to be charged up before use.

▲ You will be expected to use a variety of ICT equipment

Preparing equipment for use in the classroom

Computers and peripheral equipment

If you have been asked to prepare computers for use, you will need to find out whether you need to book or timetable them for use by your class. Your school may have procedures for this and you may need to find out about these from the class teacher or ICT subject manager. You will also need to make sure that you have set up any computers which are used within your own classroom, and are able to access any CD-ROMs or printers which are needed. If you are going to use computer suites with or without the class teacher, you will need to know how to access equipment and the use of any passwords. Always make sure that there are no safety issues which need to be addressed, for example the length of time a child should spend looking at a screen.

Recording and playback equipment

You will need to make sure you have access to this equipment when it is required and know how to use it. You may need to prepare recording equipment such as videos for use in the classroom, which may involve booking or unlocking from storage, and

▲ Children need to be given opportunities to develop their ICT skills in the classroom

finding the correct place on the tape. If children are using items such as tape recorders, they should be taught how to use them from an early age. It is important that they learn how to operate the tape recorders, by switching on and off and learning vocabulary such as eject, rewind, record, and so on. This will involve teaching groups of children so that they can show others, and will develop their self-help skills.

Overhead projectors and screens

You may be asked to prepare overhead projectors for use in the classroom or other areas in the school such as the hall or staff room. This will involve removing the equipment from wherever it is stored and setting it up so that it is ready for use. You will need to ensure that there are no safety issues to be addressed, such as trailing cables around the projector.

Roamers, pixies and other directional equipment

These are used for developing concepts such as programming and directional skills. They will need to be kept in a centralised area in school and may be time-tabled for use by different classes. You will need to know how they work and make sure that you have a suitable area to work in.

Checking for and reporting equipment faults

Electrical equipment which is used in school should always have an annual safety check, but if you find any faults in the equipment while preparing it for use, you should always report them, however minor. The school should have its own procedures to follow, such as writing in a maintenance book, but you should also inform the teacher and whoever is responsible for repair or maintenance. Faulty equipment should then be labelled and isolated from any power source.

Following manufacturers' instructions

It is important to ensure that instruction booklets for individual items of equipment are easily accessible. Staff need to be able to make sure that equipment is being set up and used correctly, and it is useful to be able to use a troubleshooting section if there are any problems.

Keys to good practice
Preparing equipment

✔ Check availability of equipment and accessories.

✔ Ensure that you know how to use all required equipment and have all the information needed.

✔ Check that you have switched on and the equipment is ready to use.

✔ Ensure you know the location of any consumables, e.g. printer ink, batteries.

✔ Make sure any safety issues are reported to the teacher and maintenance officer.

Supporting the use of ICT equipment in the classroom

When supporting pupils in the use of ICT, assistants should have an awareness of the types of skills which are being developed in pupils of different ages. There should be a clear progression from the expectations of the Foundation Stage through to children at the top of the primary phase at Year 6.

Types of skills to be developed in pupils of different ages

Children's stage	ICT skills
Foundation Stage	ICT comes under the Foundation Stage area of 'Knowledge and Understanding of the World'. Children will start to become aware of technology in the home and school environments. They will start to use ICT equipment such as computers and programmable toys, and develop their language to use related vocabulary.
Key Stage 1	Children at this stage will need to develop their knowledge, skills and understanding through working with a range of ICT skills and tools. They will need to learn how to access, enter and save as well as retrieve information. Pupils will also start to plan and give instructions, and use a variety of forms to present information.
Key Stage 2	At this stage, children will use ICT to support work in other subjects. They will need to find, prepare and interpret information using ICT, be aware of their audience and review what they have done. To do this they will need to be able to use a variety of software and the Internet, and interpret information as to its accuracy.

 Find out about...

How teaching assistants in your school are used to support activities in ICT. Perhaps you could devise a questionnaire to find out the following:

▶ How much training is available to them? Would they use it if more were available?

▶ Do they feel confident when they are asked to work in a computer suite or with groups of children using other equipment?

▶ Are there any other issues they have which they would like addressed concerning ICT?

School policy for the use of ICT

The school should have an ICT policy which will give guidelines for using and working with ICT in the classroom. There may be set routines and guidance for the use of equipment which all individuals should use, for example children to sign a checklist to say when they have used equipment. The school policy should give the aims and objectives of the school with regard to the children's experiences and opportunities in ICT.

There will also be requirements for safety, and for storage and security of ICT equipment. There may be a borough or school policy on use of the Internet and the availability of websites which are suitable for schools.

Knowledge into action

Find out about what measures your school has in place for preventing the spread of viruses through the school computers.

Legislation and regulations relating to the use of ICT

Several legal requirements exist which are relevant to the use of ICT in schools. Assistants should be aware of these and make sure that any information which is confidentially held or seen is not passed onto others. If you have access to school computers containing information about children for example, it is important that you only use them as they are intended, and do not leave computer screens on for others to read.

Relevant legislation for the use of ICT in schools

Data Protection Act 1998 This has implications for the use of data which is held on school computers and how it is used. Individuals have the right to know what information is held, and any information about the children in the school should only be used by the school and not passed on to a third party (see also Unit 3-6 page 126). Any data which the school holds should be protected against unauthorised access by appropriate security measures.

Child Protection The 1989 Children Act outlines a set of principles which everyone should follow when children are involved. These are to ensure that the welfare of the child will always come first. The local authority may have guidelines for child protection and how information is kept on computers. Staff should ensure that any information which is held about children is kept confidential within the school, and any work or results which are published do not contain children's names or other personal information.

Copyright If the school has CD-ROMs and other software, these must only be used by the school and not by other parties, and multiple copies of programmes should not be made.

Software licensing This is important in the case of schools as they should be aware of which licences they should have with regard to software held in school. There are different kinds of licence depending on the intended use of the software, for example single use or across a network.

How to support the development of ICT skills in pupils

Staff will need to understand and follow the Foundation Stage and National Curriculum for ICT when working with pupils. The class teacher will have long-term, medium-term and short-term plans (see Unit 3-3, page 68) which will highlight the skills to be taught in ICT and how pupils should be supported. Assistants should support pupils while developing their confidence and independence when using ICT equipment.

They should do this by developing a variety of skills including the following:

▷ **Basic user skills** – sometimes it is tempting to intervene when pupils are using computers and other equipment, especially if they are just starting to learn how to use them. You should try to ensure that you guide them while allowing them to operate equipment independently. You can do this by guiding them through the task verbally, or by showing them first and then asking them to repeat what you have done. In this way they will start to develop skills such as using a mouse or keyboard, switching on and closing down equipment, and following on-screen instructions.

? Think about it

You are working with a class of Reception children using a 'Firstpaint' program, two at a time. This involves the use of a mouse which they have not experienced before in school. The first two children with whom you work have obviously used a mouse before at home, but the second pair have not and are having difficulties.

How could you help them with their mouse skills without doing the work for them? Do you feel that this kind of program is appropriate for Reception? Why?

▷ **Selecting and using appropriate software packages** – the class teacher should give guidance when selecting software for use in the classroom, as it will usually be related to other work which the children are doing. For example, if using the computer during the Literacy Hour, you may be supporting children who are working on a spelling program. For work on mathematical programs, the children may be using databases or spreadsheets. You will need to use their own existing knowledge as a starting point when helping them to use appropriate software for the task. The program selected should be straightforward for the children to use and not too time-consuming or too short for realistic use in the classroom. Some programs are unsuitable as they take too long to complete, or require adult input to restart at frequent intervals.

▷ **Accessing and using learning programs** – you will need to be able to use computer programs without needing assistance, as this will interrupt both the teacher and the pupil you are supporting. Most programs will be straightforward if aimed at the primary age range, but you should have had sight of them before you start. Some of these will be CD-ROMs and programs which are already on the school's computer, but there will also be a selection of primary age materials through the Internet, which are easy to access (see websites at end of unit). Children may need support when accessing learning programs from CD-ROMs and computer disks, and you should do this by talking them through each stage if they are unsure. Older children may need to write themselves reminders for accessing programs. You may also need to demonstrate to children how to use tapes and videos and how to find the correct place using the counters on machines.

▷ **Accessing information** – children will need to learn how to access information from computer files, CD-ROMs and the Internet. You will need to help them to build up these skills gradually as they use computers to help them in their work in other subjects.

▷ **Using electronic communication systems** – pupils will begin to use the Internet and e-mail towards the end of Key Stage 1 and throughout Key Stage 2. They should be encouraged to use their research skills through finding out specific information, for example 'What can you find out about whales?'. This will give them a focus and help them to interpret the information in their own way. You can support them by showing them steps which they should work through to reach the information they need.

Safety when using ICT equipment

When using all these methods to develop ICT skills in pupils, assistants should also be aware of the risks associated with using equipment and how these can be minimised. Equipment should be safe as long as it is used properly and checked regularly. Children should always be taught to shut down computers correctly after use as they can be damaged if turned off incorrectly.

✓ Keys to good practice
Using ICT equipment

✔ Check the equipment regularly and report any faults.

✔ Use only the correct accessories with each item of equipment.

✔ Never overload plugs.

✔ Ensure that the equipment is being used safely and intervene when it is not.

✔ Store equipment safely when not in use.

End of unit test

1 What sort of ICT equipment might be found in primary schools?

2 What should you consider when preparing ICT equipment for use?

3 What types of ICT skills would you expect from a child at the end of the Foundation Stage?

4 What sort of ICT programmes might you give to children in Reception?

5 What skills will adults be helping to develop in children in the use of ICT?

6 What should you do if you find any faulty equipment?

7 What relevant legislation exists for the use of ICT in schools?

References

Curriculum Guidance for the Foundation Stage (QCA, 2000)

National Curriculum Document (QCA, 1999)

Scheme of Work for Information Technology (QCA, 1998)

The *Times Educational Supplement* has an IT section which has useful and up-to-date websites and information.

Websites

BECTA (British Educational Communications and Technology Agency): www.becta.org.uk/technology/software/curriculum/licensing/

National Curriculum Website: www.nc.uk.net

Children Act 1989: www.fnf.org.uk/childact.htm

Data Protection Act: www.legislation.hmso.gov.uk/acts/acts1998/19980029.htm

Guidance on the use of ICT in the classroom: www.mape.org.uk

Help pupils to develop their literacy skills

This unit will help you to support pupils when developing reading, writing and speaking and listening activities. You will need to know the different ways in which the teacher plans for learning activities within the Foundation Stage and during the Literacy Hour, and the support you are required to give different groups and individuals. Assistants will need to work under the direction of the teacher to help children to achieve the learning objectives of the lesson. They will need to report back to the teacher as to pupils' achievements in reading, writing and speaking and listening.

The structure of the National Literacy Strategy

As with other subjects, the English policy will need to relate to local and national frameworks and policies for English. This covers pupils' reading, writing and speaking and listening skills. The National Literacy Strategy is a non-statutory document for Key Stages 1 and 2, and will be a requirement in many primary schools. The Foundation Stage will follow the framework of the strategy, although pupils will not have a Literacy Hour, and will follow the Early Learning Goals. It is not possible or appropriate to reproduce large sections of the Literacy Strategy here, but assistants should be aware of how it is broken down and the kinds of tasks which they may be asked to do with groups or individual children.

The interactive use of speaking, listening, reading and writing

When pupils are developing their language skills, they are learning to communicate with others. The three areas of language interact with each other to promote the child's self expression and imagination. Through the English curriculum, pupils explore the ways in which language works so that they can use this knowledge in a variety of situations.

The way in which English is taught in Key Stages 1 and 2 will vary slightly, but the purpose behind the Literacy Hour is to give structure to the way in which pupils are taught in primary schools. The Literacy framework then gives details of what should be taught during that time.

1 Whole class (15 minutes) Key Stages 1 and 2 – this should be shared text work using a big book or equivalent, and should be a mixture of reading and writing as a class.

2 Whole class (15 minutes)
   Key Stage 1 – this session should be focused word work, which concentrates on an aspect of the Literacy framework to be covered during the term, for example looking at the spelling pattern 'ow'.

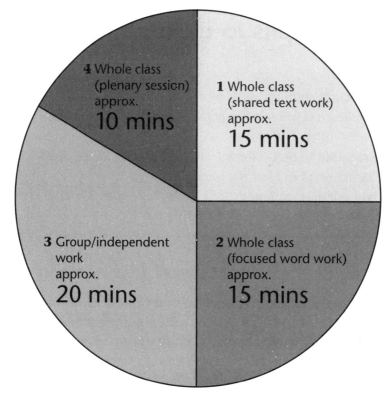

▲ Structure of the Literacy Hour

Key stage 2 – this session should be a balance of word work and sentence work over the term.

3 Group/independent work (20 minutes).

Key Stages 1 and 2 – children should be working independently on reading, writing or word/sentence work. The teacher should be working with one or two groups each day on guided text work, which can be reading or writing. Assistants may also be working with a group to support the day's learning objectives.

4 Whole class (10 minutes).

Key Stages 1 and 2 – this plenary session gives the class a chance to review and think about what they have learned during the session. It is also a good opportunity to show others the work they have done.

➜ *Knowledge into action*

Ask your class teacher for a copy of the National Literacy Strategy Framework for teaching. Find your year group's medium-term plan, for example Year 3 term 2 on page 34. Can you find some examples of work you have done during the term in the sections word, sentence and text level work?

Help pupils to develop their reading skills

Assistants working in primary classrooms should expect to be asked to hear children read. They will need to know and understand the school's English policy in order to support the children, and be sure of the methods which are used by the school to develop children's reading skills. These should be set out under the school's objectives for reading; for example, see the box below.

Maplewood Primary School English Policy

Objectives for the teaching of reading:

▷ to encourage an interest in books and the enjoyment of reading

▷ to help the children become fluent, confident readers by teaching that the understanding of the text is of prime importance and by introducing the various strategies needed to decode unknown words

▷ to ensure that the children experience a wide range of literature, including fiction, non-fiction and poetry, as well as a variety of genres

▷ to become confident when handling books and to develop the knowledge which enables them to be used as a learning tool

▷ to have an interest in words and their meanings.

Basic principles of how children learn to read

You should have some idea of the basic principles by which children learn to read so that you are able to support their development of reading in the learning environment. Children are taught a range of strategies to enable them to make sense of what they are reading.

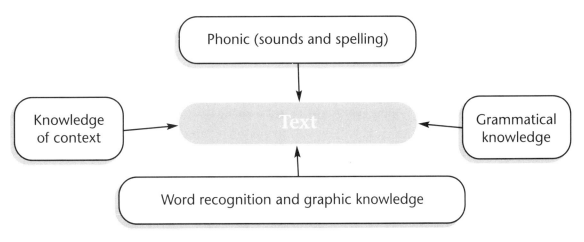

▲ Strategies for learning to read (from *National Literacy Strategy Module 4 – Teacher's Notes*. DfES 1998)

▷ **Phonic cues** – children start by learning initial sounds so that they can begin to word build using phonics at an early stage of reading and writing. They need to be taught their sounds using phonics rather than letter names so that they are able to 'sound out' words. For example, the word 'cat' is sounded out easily using phonics once children have learned to link the sounds together. Teachers may tackle phonics in a variety of ways but will need to be constantly revising sounds already learnt so that the children will retain them.

▷ **Contextual cues** – children will also learn through thinking about the setting of the text and the kinds of words which may be used as a result. For example, in a book about animals they may recognise the word which is to follow 'the cat ran after the' simply because they know that cats chase mice, and that the sentence will then make sense.

▷ **Grammatical knowledge** – children will be able to make sense of the text through their knowledge of grammar and syntax.

▷ **Picture cues** – these should especially be used when the child is at the early stages of reading as they will give the child more confidence when learning to read. It is important for children that they are able to see the pictures to involve them in the text straight away.

Knowledge into action

Look at this sentence:

The brig was wuffling snickerly at the linp.

Can you see find the subject, object, verb and adverb in the sentence?

Although the sentence does not make sense to you, you will understand who is doing something to something else, through the way in which the sentence is constructed. Through the kinds of strategies we teach children when learning to read, we are building up these skills so that they can make sense of text even if they do not understand some words.

All of these cues will help the child to decipher the text through forming a system through which they can decode the meaning. When children are starting to learn to read and remember sounds, they are constantly renewing the skills they have already developed. The skill of reading is therefore one of constantly revising up and building a bank of sounds and then words, so that the child will be able to gradually build on previous knowledge. The support the child receives in school through the Literacy strategy will promote the development of these skills through focusing initially on 45 high frequency words and building up to 150 words to be learned between Years 1 and 2. The Literacy Strategy also outlines the development of phonics during Key Stage 1. By Key Stage 2, the focus changes to medium frequency words and their spelling, blending phonemes together, and grammar.

You should also be aware of the different stages to expect from different ages of children in school. Remember that this is an average and that some children will develop these skills more quickly or slowly than others.

Stages of reading skills development

Age	Stage of development
1-2 years	Children will enjoy looking at simple picture books. They will like identifying recognisable items in the pictures.
3-4 years	Children will be able to listen to stories and will enjoy having the same stories repeated to them. They will have favourite books and may start to 'read' books independently.
5-7 years	Children will start to recognise more words and will start to be able to read simple sentences and books. They will enjoy books for a range of purposes, for example non-fiction and poetry as well as stories.
7-11 years	Children of this age will still enjoy a variety of texts and also listen to stories being read to them. They will develop their reading skills by extending their vocabulary and understanding.

Strategies for supporting reading development

Teachers, parents and assistants should all be working together to encourage children to enjoy and benefit from reading. The main focus of development will be through the Literacy Hour, although reading will be promoted through all areas.

Strategies for supporting reading

You should know the different kinds of reading which take place in school so that you are able to deal with reading in a variety of situations.

▷ **Shared reading** – this will take place in the class situation and everyone will be able to look at an enlarged text together. These texts should be books on a variety of subjects and themes, and will be used over the week. The teacher will usually go through the text, involving all the children, and practising basic skills. These may be:

 – practising word recognition in context

 – identifying sentence structure and punctuation

 – teaching reading strategies, for example by using contextual cues.

▷ **Guided reading** – this will take place in small ability groups (usually 6 children) using a set of books which are the same. The books should be slightly challenging so that the children need to think about some of the words. Children will then read the books independently while the teacher or assistant supports them. During this time the children will be looking at a variety of cues to help them to decode the text. It is important that during guided reading, teachers and assistants help children by encouraging them to use all these cues together. When supporting individual children by hearing them read, you should help them by:

 – using phonic and word recognition strategies

 – encouraging self-correction of their own reading mistakes

▲ Shared reading is a valuable whole class activity

    – checking that their reading makes sense

    – learning new words.

▷ **Individual reading** – this will usually be re-reading shared books from the classroom, books which have been used during guided reading, or those which can be read by the child without adult support. The child will read independently without help from an adult.

▷ **Paired reading** – this will be two children reading together with one supporting the other. The children may be the same age, or sometimes infant children working with juniors for paired reading.

Working with groups

The teacher may also use a range of questioning strategies which take into account the differing abilities of children within the class. You should remember when you are dealing with groups of children, to use strategies to involve all children, particularly those who are quiet and reluctant to discuss what they are reading. Remember that it is very important for these children to have as much praise and encouragement as possible to build up their confidence.

Case study

You are working with a group of Year 3 guided readers and reading an information text about spiders. The group are very interested in the book and are enjoying looking up some of the more unusual information. One of the girls is not so interested in the book and is unsure what information she would like to look up.

1 How could you encourage her to become more interested in the book?

2 What would you do if you could not involve her in the text?

Working with individuals

If you are working in a class to support a particular child under the direction of the teacher, you will need to ensure that you understand your role within the classroom organisation. You should be clear on the needs of each child you are supporting, for example if a child has Special Educational Needs, you should be aware of what these are. If the pupil needs to work on specific language targets, these can be worked on while you are hearing the child read. A partially sighted child may need particular resources, such as a magnifier or enlarged text, to enable them to use the school's resources.

Case study

Joseph is in Year 2, has special needs and is at stage 'School Action' on the SEN register. He has been quite slow to develop his reading skills and the teacher feels that he would benefit from extra reading sessions on an individual basis as often as possible. Joseph has been working on learning the list of high frequency words to help him to make more progress. You have been asked to hear Joseph read.

1 What strategies would you use when hearing Joseph read?

2 How could you encourage him when he reads well?

Problems when supporting reading development

You may find that while you are supporting children in the learning environment you face problems to do with the resources you are using, the environment, or the pupil's ability to learn. If you find that there are difficulties which mean that you are unable to continue with your task for any reason, you should speak to the class teacher if possible. There is not always an option to do this if the teacher is busy or elsewhere: you may have to decide what to do. If there is a problem with resources, for example you do not have enough books or they are inappropriate for the group you are with, you may need to find them another literacy-related activity to do, such as a word game, and speak to the teacher afterwards. If there are problems with the learning environment, for example there are too many distractions where you are sitting, the best thing would be to move to a quieter area or abandon the task. It is not possible to work if the children are unable to concentrate on their reading or on what is being said. You may find that if you are supporting guided readers, there is one child who finds the book too difficult or too easy – in this case you can give the child alternative activities relating to the text. Where pupils are causing the concern, for example due to behaviour problems, you should not attempt to continue unless their behaviour improves. If it does not, they should be sent back to the class teacher.

Supporting children who speak English or Welsh as an additional language

Children whose first language is not English may find reading and writing more difficult to pick up than spoken language, and will need more support when reading. You may be able to use dual language texts which your school may have, or speak to the local EAL (English as an Additional Language) Unit about borrowing some of these. It is also helpful to use commercially or school produced taped stories which have text for the children to look at while listening, so that they can see and hear what is being read at the same time. For other ideas see also Unit 3-12 – supporting bilingual and multilingual children.

Different resources available

Schools should have a variety of books which are accessible and relevant to the age range. Most schools have their own libraries where children can spend lesson times and are able to borrow books to take home. There should also be other resources which are available for teachers and assistants to use during and outside the Literacy Hour.

Different resources can include:

▷ big books for sharing texts as a class

▷ a good variety of fiction and non-fiction texts

▷ reading schemes

▷ poetry and plays

▷ tapes of stories and rhymes

▷ sets of books for guided reading

▷ story sacks – these are sacks containing characters from books

▷ computer programs to develop reading skills – for example, to support a specific programme.

Help pupils to develop their writing skills

Assistants may also be asked to help pupils in primary classes to develop their writing skills. This may again take place during the Literacy Hour, or at other times prescribed by the class teacher. Assistants will need to have read and understood the school's policy for the development of children's writing and if asked to mark children's work, the marking policy (see, for example, the box below).

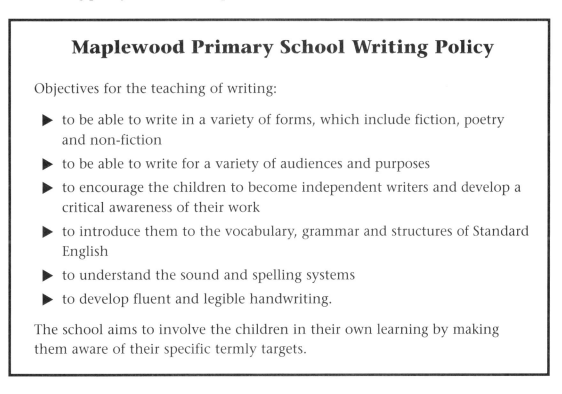

Maplewood Primary School Writing Policy

Objectives for the teaching of writing:

▶ to be able to write in a variety of forms, which include fiction, poetry and non-fiction

▶ to be able to write for a variety of audiences and purposes

▶ to encourage the children to become independent writers and develop a critical awareness of their work

▶ to introduce them to the vocabulary, grammar and structures of Standard English

▶ to understand the sound and spelling systems

▶ to develop fluent and legible handwriting.

The school aims to involve the children in their own learning by making them aware of their specific termly targets.

The way in which children learn to write differs from reading as they need to remember a greater amount of information. In reading, children have the cues on the page in front of them to work on, but in writing they will need to formulate and structure ideas for themselves. The Literacy Strategy structures and builds on the knowledge they already have, so that by the end of Key Stage 2 they will be experienced writers.

Stages of writing development

The table below shows approximate stages of writing development in children. Children's writing however does develop at an individual pace and some children may be faster or slower than others at developing these skills. Teachers and assistants will need to be aware of those children who are working above or below the class average.

Approximate stages of writing development

Age	Stages of writing development
3-4 years	Children will start to have more control over their fine motor skills. They will be able to control a pencil or crayon and make deliberate strokes on a page.
4-5 years	Children may be able to write their name and will start to write some letters and words, although these may not be correctly formed or oriented. They will start to learn that letters relate to spoken sounds. Progress may still be limited to the mechanics of writing.
5-6 years	Children will make progress in writing and start to put more words together. At this stage, progress may be quite different between children.
6-7 years	Children will begin to focus on the context and setting of their writing. They will start to be more aware of points such as grammar and spelling strategies and begin to use dictionaries.
7- 9 years	As children become more experienced writers, they will need to take into account audience, text structure, and effective use of vocabulary.
9-11 years	Children should have learned how to look constructively at their own or others' work and be able to check and redraft.

Strategies for supporting writing development

The school will teach writing according to the Literacy Strategy, which is through shared and guided writing. Assistants should understand the difference between the two, and their expected role during writing activities. You will need to clarify exactly what you have been asked to do with the class teacher, so that you are able to report back at the end of the session which children have achieved the learning objectives.

In **shared writing**, pupils will work as a class to compose pieces of work and discuss language, punctuation and grammar. Teachers will work through the different aspects of writing to enable children to structure and formulate their work while focusing on technical and phonic knowledge. They may then use this as a basis for the work they carry out independently. Shared writing may be carried out two or three times a week, and the teacher will usually act as scribe for the children's ideas. Assistants who are supporting individual children may need to sit with them at this stage to keep them focused on the activity, and help them to remain involved with what is being said. Assistants who work in the classroom may be less involved at this stage, although if they are to work with a group they will need to know what the focus of the session has been.

In **guided writing**, the children will be grouped and have more ownership of their work. It is designed to complement shared writing, and to act as a link between shared and independent work. Teachers or assistants may work with children of the same ability to support the development of specific targets or objectives. During guided writing, children will also have more specific support to help them to develop their own ideas. Assistants may need to help those children who are less confident about putting their ideas forward and contributing to the group. They can do this by prompting and asking these children about their work. If they are at the early stages of writing, it is not appropriate to correct all errors which are made, since this will discourage the children in their writing. It is better to point out any errors which are related to the focus of the lesson, for example if this has been on using capital letters and full stops and these have been omitted.

Individual writing

At the earliest stages of writing, support will focus on pencil grip and the formation of letters. If there is a problem with holding the pencil, children are sometimes provided with a pencil grip or a wider pencil so that it is easier to hold. Staff should encourage pupils to follow the correct letter formation so that they start to write more fluently. As they learn their letters and sounds, children will start to use phonics to help them break words down and, eventually, write independently.

▲ Letter formation is important from an early stage

As pupils become more confident and able writers, they will be able to concentrate more on the development of ideas. Through shared and guided writing, they will learn how to put these ideas into words and sentences. They may need to be given support such as writing frames when they reach this stage, to guide their ideas into a structured format. This may also help children with special needs such as autism.

When working on individual writing, pupils will need to have a clear idea of what they have been asked to do, and any support prompts which are available to help them. There may be class lists of words on the wall for children to refer to, and some children may have access to dictionaries or word banks. There may also be specific word prompts relating to the topic or book which is being studied during the week; for example, if they are reading an information book about 'My Body' these could be body words.

Beginning of story	Middle of story	End of story
Children should have some ideas about the setting of their story, how it will start, and what their characters are like.	This should include what happens in the main part of the story and how it affects the characters.	This will be how the story ends and what the characters feel about what has happened.

▲ Example of a writing frame for a story

Case study

Rania is an assistant in an infant school. She is working with a group of Year 1 children during the Literacy Hour. It is the third session of the hour and she has 20 minutes with the group who are starting to retell a story in their own words. The children need to remember to include the points which were covered during the whole class session. These were:

▶ to think about what happens at the beginning, middle and end of the story
▶ to remember full stops and capital letters.

1 Give some examples of how Rania might start this session.
2 What kind of encouragement or help could she give to children who were finding the task difficult?

Knowledge into action

Ask for the opportunity to observe writing sessions in different year groups.

▶ Find a variety of forms of writing, and different purposes.

- What progression can you see?
- From what you have seen, do you think that the Literacy Hour is having an impact in primary classrooms?

Problems when supporting children during writing activities

These may be the same kinds of problems as those during reading activities, concerning resources, the learning environment, or children's behaviour and ability to complete the task. Where you have any concerns you should always speak to the class teacher.

Supporting SEN children

If a child you are supporting has Special Educational Needs, you will need to make sure that you understand what these needs are with the teacher. You should always agree the strategies which are to be used with children who need extra help or who have specific educational targets or an Individual Education Plan (IEP). If the child has problems with writing skills, these may be addressed in the form of more individual help to prompt the child to think about points which have been discussed in class. These may take the form of specific writing support programmes or small targets which are to be built up. The school may have the resources to provide small group work for some of these children, so that they have more focused help.

Supporting bilingual and multilingual children during writing activities

Children who speak English as a second language may need more encouragement and support when undertaking writing activities. Assistants and teachers should be aware that they may lack confidence and need to have more time to think about the task. These children would benefit from being read to at a slightly slower pace, and have previous work recapped before carrying on. It may help them to have a model or writing frame before starting, so that they can clarify mentally what they have been asked to do. See also Unit 3-12 – supporting bilingual and multilingual children in the classroom.

Resources

Since the introduction of the Literacy Hour, schools have many more and varied resources for supporting the teaching of reading and writing. Teachers will often have access to useful ICT programs which are becoming widely available and can develop skills such as phonics, sequencing, and spelling. The school may have specific handwriting resources, which give guidance for joined letter formation.

Keys to good practice
Supporting reading and writing in the classroom

✔ Confirm the children you will be working with and agree organisation.

✔ Clarify your understanding of pupils' learning needs with the teacher.

✔ Agree any strategies to be used.

✔ Obtain any resources needed.

✔ Encourage and praise the child where appropriate.

✔ Monitor pupils' progress and report back to the teacher.

Help pupils to develop their speaking and listening skills

During the Foundation Stage, the Early Learning Goals for Communication, Language and Literacy are at the heart of their learning experiences. Children need to experience interactions with others in a variety of situations:

▷ attentive listening and responses

▷ using language to imagine and recreate roles and experiences

▷ interacting with others both in play situations and to accomplish tasks.

The National Curriculum for Speaking and Listening sets out the skills which are to be developed over Key Stages 1 and 2. During Key Stage 1, as children develop their use of language, they will learn to respond appropriately to different situations, and to listen carefully to others. By the end of Key Stage 2, children should be able to adapt what they say to the purpose and to their audience.

The school's English policy should outline the shared objectives for developing children's speaking and listening skills (for example, see below).

Maplewood Primary School English Policy

Objectives for the teaching of Speaking and Listening:

▶ to develop knowledge and understanding of the spoken word
▶ to develop the ability to listen to others
▶ to encourage the children to express themselves effectively in a variety of situations, enabling the children to match response and style to audience and purpose
▶ to develop a growing vocabulary and an enjoyment of words and their meanings
▶ to develop imagination and inventiveness
▶ to be able to give and receive instructions
▶ to be able to use speaking and listening skills when participating in a range of drama activities.

The National Literacy Strategy also offers a structured framework which outlines teaching objectives, focus for teaching and strategies for extending and reinforcing speaking and listening skills.

Providing opportunities for speaking and listening

Although all classrooms will offer children opportunities for speaking and listening, staff will need to be aware of how they can make these beneficial for all children. It is important to observe and make a mental note of those children who are not comfortable in these situations and are reluctant to contribute, as well as children who are over-enthusiastic about their own contributions but do not listen to others. Sometimes children may put forward negative comments about the contributions of others during discussions. Adults should always intervene to prevent this kind of intimidation, as it may stop children from speaking in front of others. If pupils speak with different accents or dialects from the majority of children in the class, they should feel comfortable speaking in front of others and should not be discouraged.

Some children may find it very difficult to speak in a class group, and will need to be encouraged to put their ideas forward. This may be due to a number of factors:

▷ Physical or emotional factors. Children may find it difficult to speak openly if they have a physical condition or speech difficulty which makes it hard for others to understand them. Adults may need to support them by repeating back what they have said to the group after they have finished speaking. You should not interrupt the child or finish sentences for them.

▷ Lack of self-esteem. Children who do not feel able to speak in front of others may lack self-esteem due to their experiences at home and school. Staff need to develop self-esteem in children by giving them opportunities to succeed and to praise their achievements (see also Unit 3-13 page 218 about developing self-esteem).

▷ A child's special needs. Children with special needs may lack confidence or feel 'different'. Assistants who work with individual children will know their child and may be able to encourage them to talk through particular interests or experiences which they have had.

▷ Child may speak English or Welsh as an additional language. If the child is not confident in the second language, this may prevent them from contributing.

Strategies for encouraging children when speaking

Children who are not confident when speaking need to be aware that we value what they have to say. We can show them that we are interested by:

▷ giving them eye-contact when they are talking to us

▷ smiling or encouraging them to continue while they are talking

▷ repeating back what they have told us, 'You enjoyed doing cooking with Mrs Briggs this morning, did you?'

▷ asking them open-ended questions to encourage them to answer in more detail.

Strategies to support children when listening

Some children will find it very difficult to sit quietly and listen to others. At a very young age, children will often need to say what they are thinking immediately and will find it hard to wait. They may find activities such as 'circle time', where they need to spend a long time listening to others, quite difficult, or easier in a smaller group. Children who lack confidence in speaking and listening situations in class, for whatever reason, should also be given opportunities to develop these skills in smaller groups, which they may find less threatening. We can develop speaking and listening skills in many different situations, although it need not be a planned event. Older children however may enjoy debates and discussions about set topics, and will be able to adapt their language and ideas.

Examples of some discussion opportunities for Reception and Year 1	
Weather	Give children opportunities to discuss different kinds of weather and how these make them feel; what clothes they should wear in different weather; how they feel when they are hot or cold; seasons; holidays to warm or cold places.
Fruit and vegetables	Naming different fruits or vegetables; where they might grow; whether we need to cook them; colours; sizes; likes and dislikes.
Visiting the school grounds	Looking at different plants and animals in the school environment, listening to sounds; reading any print or numbers; counting.

We can also encourage activities such as board games, and give opportunities for play so that children are able to use their language skills in different situations.

Keys to good practice
Developing speaking and listening skills with children

✔ Make eye-contact with children.

✔ Listen carefully to what they are saying.

✔ Ask open-ended questions.

✔ Praise children for appropriate language.

✔ Give a variety of opportunities for children to use their language skills.

End of unit test

1 How does the Literacy Strategy encompass reading, writing and speaking and listening?

2 Name some of the cues which children use when learning to read.

3 What stages do children progress through when learning to read?

4 Name some of the different ways in which reading is tackled in school.

5 What should you do if a child you are supporting has Special Educational Needs?

6 What is the difference between shared and guided writing?

7 What strategies might we use to encourage a child who finds writing difficult?

8 What is a writing frame?

9 Why is it important for children to learn to listen to one another?

10 Why might children feel uncomfortable speaking in front of others?

11 How can we show children that we value what they have to say?

12 What opportunities can we give children to develop speaking and listening skills?

References

National Literacy Strategy, *Framework for Teaching YR to Y6* (DfES, 1998)

National Literacy Strategy, *Teachers notes modules 1-6* (DfES, 1998)

National Literacy Strategy, *SEN Resource Folder* (DfES, 1998)

Curriculum Guidance for the Foundation stage (QCA, 2000)

Websites

www.standards.dfee.gov.uk/literacy/

Unit 3-19 Help pupils to develop their numeracy skills

This unit will help you to support pupils when developing numeracy skills. You will need to know the different ways in which the teacher plans for learning activities within the Foundation Stage and during the Numeracy lesson, and the need to work under the direction of the teacher to help children to achieve the learning objectives of the lesson. Assistants will need to report back to the teacher as to pupils' achievements in Numeracy activities. Some of this may take place during the plenary section of the Numeracy session.

The structure of the Numeracy Strategy

The Numeracy Strategy is a non-statutory document which will be a requirement in many primary schools. Assistants should therefore have some training or understanding of the way in which this works. The Foundation Stage will follow the framework of the strategy and the Early Learning Goals for Mathematical development. Although it is not possible to reproduce large sections of the strategy here, you should be aware of the way in which it is broken down and the tasks you may be asked to do with groups or individual children.

Assistants should be aware that maths may be taught very differently from their own experiences in school. This is because there is now a much greater emphasis, particularly in the early primary phase, on teaching children different methods of arriving at an answer, and showing them different methods of working. The National Numeracy Strategy is designed to give children a solid grounding in number from which they will be able to base their working. For example, instead of giving a child a page of sums with set answers at all times, we may be sometimes giving them tasks such as, 'The answer is 12. What is the question?' and seeing how many they can devise.

The daily lesson will be between 45 minutes and one hour, and from Years 1 to 6 will have the same structure:

1 Whole class oral and mental work (5 to 10 minutes), to sharpen and develop children's oral and mental skills .

2 Main teaching activity (30 to 40 minutes) – this will usually start with the whole class, and then children will move into groups, pairs or individually to work on the focus of the lesson.

3 Plenary (10 to 15 minutes) – a whole class activity to finish the lesson and summarise what has been learned, perhaps leading on to homework.

During Reception, children will usually learn numeracy skills through part of an integrated day, working towards a structured Numeracy lesson in Year 1. They will start to learn a variety of mathematical skills such as sorting, matching, finding patterns, using number and looking at shape, space and measures. Children will need to have as much practical experience as possible so that they will find it easier to later relate this to more abstract ideas.

The Numeracy Strategy framework gives a list of Key Objectives for each year group from Reception to Year 6. Children are therefore working through a progression of skills development throughout their primary years.

Examples of some of these skills in Reception are:

▷ recognise numerals 1 to 9

▷ use language such as more or less, greater or smaller, heavier or lighter, to compare two numbers or quantities

▷ talk about, recognise and recreate simple patterns.

By Year 6, examples of the skills children are learning are:

▷ order a mixed set of numbers with up to three decimal places

▷ solve simple problems involving ratio and proportion

▷ solve a problem by extracting and interpreting information presented in tables, graphs and charts.

(Source: *National Numeracy Strategy Key Objectives*)

You will need to have an awareness of the skills that children in your class will be working towards in order to support them fully and help them to access the curriculum. The Numeracy Strategy clearly sets these out in the teaching programmes for each year group, and each term. It also gives examples of the activities which teachers can use with children.

Knowledge into action

Find out how your class teacher uses the Numeracy Strategy to plan for and teach pupils in your class. Find the Key Objectives, teaching programmes and supplement of examples for use within your class age range.

The school's mathematics policy should give a breakdown of the aims and objectives of the school's teaching of maths. Staff should refer to the maths policy and Numeracy Strategy, which give guidelines for the way in which maths is to be taught in the school.

St John's Infant School

Maths Policy

Aims

We aim that by the time children leave our school, they will:

▷ have developed a positive attitude towards maths and see it as relevant to their daily lives

▷ understand and use mathematical language to talk confidently about maths

▷ be able to use a variety of mental and other skills to confidently tackle maths problems

▷ look for and recognise patterns and relationships to help them solve problems

▷ be able to work both independently and collaboratively

▷ have high self-esteem and value the approaches and achievements of others.

Objectives

We will follow the National Numeracy Strategy in order to fulfil the requirements of the National Curriculum. In accordance with the framework, teachers will use a variety of strategies, approaches and experiences to deliver the curriculum. This will include ICT.

Children will:

▷ develop their knowledge and understanding through practical activity, exploration and discussion

▷ learn to count and read, write and order numbers to 100 and beyond

▷ develop a range of calculation skills

▷ learn about shape, space and measures through practical activities which build on their understanding of their immediate environment

▷ learn and use mathematical vocabulary

▷ talk about their methods and explain reasoning when solving problems.

▲ Example of part of a maths policy

Help pupils to develop their understanding and use of number

Assistants will be asked to work with groups of children and individuals to help them to understand and use number. When working on number activities with children, assistants will need to work with class teachers to ensure that they understand the learning objectives of the lesson, and are clear about how activities are to be taught. They will also need to know how what they are doing fits in with the rest of the class.

The teacher is responsible for informing assistants about individual children's learning needs. They will need to have up-to-date information about pupils' current ability to understand and use number. This may come from the class teacher, from their own observation and knowledge of the pupil, or from written records or assessments. Assistants will need to know if they have number targets to work on, either as a group or as part of an IEP – see the example below. The strategies which assistants use should be agreed with the teacher before the start of the lesson.

Individual Education Plan	
Name: William Mullenger	**Class teacher:** Mrs Collett 3NC
Date: September 2002	**Review:** December 2002
Targets To be able to remember number bonds to 10. To develop mental strategies when using number.	**Review**

▲ Part of an IEP for number

The strategies which assistants may need to use with pupils may range from explaining tasks and following instructions, to questioning skills or giving children extension activities if they finish their task. Some IEPs may include suggested strategies for adults to use with pupils. At the end of the lesson, assistants will need to give feedback to the teacher about the pupil's achievements to enable them to amend and maintain records and reports.

Helping pupils to interpret and follow instructions

Pupils may find that they do not understand what they have been asked to do, and this may be for a variety of reasons. Some pupils may have special needs and require help to understand the task through further explanation or work that is more specific to these needs. Others may have not been listening to what the teacher has said, or have found the explanation hard to understand. Assistants must be able to explain what their instructions mean and clarify tasks, through finding out exactly how much the child did understand as a starting point.

Case study

Year 3 are starting to learn about division and how it is the reverse of multiplication. Their task is to work through a series of division questions through using multiplication strategies, for example 'Solve 28 ÷ 4 by saying how many fours make 28'. You are working with Jack, who has grommets in both his ears and found part of the lesson hard to understand as he did not hear clearly. How would you go about explaining the task to Jack?

Questioning and prompting pupils

Pupils will need to be questioned when working on maths activities, and assistants should know the different ways they can do this. The Numeracy Strategy booklet 'Mathematical vocabulary' gives ideas for these, and gives examples of different types of question:

▷ Recalling facts, e.g. 'What is 5 add 6?'

▷ Applying facts, e.g. 'Tell me how you would find out how far it was from one side of the playground to the other'

▷ Hypothesising or predicting, e.g. 'Estimate how many multilink cubes will fit in the container'

▷ Designing and comparing procedures, e.g. 'How could you subtract 47 from 93?'

▷ Interpreting results, e.g. 'What can we see when we look at the hundred square for numbers ending in 7?'

▷ Applying reasoning, e.g. 'How many different ways can 3 eggs go into an egg box?'

These different types of questions show the ways in which we can challenge children by giving them open as well as closed questions when engaged in maths activities. You should always try to ask the child as much as possible by guiding them round the task rather than giving them direct instructions.

Think about it

Think of how you could question a Reception child who is finding it difficult to understand the principles of addition. She has completed some practical tasks using counters and is now making small numbers to put together.

Helping pupils to select and use appropriate resources

Assistants should make sure that they are always familiar with and know the location of any resources that they have been asked to use. Pupils may need help with this if they have been asked to carry out an activity and are unfamiliar with mathematical resources. Children with whom you are working may not have used some items before and younger children should be given the opportunity to look at and explore them before starting to use them.

▲ There are various resources to help with different maths activities

Reinforcing mathematical vocabulary

Assistants may need to reinforce the use of any vocabulary which has been used by the teacher while explaining new concepts. This will help children to absorb new words while working on mathematical ideas. For example, while working on calculations, Year 4 pupils may be required to learn any of the vocabulary shown in the box below.

Mathematical vocabulary for Year 4

Add, addition, more, plus, increase

Sum, total, altogether

Double, near double

Subtract, take away, minus, decrease

Leave, how many are left/left over?

Difference between

Is the same as, equals sign

(Source: *National Numeracy Strategy, Mathematical Vocabulary* – DfES, 1999)

The National Numeracy Strategy publication on mathematical vocabulary also gives details of the vocabulary which should be used with pupils at each stage from Reception to Year 6. Assistants should be aware of the vocabulary which they can use so that they can reinforce and extend the children's learning.

Introducing follow-on tasks to reinforce and extend learning

Assistants may be asked to use follow-on tasks for those children who finish their work and have a good understanding of the concept on which they are working. These should relate to the learning activity which they have completed. For example, a Year 5 child who has just completed an exercise about odd and even numbers could be asked to carry out an investigation to find out about number patterns when using them for calculations.

Using praise to promote further learning

When you are supporting children in their mathematical development, you should always remember to use praise and encouragement, as children may become quickly discouraged if they find a concept hard to understand. Children will need to experience success at their own level in order to remain motivated and on task. You will need to be able to give them constructive feedback to help them to build on what they know and encourage them in their work. This should always be appropriate to their age and area of achievement.

Case study

Look at these two conversations:

Katrin: I have added these two numbers together but I don't think the answer can be right, it looks too big.

Assistant: How did you get such a big number? You have obviously done something wrong there.

Katrin: I have added these two numbers together but I don't think the answer can be right, it looks too big.

Assistant: You're right, well done for spotting that. How could you check the answer?

1 Which assistant has used the wrong method of questioning with Katrin?

2 How will the correct method encourage Katrin despite her mistake?

Using calculators

Pupils should always be aware that the use of calculators is as a learning aid and not as a matter of routine. Children should be taught how to use efficient mental strategies before using the calculator. They should have their own methods for checking whether their answer is correct. (See also the *Numeracy Strategy Framework* page 8 – The role of the calculator.)

Case study

Lucy is a teaching assistant in an infant school. She has been asked to work with a group of Year 1 children during the second part of the Numeracy lesson. The group are working below the class average and have been asked to carry out a number investigation to find out how many different ways they can find to make the number 10. Think about the resources and ideas Lucy could use with the group while doing this activity.

Help pupils to use and understand shape, space and measures

The terms 'shape, space and measures' apply to a range of mathematical activity in primary schools. Through this area, pupils will be learning to develop their skills in learning about shape, length, capacity and weight and time. They will also need to be able to estimate, measure and compare in these areas. Teachers and assistants will need to be able to work together to develop children's knowledge and understanding when undertaking these tasks. As with number activities, you will need to know the learning outcomes of tasks you are doing with pupils so that you can work on these together.

The National Numeracy Strategy gives the structure of how shape, space and measures are to be worked through within the Numeracy lesson. Pupils will learn how to use the vocabulary related to shape, space and measures, and to use different units of measurement. It is useful to be aware of the progression which is expected of pupils between Reception and Year 3, for example, when thinking about measuring time, as shown below.

Reception: Starting to look at the vocabulary of time through learning the days of the week, thinking about times of day such as morning, afternoon, playtime, bedtime. Children will start simple sequencing activities, through listening to stories and thinking about their own experiences. They are beginning to be aware of important times of day, e.g. coming to school at 9 o'clock, going to bed at 7 o'clock.

Year 1: By Year 1, pupils will be aware of different units of time and how they fit together. They will start to be able to order days of the week and the seasons. Children may also be able to read o'clock and half past on an analogue clock.

Year 2: In Year 2, pupils will start to extend their vocabulary to the names of the months and recognise when their own birthday falls. They may know other words such as fortnight, minute and second. Children will start to know that one week is seven days, a day is 24 hours and so on. Children may start to estimate how long things will take, for example what might take an hour?

Year 3: By Year 3, children should be able to read the time on a digital or analogue clock to the half or quarter hour. They will continue to extend their vocabulary and estimating skills.

By Year 6, pupils will be using their skills at measuring time to solve problems.

Building on children's prior knowledge

Assistants will need to know the stage which pupils have reached in order to build on the skills they have. Children will then need to be given opportunities to use the skills which they are learning and apply them in a variety of situations. Ways in which assistants can find out about pupils' previous level of understanding include the following:

▷ Through the teacher. You may be informed of a child's or group's understanding of a concept or stage of understanding through speaking to the teacher about work they have already completed.

▷ Through observing the pupil. You may know more than you think about a pupil's ability, and already be aware of the child's capabilities, through working with and watching them in class. You may also be asked to observe a child or group of children to see how they work when they are not being supported.

▷ Through teacher or class records. The child may already have specific learning targets or difficulties when working on shape, space and measures and you will need to be aware of these, as the pupils may require particular strategies to help them work on their targets.

Assistants will also need to provide feedback to the teacher after the task has been completed so that the child's or children's records can be maintained.

Support strategies when working on shape, space and measures

Teaching assistants will need to use the same types of strategies when supporting children using shape, space and measures as they do with number activities (see page 258). They should have a range of strategies which are agreed with the teacher, and ensure that they have sufficient resources to carry out activities with the children. The resources which may be needed will include such equipment as scales, rulers and height charts, trundle wheels, clocks and timers, measuring jugs and so on.

Resources may be kept in classrooms, or if they are to be shared between classes in a central area to which everyone has access. You will need to find out whether items need to be signed out when they are removed.

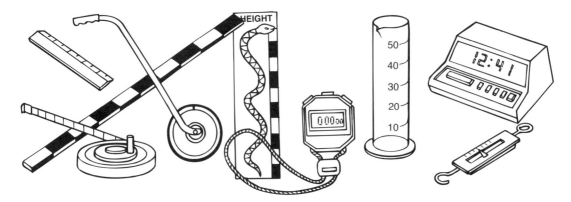

▲ A variety of measuring equipment will be needed

? **Think about it**

Think about how you might help a group of Year 2 children in the following activities:

▶ Estimating and measuring the length of the corridor
▶ Estimating and timing the length of time it takes to get changed for PE
▶ Estimating and finding out how many unifix it will take to balance a pair of scissors

What types of questioning might you use?

How could you draw on their past experience to help them with the tasks?

Children will also need to learn to differentiate between different types of units of measurement, and will need to have plenty of practice with each.

In order to maintain pupils' interest and concentration in the task, assistants must remember to use encouragement and praise. These areas are interesting to children as they often include practical activities which will hold their interest. When working with younger children with equipment and practical tasks, it is worth giving them the opportunity to look at and handle shapes and equipment before starting the task. This will give them the chance to explore and become used to the equipment, so that they can focus on the activity later. However, they will still need to be kept on task and complete the learning objectives for the session.

Working with children who have special needs

Children who have a Statement of Special Educational Needs may be working at a very different level from others in the class. You may find that you are supporting a child, or children, who needs specific help with mathematical tasks. The special needs which you may experience in mainstream schools may cover a wide range of difficulties, and it is not possible to include them all here. The child may need specific help with vocabulary, or have a visual impairment which makes it difficult to use some mathematical equipment. Your class teacher will need to seek advice from the school's SENCo and other agencies outside the school for the best strategies to use with particular children. (See also Units 3-13 to 3-16 for supporting children with special needs.) The DfES has produced a useful publication for supporting pupils with specific needs during the daily mathematics lesson (see page 268 for reference).

Problems when supporting mathematical development in number and shape, space and measures

The different problems you may find when supporting children with mathematical tasks may be related to any of the following.

The child's own concept of working with mathematical tasks

From an early age, teaching staff should present children with positive and fun methods of working with mathematical tasks so that they do not think of them as 'difficult' activities. Children should be given plenty of opportunities to use games, investigations and other forms of maths which will develop their skills while encouraging them to be independent. Where children have trouble understanding concepts, staff must always give them the opportunities to talk about their understanding and any concerns that they might have. This may be more likely to happen in a group situation rather than a whole class. Children can very quickly start to feel that they can't 'do' maths and lose self-esteem when attempting mathematical tasks.

It is important not to let any negative feelings or experiences from the past about maths to overflow into verbal or non-verbal language with the children. They need to know that 'Maths is fun!'. Regardless of our own feelings or maths background, we can competently support children in this area.

Case study

Hiab is in Year 4 and the class has just had a Numeracy lesson on finding the area of a circle. She is a quiet child and does not have enough confidence to put up her hand when the class teacher asks if there are any questions. You are later working with her group and notice that she is having difficulties.

1 How could you talk to Hiab without damaging her self-esteem?

2 What would you say to the class teacher?

▲ Children need to be given opportunities to play mathematical games

The child's ability to learn

It may be that the child is unable to complete the task because it is simply too difficult, or the child has special needs which make the task very hard to complete. You may need to adapt the child's work so that they have a more realistic chance of completing it and maintaining their confidence and self-esteem.

Case study

Adrian (Year 1) has been diagnosed with pervasive developmental disorder, a mild form of autism. Although Adrian is usually able to join in with whole class activities and does not have his own support assistant, he finds some activities difficult. You are working with his group who are measuring the length of a table using their handspans. Adrian has become anxious because he can see that this will not be an accurate way of measuring the table.

1 How could you reassure Adrian if he continues to be distressed?

2 What would you do with the rest of the group if Adrian needed to be removed from the activity?

If the child has difficulties with behaviour and staying focused and undisruptive, you may need to speak to the class teacher, so that others are not disturbed. If the teacher is busy you will need to remove the child from the activity by sending them to work alone to enable you to work with the group.

The learning environment

Children can be easily distracted, especially at a very young age, and they will need to have an environment which maximises the opportunities for learning. The area will need to have sufficient space and be comfortable for everyone to work in. There should be a minimum amount of noise, and children or support staff should not be disturbed by others when carrying out tasks. Children need to be encouraged to be as independent as possible when they are not working in a group with the teacher or assistant so that this is less likely to happen.

Resources

Children must have access to the resources they need when they are working. Staff must also ensure that any equipment they need to use is in working order, has live batteries and so on. If items are broken or missing, this should be reported straight away so that they can be mended or replaced as soon as possible. Time can be wasted when staff have to spend lesson time sorting out these issues which should have been checked beforehand.

End of unit test

1 What is the structure of the Numeracy lesson in Years 1-6?

2 How will Reception children learn maths during the Foundation Stage?

3 How will teachers plan for Numeracy activities?

4 What sort of strategies might assistants use when working with children on number activities?

5 What are some of the questioning strategies assistants might need to use?

6 What do 'shape, space and measures' refer to in mathematics?

7 How might assistants find out about children's previous level of understanding?

8 What different equipment might children need to use when looking at shape, space and measures?

9 How might you find out about how to help a child who has a Statement of Special Educational Needs with mathematics?

10 What type of problems might you face when supporting children with mathematical tasks?

References

Aplin, R., *Assisting Numeracy: A Handbook for Classroom Assistants* (Beam, 1998)

National Numeracy Strategy: Framework for Teaching Mathematics (DfES, 1999)

National Numeracy Strategy, Teaching Mental Calculation Strategies at Key Stages 1 and 2 (QCA 1999)

National Numeracy Strategy, Mathematical Vocabulary (DfES, 2000)

Guidance to Support Pupils with Specific Needs in the Daily Mathematics Lesson (DfES, 2001)

Planning, Teaching and Assessing the Curriculum for Pupils with Learning Difficulties – Mathematics (QCA)

Unit 3-20 Help pupils to access the curriculum

This unit is to help assistants who provide literacy and numeracy support to help pupils to access the curriculum. Children will need to have skills in literacy and numeracy before they can fully participate in learning activities in other curriculum areas. You will need to be able to support children individually and in groups while helping them to develop subject knowledge and skills in other areas. You should be aware of the problems which may occur when providing learning support to these children and know how to deal with them.

How the school's policies and procedures support pupils with literacy and numeracy related learning needs

Within the school setting, there will be different policies with which you should be familiar to give you an understanding of how the school plans and provides for children who need extra support in these areas.

▷ **English or literacy policy** – this will give staff information about how English is to be taught in the school; see also Unit 3-18 page 239 for an example of an English policy.

▷ **Mathematics policy** – this will give staff information about how mathematics is to be taught in the school; see also Unit 3-19 page 257 for an example of a maths policy.

▷ **Special needs policy** – this will give information about how the school provides for pupils with Special Educational Needs across all curriculum areas.

▷ **Early years policy** – this policy will outline how the school provides for children in Nursery and Reception classes and how their work links to the Early Learning Goals. It is unlikely that children who are at this stage will have extra input with literacy or numeracy activities unless they have specific learning difficulties.

▷ **Other curriculum policies** – these will be the policies which the school has for subject areas such as geography. They will give guidelines for how the different subjects are taught within the school and may provide curriculum links with other subjects.

Find out about...

The different policies which exist within your school and which of these you think are particularly relevant to your work with children.

Planning and implementing learning activities

The class teacher will normally plan and provide for children within the class, some of whom may have special needs and individual learning targets. As part of this provision, you may be asked to assist with planning. This extra involvement is valuable for several reasons:

▷ You will have a greater understanding of the reasons why children are being asked to carry out certain activities.

▷ You will have more confidence in carrying out the task effectively.

▷ You will have longer to consider activities which you are to carry out with children.

▷ You will have greater ownership of the curriculum.

▷ You will be able to contribute your own ideas.

▷ You will be able to prepare more thoroughly for learning activities.

Assistants will also need to have up-to-date information about pupils' learning needs when planning, and if this is done in co-ordination with the class teacher there will

▲ Planning with the class teacher will give you more opportunities to prepare for learning activities

be opportunities to discuss progress. It would still be advisable however to find out more about individual children through looking at records and speaking to the Special Educational Needs Co-ordinator (SENCo). There may be different information available about some children, and you may need to discuss some of this with others in the school.

How to provide literacy and numeracy support to help pupils to access the curriculum

The term 'literacy' is used to describe the skills of reading, writing, speaking and listening in schools. 'Numeracy' incorporates not only the use of number but also a variety of other topics such as weight, time, length, shape and money. Pupils will need to be able to use and incorporate the skills which they learn in literacy and numeracy into all areas and subjects which they learn in school. When pupils are not making the kind of progress which is expected at different stages, assistants may be asked to support them, although this support could also take place as and when it is needed. These children may or may not have a Statement of Special Educational Needs. Their support may take place either through a structured programme such as the ELS (Early Literacy Support Programme) or through other interventions within and outside the literacy and numeracy classes. You should also read Unit 3-18 Help pupils to develop their literacy skills and Unit 3-19 Help pupils to develop their numeracy skills. These units will give you an indication of how your work with pupils fits into the structure of the Literacy and Numeracy Strategies as a whole.

The Early Literacy Support Programme

This programme was introduced into schools in 2001 and was first implemented in the Spring term 2002. It is designed to support children at Key Stage 1 but is not for use during the Literacy Hour. The intervention is to be used by teaching assistants and provides learning materials and lesson plans for 60 20-minute daily sessions to be used with Year 1 children who are not making the same progress as their peers. The children are given opportunities to revisit the key objectives from their work in Reception. At the time of writing, it is hoped that these children will be able to 'catch up' with others in their class after the 12-week programme. Year 1 teachers and teaching assistants who are using the programme will need to have comprehensive training so that they can deliver effective intervention. In some schools the programme is delivered alternately by the teacher and classroom assistant who hand on information to each other each time. This gives them a good idea of children's progress and relies on good teamwork.

How the ELS is structured

▷ Screening for the programme takes place during the Autumn term. Year 1 teachers, assistants, the SENCo and Literacy co-ordinator support the selection of the group.

▷ After selection, assistants work with groups of up to six children for 3 sessions to get to know them before the programme starts.

▷ Programme starts in the Spring term of Year 1. Resources and plans are provided and sessions can be at any time of day apart from the Literacy Hour.

▷ Progress of individual children will be checked by the assistant and class teacher after each four-week block of sessions.

▷ Parents are encouraged to support their children's learning at home.

▷ Class teacher uses weekly notes from the sessions to promote the children's new learning through the Literacy Hour.

This strategy for literacy intervention is designed to help children who are finding the acquisition of these skills difficult. The reason for it is to help them to develop the important basics of reading and writing. The literacy base will then be a good foundation on which to build other subjects across the curriculum.

The **Additional Literacy Support** programme was introduced into schools in September 2001. This programme is designed for use with Year 3 children who are not quite reaching national targets but should do with a little additional help. It is structured in a similar way to the ELS and is again run by teaching assistants. This intervention is designed to take place during the Literacy Hour and children have ongoing assessments and regular checks.

The **Further Literacy Support** programme, or FLS, will be aimed at supporting children in Year 5 who still need extra help with their literacy skills. At time of writing, schools are due to receive information during the Autumn term 2002 for implementation in January 2003.

None of these programmes are a statutory requirement but it is hoped that schools will take advantage of the programmes and the teaching materials.

Find out about...

Whether the ELS or ALS have been implemented in your school. How successful have they been in their objective of helping children to reach their targets?

Other strategies for supporting pupils' literacy needs

Pupils who have literacy needs but who are older may need support with one or more of the three areas of speaking and listening, reading and writing. These areas all interact with one another when children are learning, and you will be required to encourage children to develop these skills within the classroom. Their needs may not be limited to literacy since it is the basis for all other subjects.

Speaking and listening

Clearly, children will need to have speaking and listening skills to enable them to access the curriculum. Where children have difficulties, this may be for a number of reasons:

▷ Shyness – children may not feel that their contributions are as valid as those of others or may be worried about 'getting it wrong'. Staff will need to be aware of these children and offer them as much encouragement as possible.

▷ Children who have difficulty listening to others and keeping still. Some children may be very enthusiastic about putting across their own ideas but less interested in listening to others. These children may need to be taught that they will have to wait for others and that their ideas are just as important.

▷ Children with special needs. These children may have a range of difficulties which make speaking and listening difficult. Children may have speech problems and be reluctant to say what they think in case others find them difficult to understand. Others may rely on signing or other forms of communication to get their ideas across or to understand what is being said. If you work with a child who has special needs in this area, it is important to ensure that they have as much opportunity as other children to put their ideas forward.

▷ Children who speak English or Welsh as an additional language. These children may not have gained enough confidence to be able to speak in front of large groups of children and may be happier contributing to a smaller group until they are more confident. You should also ensure that they have understood any oral or written instructions which have been given out.

⊙ Think about it

Think about children in your class who do not contribute as much as the others. How does the teacher try to involve them in whole class discussions and group activities? Can you think of other ways in which they could be encouraged to participate without making them feel more self-conscious?

Reading and writing skills

Reading and writing skills are important in all areas of the curriculum. Children who need to have support in these areas may be very aware of their difficulties and it is important for staff to be sensitive when working with them. You should always remember to use praise and encouragement so that they do not feel that their achievements go unnoticed. The support you may be asked to give with reading and writing could include the following:

▲ Assistants may be asked to help or support children who speak English or Welsh as an additional language

▷ Helping children to interpret and understand instructions. Children may have difficulty in reading and interpreting instructions if they have not been given or reinforced verbally. You will need to make sure that these children have a clear idea of what they have been asked to do.

▷ Looking out for situations which could prove difficult for children who need literacy support. You will be aware of these children, but may need to think carefully in different situations about whether they are able to participate in activities without support.

▷ Observing and monitoring children's progress. The class teacher may ask you to watch and record how some children get on when they are left to work independently. This could be in any curriculum subject area but may have a particular focus – for example, reading through and checking in a comprehension exercise.

▷ Differentiating and modifying children's work where necessary. Children may sometimes have difficulties with the task itself and assistants may need to simplify what they have been asked to do.

Strategies for supporting children with numeracy needs.

As well as having literacy needs, children may have difficulties when carrying out mathematical tasks in other areas of the curriculum. The strategies which you use to support these children will depend to a large extent on the difficulties which they have; for example, a child with autism may find it hard to explain the methods they have used to complete a calculation. A child who has a speech and language disorder may find the same calculations difficult because of finding it hard to associate symbols with the type of calculation.

Children who need support with numeracy activities may need help in any of the following areas.

Numbers and the number system

Pupils who have difficulty with number may be said to have 'dyscalculia'. This is a condition which affects the ability to acquire arithmetical skills. It is quite common for children with this condition to suffer from dyslexia as well, and have difficulty understanding and learning number facts. They will benefit from having additional practice with counting orally and using objects as they do so, so that their counting is organised. They will also find it useful to learn patterns in number so that they can use these as a memory aid. Other pupils may also find it difficult to process number and will require as much visual representation (number lines and grids) and practical experience as possible.

Calculations

Some children may find it difficult to write calculations on paper while being able to perform them mentally. They may need to do this by first transferring their mental method to paper. (See also Unit 3-19, page 261 for advice on calculators.)

Problem solving activities

These may be difficult for children and it is important to ensure that the context of the problem is realistic for the child so that they are able to relate it to their own experience. Assistants can help by checking that children understand what is being asked, perhaps identifying key words or drawing pictures relating to the problem.

Shape, space and measures

Children may use this in other subject areas and will need to be reminded about how to use measurements and what unit is used to measure weight, for example.

Data handling

Children often have difficulties with data handling and it is regularly used in other subject areas, such as geography, science or ICT. They need to make sure that they have the correct information and that they have made clear recordings so that they can use this information accurately. You might have to offer support, particularly if the children need to represent the information in a mathematical form such as a graph, which they may not remember how to draw.

Assistants should also be aware that these areas should be developed wherever possible, and that they should make as much use as they can of opportunities to develop children's experience of mathematical activities.

Knowledge into action

Select one of the above areas in any year group and ask the teacher if you can work with a group of children who may be having difficulties.

▶ What sort of problems are they having?

▶ How do you set about helping them?

▶ Any other comments?

Working with the teacher to support literacy and numeracy needs

In order to ensure that all children in the class have full access to the curriculum, you must be aware of the learning objectives of each lesson. You will also need to have a clear understanding of the literacy or numeracy demands of any activities which are being undertaken so that you will be able to target those children who are finding these areas difficult. You will need to work with the teacher to make sure that you are aware of specific areas which children may find difficult.

Pupils who speak English or Welsh as an additional language

These pupils will have different learning needs from others in the class, particularly if they have recently started to learn English as a second language. You may find that they understand more than they are able to speak, and staff must be careful when giving them tasks that they are being sufficiently challenged and are grouped by ability rather than knowledge of English, particularly during mathematical tasks. It is important to remember that these children do not have learning difficulties (and indeed may be very bright) but will have different learning needs from other children. (See also Unit 3-12 Provide support for bilingual/multilingual pupils for strategies for supporting them.)

In order to distinguish between these different types of learning support, it is important that staff consider the difference between bilingual children and those who have learning difficulties. Although some areas will overlap, such as the development of vocabulary and language skills, some may be specific to EAL children:

▷ development of self-esteem through social and cultural reinforcement

▷ giving children more time to listen and process information

▷ providing dual language texts to enable children to develop verbal and written language together

▷ using pictures to support comprehension.

Bilingual children will need to have support not only with academic areas but also with social issues so that they are able to retain their own identity. Staff should monitor whether the support given for bilingual children is showing clear progress within their individual targets. If pupils have had a good deal of support over time, and are not seen to be making progress with their language skills, it is possible that they have a learning difficulty. In this case it is advisable to speak to the school's SENCo to see whether an assessment is possible with the educational psychologist.

Problems when providing learning support in literacy and numeracy activities

The problems which may be found when supporting children with literacy and numeracy activities have been looked at in Units 3-18 and 3-19. You may also find that pupils have difficulty relating the work that they are doing in other curriculum areas with literacy and numeracy. However, if you find that a pupil is experiencing difficulties which you do not feel able to resolve, you must inform the teacher as soon as possible.

End of unit test

1 What are the policies which you should be aware of when supporting pupils' curriculum needs?

2 Why should assistants be involved with planning as much as possible?

3 How can you find out about pupils' learning needs?

4 Why do children need to develop their literacy and numeracy skills as much as possible?

5 What is the Early Literacy Strategy and when is it used?

6 How might you involve children who are reluctant to contribute in class?

7 How can you support children who have reading and writing difficulties?

8 Why might children who have numeracy difficulties need different strategies to help them?

9 Why would a bilingual child still need support after receiving it over a period of time?

10 What should you do if you do not feel that you have enough experience to deal with a particular problem when supporting a child?

References

National Literacy Strategy, *Early Literacy Support Programme. Session materials for teaching assistants* (DfES, 2001)

National Literacy Strategy, *Early Literacy Support Programme. Materials for teachers working in partnership with teaching assistants* (DfES, 2001)

Guidance to support pupils with specific needs in the daily mathematics lesson (DfES, 2001)

Websites

All information in the ELS file and book may also be found at:

www.standards.dfes.gov.uk/literacy

www.dfes.gov.uk

Set D

Unit 3-21 Support the development and effectiveness of work teams

In this unit you will learn about the importance of taking an active role as part of a team. Teams in schools may be different groups of people who work together in order to achieve shared objectives for supporting individuals or groups of children. You will need to be able to contribute to the effectiveness of the team and work alongside others for the benefit of pupils. This means that you will need to be aware of the ways in which you can recognise and respond to issues affecting team effectiveness. You should also be able to contribute in your own way to the development of the team through providing support and advice to others.

Principles underlying team effectiveness

There have been many different areas of research surrounding the effectiveness of work teams. Most agree that there are certain stages which groups pass through before they can operate effectively. One of the most succinct definitions has been reached by Tuckman (1965) and others, who believed that all groups need to go through a process of maturing before they are able to function efficiently. The process has been divided into four stages: Forming, Storming, Norming and Performing. (See also the section on development of groups on page 46.)

▷ At the **Forming** stage, members of the team are just starting to get together and a leader emerges. Members of the group will need to have a clear sense of identity and purpose.

▷ When **Storming**, members will start to view themselves as more of a team and will have reached an understanding of what is expected of them. There may be a challenge to the leader during this stage. Individuals will need to have clear roles and opportunities for participation within the group.

▷ **Norming** defines the stage at which the team organises itself into work groups and starts to develop different areas of activity. At this stage, the group will need to establish a culture around shared norms and values that they all agree on.

▷ **Performing** is the ideal state to which all teams aspire. The group are comfortable with one another and work effectively together.

These four stages may not have clear boundaries and teams may sometimes become 'stuck' at a particular stage, or go backwards and not develop fully. John Adair, in his book *Effective Teambuilding*, suggests that there may also be a fifth phase of development, the **Dorming** phase, when the group may fall into a state of complacency about its achievements and does not continue to move forward. This is usually avoided through consistent planning.

 Think about it

Think about different groups in which you may have worked in the past. What might it feel like to be in a group at each of the four different stages?

Skills that are needed when working within a team

Within the team, individuals will also need to have effective communication, interpersonal and collaborative skills. This will enable the team to function more efficiently.

Effective communication skills

Good communication is an essential part of working as a team. The principles of effective communication include the following:

▷ Listening to what others have to say. This is important: often people listen to one another but do not really hear what others are saying. This may be because they are thinking about something else or are too eager to put their own point of view across.

▷ Making sure that you contribute to team discussions. You may not feel confident in volunteering your ideas: perhaps you are new to the team or find it difficult to put ideas forward. You should remember that all contributions are important, and your point of view is as valid as anyone else's.

▷ Providing regular opportunities for talk. This is important in a school, where everyone is busy and may not have time for discussions when one member of the team needs to talk about a particular issue. For teams to communicate effectively within a school, there will need to be systems in place which contribute to this. These may be through clear staff structure and clearly defined roles, which will make it easier for individuals to see where they fit into the school as a whole and how their role is defined. It should also take place through meetings between different groups within the school, for example the senior management team, the teaching staff, the year group, teaching assistants, individual support assistants and those working within a particular class. These meetings provide regular opportunities for discussion and exchange of information, which may be written or verbal.

▲ Meetings will give individuals within a team opportunities to contribute their ideas

Effective interpersonal skills

These are sometimes the most difficult skills to have as within any team there will be a number of personalities. Individuals will need to have the skills to relate to one another well and be sympathetic, supportive and helpful. Members of the team should be sensitive to the needs and feelings of others, and encourage those who they know are finding work challenging or difficult. This may be due to other issues which they have to deal with outside school.

There may be a combination of factors which makes it difficult for individuals to focus and tackle problems in the work environment. This may mean reading others' body language at times or realising that now may not be a good time to approach another member of the team with a problem. There may also be a member of the team who is much more of a speaker than a listener. This can be a problem if the person does not give others the chance to have their say.

? Think about it

Have you ever been in a group, perhaps when you yourself were at school, where one or a group of individuals was always the first to put their ideas forward? What kind of effect did this have on you and others within the group?

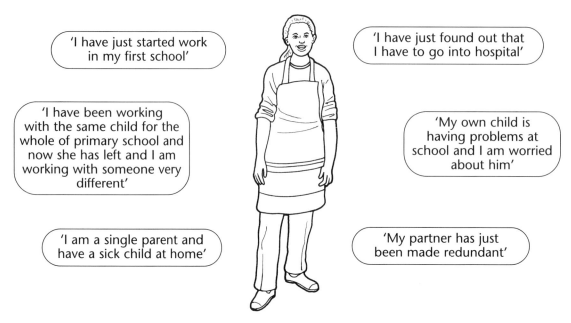

▲ Issues outside school may make it difficult to concentrate on problems in the work environment

Effective collaborative skills

Members of the team will need to be able to work together. In his *Team Development Manual*, Mike Woodcock outlines nine 'building blocks' which lead to team effectiveness. These are:

▷ have clear objectives and agreed goals

▷ be open about facing issues and resolving them

▷ work in an atmosphere of mutual support and trust

▷ have appropriate leadership which suits the task, team and individual members

▷ conduct regular reviews to reflect on their performance as a team and their performance as individuals

▷ have good relationships with other groups

▷ have sound procedures for working together and taking decisions, with all members being consulted and involved

▷ encourage and foster individual development of all team members

▷ work together cohesively but be free to disagree when necessary, i.e. allow both co-operation and conflict to get results.

Teams within a school should be able to apply these skills to their own environment and experience to ensure that they are supporting other members of their team. It is important to remember that although you are working as a team, individuals will have their own strengths and should be valued.

▲ Collaboration is an important part of team work

 **Think about it**

John is a teaching assistant in a primary school. He has been told that he is to have a staff appraisal the next day but has not been told about appraisal before. How could the school have adapted some of the building blocks into their practice to help John as a team member to prepare for appraisal?

Helping and advising others

You may find that you are in situations where other team members need your help and advice. If you are the most experienced teaching assistant, others may come to you in this situation. You should always think about your role and theirs within the team when doing this, while remaining supportive. Where you do not feel that it is appropriate for you to deal with a particular issue, you may need to refer to someone else within the team. You must remain non-judgemental about others and not allow your own opinions to intrude or cloud any decisions you may have to make.

Penny is an individual support assistant in a junior school. She has been supporting Ryan, who has Asperger's Syndrome, for two years but is finding it difficult to work with the teacher with whom she is placed at the moment, as the teacher often gives her last minute plans and asks her to carry them out with Ryan. As he needs to have plenty of structure and routine to his day, Penny is finding this hard as Ryan often becomes distressed if there is a change to what he is expecting. Penny has discussed this with you as she feels that you are the closest member of the team.

1 What advice would you give to Penny?

2 How do you think the team as a whole could help in this situation?

The relationship between your role and the role of others within the team

You may find that there are a variety of different teams in which you work within a school on a short-, medium- or long-term basis. Although your role may be the same within each, these different teams will be focusing on different areas within the school. These may be:

▷ supporting a particular child – assistants who work with individual children may work alongside others such as the SENCo, or other professionals who come into the school to support a child who has Special Educational Needs (see Unit 3-4, page 95 for the types of professionals who may come in to schools)

▷ within the class – assistants will work with the class teacher but there may also be other adults or assistants within the class who work together

▷ within a year group – the school may be large and have 3 or 4 classes within a year group. Year groups may work very closely together and support one another in planning and moderating children's work

▷ within the school – all members of staff within a school are part of a team and will support one another. For example, the maths co-ordinator will be able to offer help and advice to any member of staff on any maths activities.

In each of these situations, members of the team will need to understand their role and how it fits in with the role of other members of the team. The most important part of any role within a team is communicating effectively with others. There should be clear and consistent methods of communication so that all members of the team feel that they are valued. (See also Unit 3-4, page 95.)

Interpersonal relationships and how these work within a team

Individuals within a team will have a range of personalities, but will need to be able to work together in order to achieve different goals. Because there are different personalities, there may sometimes be areas of conflict or disagreement which may occur at different levels. This can cause problems where individuals have very different ideas about how things should be done (see page 286.) Having good relationships with others means being able to listen to others and respect their ideas and opinions. Your own personal feelings about people should not interfere with your role as a member of the team.

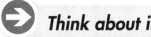

Think about it

Think about your own experience of working within a team. Do some members of the team always put their ideas forward while others are very quiet?

Working together for the benefit of the team

Although you will have your own agenda, you will also need to be aware that other members of the team should have information about what you are doing in case they need to take over from you. In a school where there are good systems in place and planning and reviewing take place on a regular basis, there should be information for others to use if they need to. Similarly, if you find that you have information which may be of help to another member of the team in what they are doing, you should be willing to share this information.

Understanding different ways of working

All schools will work slightly differently and it may take some time for you to become used to different styles of teaching and learning. You may also be moved to a different class or classes within the school and have a variety of teachers to work with who may also have slightly different approaches. It is important to be able to work in different situations.

Case study

Marguerite has been working as a classroom assistant with the same teacher for three years. The teacher has left and Marguerite has to work with a new teacher although she is in the same year group. The new teacher asks Marguerite if they can spend Thursday lunchtimes planning for the following week, but Marguerite is not paid for working in her lunch hour and is unwilling to stay.

1 Do you think that Marguerite should speak to the teacher or another member of the year group? Why?

2 How would you suggest that this problem be resolved?

Professional and personal relationships

When working with others as members of a team, it is important to be able to recognise the difference between working and personal relationships. When individuals work together as professionals, it is important to establish good working relationships first, although people often become friends through working together. In order to establish good working relationships with others, you will need to ensure that you consider the keys to good practice (see below).

You will also need to be aware of ways in which you contribute to the development of that team. Apart from areas already discussed, such as being aware of how you can support others, you will need to be able to develop other strategies for your contribution to the team.

Keys to good practice
Establishing good working relationships within a team

✔ Be considerate towards others within your team.

✔ Carry out your duties well and cheerfully.

✔ Do not gossip or talk about other people in your team.

✔ Speak to the appropriate team member if you need help.

✔ Prepare for and contribute to meetings.

✔ Acknowledge the support and ideas of other team members.

? Think about it

How much do you feel part of a team as a teaching assistant? Do you tend to mix only with other support staff or do you feel part of the school as a whole? Why do you think this is?

Problems which may occur when working in teams

Apart from clashes of personality, there are other areas which may cause problems within a team. One of the main areas is that of conflict. Members of an effective team will need to confront any differences they have rather than ignore them. In his book, *Managing Disagreement Constructively*, Herbert Kindler identifies four main areas of conflict which occur within teams. He defines these as follows:

▷ Having inaccurate or incomplete information – in this situation, members of the team may have access to different information and feel that they have not been fully informed as to what is happening. This may also cause them to interpret information in different ways. This emphasises the importance of openness within teams.

▷ Having inappropriate or incompatible goals – staff may feel that they do not agree on strategies for managing one area of their work. However, if everyone in the team ensures that they have the same aims at the outset, these types of conflicts should be avoided.

▷ Having ineffective or unacceptable methods – it is important for the team to have shared values so that some members do not seem to say one thing and do another. This again makes it important for members of a team to share values and be consistent in their practice.

▷ Having antagonistic or other negative feelings – this is usually due to left over resentment which has built up over time. Conflict which is caused by old wounds is difficult to diagnose for this reason and often difficult to heal or resolve.

The school may have policies and procedures in place for dealing with difficulties and conflicts within working relationships. This will include areas such as confidentiality and all members of teams should be aware of issues surrounding the exchange of information. You should be aware of who you need to speak to on a professional level if you find that there are problems within your team or group which are affecting your work. Kindler also states that conflict exists at six levels:

▷ **Conflict within the individual** – this means that one person has to choose between actions or goals which are incompatible with one another; for example, an assistant who has been offered ICT training after school each Thursday but has other commitments at home.

▷ **Conflict between two people** – this may be when individuals disagree about joint outcomes. It is most likely if members of the team do not have the same ideas about the team's objectives when working together.

▷ **Conflict within a group** – members of the group or team may disagree on important issues, such as which topic or area to plan for the term.

▷ **Conflict between groups** – different groups or teams within the school may disagree about the way in which something is done; for example, year groups who would prefer to do things in a different way from one another.

▷ **Conflict within an organisation** – a school may find that members of staff do not agree with a particular decision which has been made.

▷ **Conflict between organisations** – this is not so relevant to schools, but an example might be when two schools which are geographically close together have an area of disagreement.

If you find yourself experiencing conflict or difficulty, try to identify what level it is and be ready to articulate it to the right person so that the problem doesn't fester and become worse.

End of unit test

1 What are the four main stages of team development?

2 What skills do team members need to have for the smooth running of the group?

3 How can team members ensure that they are communicating effectively?

4 What should you do if another team member approaches you for advice?

5 What types of different teams will you find within a school setting?

6 How is a working relationship different from a personal relationship?

7 Why does conflict occur within teams? What are the different types of conflict which occur within organisations?

8 How can you ensure that you establish good relationships and working practices within a team?

9 How can you ensure that there is a good system for the exchange of information within teams?

10 What should you do if someone within your team approaches you with a problem you do not feel able to resolve?

References

Adair, J., *Effective Teambuilding* (Pan, 1987)

Kindler, H. S., *Managing Disagreement Constructively* (Crisp Publications, 1996)

Woodcock, M., *Team Development Manual* (Gower Publishing, 1989)

Develop and maintain working relationships with other professionals

In this unit you will look at the ways in which assistants can support the work of other professionals in schools. You will need to be able to work with others in a way that is likely to inspire confidence and trust. You should also make sure that you make the most of any opportunities that become available to you to observe the good practice of others so that you can extend your own knowledge. Assistants must be able to maintain positive relationships with others and be willing and able to share their own knowledge.

Your role and the role of others inside and outside the school

When you are working in a school environment, you will find that there are many different professionals who work both inside and outside the school. Depending on how much you are involved with a particular child, you may get to know some of these people on a regular basis. Alternatively, working as a classroom assistant and having limited hours in school, you may find that you come into contact with very few people other than teaching and other support staff. You will need to be able to show that whoever you work with feels that you are a trustworthy and competent member of staff. (See also Unit 3-4 for more detail on the role of the teaching assistant and others within the school.)

Members of staff with whom you may come into contact regularly

▶ Other assistants – you may meet formally and informally to discuss issues

▶ Teaching staff – you will work with on a daily basis

▶ Year group leaders – you may meet to discuss ideas as a year group

▶ Special Educational Needs Co-ordinator – you may have regular contact with the SENCo if you are working as an individual support assistant

▶ Assistants' manager or co-ordinator – you should have regular meetings with other assistants to discuss school issues

▶ Headteacher/deputy head – you should have some contact with senior management which may take the form of meetings and exchanging information

---

Professionals from outside agencies will probably visit the school in order to work with and advise on children who have Special Educational Needs. If you are an individual support assistant, you may be asked to join in with meetings and discuss the child's progress. Professionals from outside school with whom you are likely to come into contact may include:

▷ speech and language therapists
▷ educational psychologists
▷ English as an additional language (EAL) support tutors
▷ sensory support tutors
▷ learning support staff
▷ behaviour support staff
▷ specialist teachers, for example for children with autism
▷ occupational therapists and physiotherapists – may also offer advice but will usually work with children outside school.

(See Unit 3-4 for a description of the roles of these professionals.)

As there are many different aspects to the role of teaching assistants in schools, your role will need to be written down clearly in your own job description so that you are aware of the different responsibilities you will be expected to undertake. There have been many changes in the role of the teaching assistant in recent years that have moved away from the traditional role of supporting the teacher to a more 'teaching' role in supporting children's learning. National Occupational Standards for teaching assistants, published in April 2001, provides a framework that schools can use to draw up job descriptions (see www.lgnto.org.uk for National Occupational Standards for Teaching Assistants). You will need to be clear about the duties that you will be expected to perform, and should also be aware of your own limitations within your role.

Case study

Sandy has just started work as a teaching assistant in a Reception class. She has been asked by one of the parents whether she can make sure that Josh can go first for lunch as he always gets very hungry by 12 o'clock. Sandy assures the parent that she will make sure he is at the front of the line. When Sandy informs the class teacher, he tells her that she should have referred the parent to him.

1 What should Sandy have done?

2 Why is it important to do this?

Observing and demonstrating good practice

Observing others

As part of your own professional development, you may be given specific opportunities to observe others in their role. However, you will also be in situations where you can observe good practice when working with others on a day-to-day basis. This will give you the chance to extend your own knowledge and to give you a greater understanding of how to work with children. In schools, assistants will have the opportunities within their own classroom to observe the class teacher. It is a good idea to keep track of any strategies or useful ideas that the teacher uses with children so that you can use them yourself. (For example, when working with young children, noticing those who are sitting and listening well before you start, rather than those who are not.) You may not realise it, but often you will pick up on good practice by being around other members of staff.

You may also be asked to be present at meetings and discussions with professionals from outside the school, particularly if you support an individual child. It is good practice to make as much use as you can of opportunities to observe others' expertise. In this way you will develop your own understanding of others' professions, and how they affect your own work.

Think about it

Ask your class teacher whether you can go into another year group for one session. Observe the different strategies the teacher or assistant uses with the children. Do you think that you will be able to use any of these strategies in your own class? Give reasons for your answer.

Demonstrating good practice

You may also be asked whether other members of staff can observe your work with children. This is a regular occurrence between teaching staff, but at time of writing is less likely to happen with teaching assistants. However, it is a useful exercise, as all staff will need to have opportunities to observe one another and look at different strengths. If you are asked whether you can be observed, you should not be anxious or wary of others observing you, as they will be looking at your skills and not being critical. It is also useful for observing and demonstrating good practice, if it is viable, for classroom assistants to 'shadow' one another for a day or more. Students might find this is a valuable exercise.

How to establish and maintain good working relationships with others

When you are working with other professionals, you will need to be able to work in an environment that is one of mutual support. In school surroundings, you will not be able to work independently of others, nor would it be practicable to do so. (See also Unit 3-21: Support the development and effectiveness of work teams.)

The support you will be required to give others will be on several levels:

▷ **Practical** – you may be working with others who are unfamiliar with the classroom or school surroundings and need to have help or advice with finding or using equipment and resources.

▷ **Professional** – you may be in a position to support or help others with issues such as planning, or you may be asked whether others can observe your work with children.

▷ **Informative** – you may need to give support to those who do not have information about particular issues. Alternatively, you may be asked to prepare and write reports about particular children.

▷ **Emotional** – it is important to support others through day-to-day events and retain a sense of humour!

? Think about it

Which of these types of support have you needed to give during the last two weeks? Why do you think they are important?

If you are working with others and are unable or unwilling to support them, you will be unlikely to be carrying out your own duties effectively. This is because you will not be working as part of a team.

? Think about it

Sasha has just started as a teaching assistant at your school. She is working in your year group. How could you help her to settle in and ensure that she starts to feel part of the school team straight away?

Providing information

When you are asked to provide information and reports about a particular child, you will need to do so in a professional manner. This means that you should always respond willingly to any requests for information and ensure that they are complete, accurate, up to date and reliable to the best of your knowledge. Reports and other requests for information should only be given to those who are authorised to receive them and you should remember to observe the school's policy on confidentiality.

There may be occasions when you are approached by professionals from outside the school who need to have access to information about a particular child with whom you are working. It is unlikely, however, that they will approach you directly, and you will be more often asked by the SENCo to produce reports. If you find that you are unable to produce a thorough report and do not feel that you have sufficient information, or if you are unsure about any aspect of what you have been asked to do, you should speak to the member of staff who has requested it. You will also need to make sure that any contact you make with professionals outside the school goes through the usual channels. If the school usually writes to inform others about meetings, it will be good practice to continue to do this rather than make a phone call. It is also useful to maintain written records of contacts made.

Keys to good practice
Providing information

✔ Provide any information requested promptly.

✔ Remember confidentiality.

✔ Ensure that details are complete and accurate.

✔ Follow the usual school routines.

End of unit test

1 Name some of the visiting professionals with whom you will come into contact when working in schools.

2 How has the role of the teaching assistant changed over time?

3 Why should you make use of opportunities to observe others?

4 Why is it important to ensure that you are aware of your own area of responsibility?

5 When are you likely to be involved with meetings with other professionals?

6 What sort of support will you be required to give others in school?

7 When are you likely to be asked for information about a particular child?

8 What should you remember to do if you are asked to provide information?

References

Working with Teaching Assistants: A good practice guide (DfES, 2000)

Fox, G., *A Handbook for Special Needs Assistants* (David Fulton, 1993)

Moyles, J., *Jills of All Trades? Classroom Assistants in Key Stage 1 classes* (ATL, 1997)

Websites

National Occupational Standards: www.lgnto.org.uk

Liaise effectively with parents

In this unit you will learn about the contact you have with the parents and carers of the children with whom you work. You will need to think about your responsibilities when sharing information with parents about their children, and how you promote positive relationships between themselves and the school. It is important that you remember to show consideration for children's home backgrounds and to report any problems in communicating information to parents with the class teacher. You will also need to know how to share the care of children with their parents. It is important to see the relationship between parents/carers and the school as a partnership.

School policies and procedures for communicating with parents

Parents are the primary carers and most important attachment that children have before they come to school. They play the most central role in the care and welfare of their children and know them better than anyone else. It is vital that good lines of communication are established and maintained between parents and staff throughout a child's time in school. This will be beneficial to everyone concerned.

▷ **Beneficial for the child** – their main role models will be seen to be forming a positive relationship, both through a formal and informal exchange of information.

▷ **Beneficial for the parents** – they will be reassured in the knowledge that the school has as much information as it can about their child. They will also know that the school is up to date with their needs.

▷ **Beneficial for school staff** – staff will need to build up an accurate and up-to-date picture of each child. Through exchanging information as much as possible, staff will be more aware of issues and when they arise.

There may be many different ways in which the school has contact with parents and exchanges information. When the child initially enters school, there may be a series of forms for parents to complete, as the school will need to collect information about the child's background. The DfES also requires that schools request information about ethnic origins, cultural background and home language.

Information provided by the school

▷ Written information such as newsletters
▷ Noticeboards

▲ There should be as many opportunities as possible for schools to exchange information with parents

▷ Prospectuses

▷ Home–school agreements

▷ Policies, for example for curriculum subjects such as history, or for issues such as behaviour

▷ School reports (annual)

▷ Accident slips – if the child has had a bump on the head

▷ Information about activities the children are going to undertake

▷ Parents' meeting (annual)

▷ Parents' evening (termly)

Information provided by parents and carers

▷ Initial information forms such as medical/allergies/emergency numbers

▷ Specific information which is relevant to the child's welfare, for example if the child is in foster care

▷ Any special needs which have been diagnosed before the child enters school

Much of the information provided by parents will be kept by the school on file or in the computer systems, so that it is accessible when needed. It is confidential and only used by staff within the school. If the school needs to pass any information onto other parties, such as outside agencies, parents should always be informed.

Other opportunities for exchange of information

When a child first enters school, there will usually be many points of contact with staff. As children progress up the school through Key Stage 1 and into Key Stage 2, this initial early contact can easily be lost and it is important to encourage parents to come into school as much as possible so that contact is maintained. Parents should feel comfortable about discussing any issues with staff as and when they happen. In the same way, teachers will find it easier to discuss more difficult issues with parents if they have already established a relationship with them.

There will also be other opportunities for verbal communication between parents and staff, which may take place at specific times during the school year. It is important for the school to make use of any time that exists for communicating with parents. These may be either formal or informal, but they are good opportunities for parents and staff to meet and talk to one another. In your role as a teaching assistant, you may find that you are involved in some of these events more than others.

? **Think about it**

Think about the times where you have been involved with the type of events shown in the diagram below. Does your school offer any other opportunities for communicating with parents?

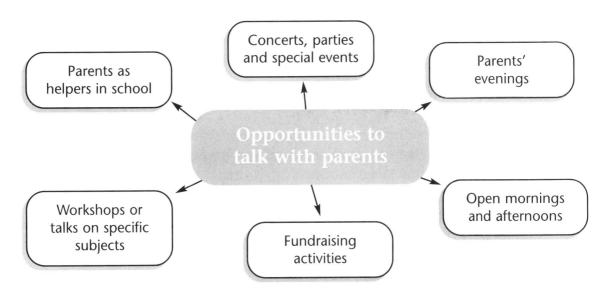

▲ It is important that contact between staff and parents is maintained

Your role when communicating with parents

In your role as a teaching assistant, you will have some contact with parents, perhaps at the beginning or end of the school day. If you are supporting an individual child, you may have more contact than this. However, it is important for you to remember that the class teacher should be the main point of contact for parents. This is because the teacher will need to have all available information at all times, and the more people that are involved, the more likely it becomes that the information will be lost.

Case study

Jackie is an individual support assistant for Katrina, who has learning difficulties. Katrina's mother sees that the class teacher is busy one morning and tells Jackie that she needs to take Katrina out of school at lunchtime for an occupational therapy appointment that afternoon. Jackie means to tell the class teacher but as she is busy she forgets all about it. When it is time to pick Katrina up, Jackie has already gone home and the class teacher has not prepared Katrina's things or told the canteen that she will not be needing her lunch.

1 What could Jackie have done to avoid this happening? Has anything like this ever happened to you?

2 Is there anything else you can think of that would have helped in this situation?

Sometimes, you may be given information by parents which needs to be passed on to another member of staff, apart from the class teacher. You may find that you are given written material to pass on, or you are asked to communicate a message to someone else. It is always best to request that the parent either writes to or contacts the person directly if possible. If you are required to pass on information, you will need to do it as soon as possible, for two reasons – first because it may be important, and secondly so that you do not forget. If there is any danger of you forgetting or not being able to pass it on immediately, then write it down.

You may also be asked by a parent if you can arrange a meeting with another member of staff, such as the SENCo or the headteacher. If a parent needs to speak to another member of staff, it is better for them to go direct to that person, or arrange a phone call through the school office. If it is an urgent request, you may be able to ask them to wait so that you can find the member of staff.

Care, confidentiality and school procedures

There may be occasions on which you have access to information about children which is confidential. This may have been given to you because it is in the child's interest that you are aware of it, for example if there is an issue of child abuse. You will need to be sure that you do not pass on any sensitive information, even if you feel that the person you are talking to is unlikely to tell anyone else. If you do not know who else is aware of this information or has access to it, you should ask the member of staff who passed it on to you.

School procedures for communicating with parents

You will need to make sure that when you are communicating with parents, you observe the school's normal procedures for doing so. This may involve making sure that any information you give to parents is:

▷ agreed with the class teacher

▷ presented in a way that is easy to understand and does not include 'jargon'

▷ consistent with your own role within the school

▷ consistent with confidentiality requirements.

? Think about it

Are you aware of any school procedures for passing information to parents? Find out whether your school has a written policy or what the normal procedures are. What kind of information are you able to communicate to parents in your role as a teaching assistant?

Addressing parents

Staff should make sure that when addressing parents, they use the preferred name or form of address. Nowadays there are many different types of family structure and staff should not assume that children are living with two parents who are married. Some parents may be married, but prefer to be known under separate surnames – some mothers would rather not be known as 'Mrs'. Other parents may have titles or modes of address which are important. These details will usually have been noted down on forms when their child enters school.

You should also be aware that in some cultures, it is not acceptable for individuals to be addressed by their forename. When writing parents' names, their surname may sometimes need to be written first. If you are in any doubt, you should always check such details in the school's records.

Difficulties in communicating with parents

Sometimes there will be problems when the school needs to communicate information to parents. There can be several reasons for this:

▷ The child may not have passed on important information, either orally or through letters: to avoid problems the school could also display important information on noticeboards and in windows, or have a set day for sending home letters so that parents always ask their child on a Thursday, for example, if there are any letters.

▷ Telephone numbers or addresses may not have been updated: parents often forget to inform the school of changes, particularly in telephone numbers. Send home regular reminders or keep a prominent notice on a noticeboard.

▷ Parents may not be able to read letters which are sent home, either because they are unable to read or because they speak English or Welsh as an additional language (see below).

▷ Contact books are not regularly checked by parents or staff. The school needs to make sure that there is a policy for checking these books to ensure that important information is not missed (also see below).

If you find that important information has not reached a parent, you may need to seek advice from the relevant person within the school about how best to deal with the problem. Usually, assistants will not need to contact parents directly, although if working with an individual child, you may have a source of communication such as a contact book, which is completed regularly. Schools may also have other books, such as homework diaries or reading records, which parents and staff need to fill in on a regular basis. This will be useful if you seldom see the parent and wish to let them know about things which have happened at school. Similarly, parents may need to inform you about what has taken place at home. You may need to telephone parents if they have not returned forms or requests for information. If you need to do this you will need to make sure you address the parent correctly and observe school policy.

If you have an 'open door' policy, you may find that some parents are over-keen to come into the school, and this can become a problem if it happens too often. If you have a problem in the classroom in which you work, you may need to refer to another member of staff, but as an assistant you should not speak to the parent about it.

Parents who speak English or Welsh as an additional language

Where you need to communicate with a parent or group of parents who find it difficult to speak and understand English or Welsh, care must be taken so that the parents do not feel isolated from others in the school. This can happen very quickly, particularly if the parents' cultural background is also different. The class teacher or another member of staff may need to refer to your local support team for those who speak English or Welsh as an additional language.

If the parents come to the school regularly with their children, it would be good to encourage them in to help and become involved with the school so that they form positive relationships with staff. If the parents do not have regular contact with the school, you may need to have help from an interpreter, particularly if there are several families within the school.

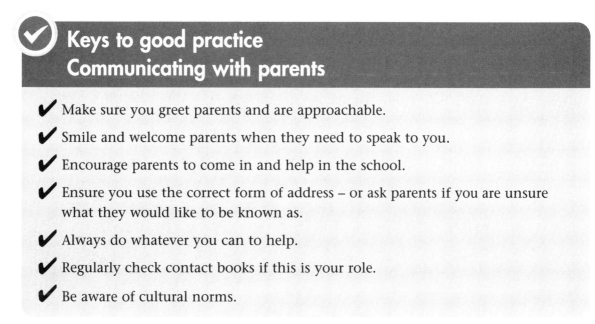

Keys to good practice
Communicating with parents

✔ Make sure you greet parents and are approachable.

✔ Smile and welcome parents when they need to speak to you.

✔ Encourage parents to come in and help in the school.

✔ Ensure you use the correct form of address – or ask parents if you are unsure what they would like to be known as.

✔ Always do whatever you can to help.

✔ Regularly check contact books if this is your role.

✔ Be aware of cultural norms.

How you share the care of children with their parents

When you are working in a school, you are taking on the role of caring for children in place of their parents. As already mentioned, parents are the most important attachment that children will have formed before coming to school. This strong attachment is a basis for their ability to relate to others. You will need to show that you take the parents' wishes into account when caring for them. Parents should feel that they can trust you implicitly and will be happy to leave their children in your care. This care should take into consideration the physical, social and learning needs of their children.

▷ **Physical needs** – this will encompass the child's health and well-being. If they are injured, fall ill or need help while they are in school, parents need to know that they will be looked after, or measures that will be taken in the case of an emergency.

▷ **Social development needs** – this part of the child's care is their social needs, or interaction with others in the school setting. This will include playtimes and lunchtimes. Parents need to feel confident that their child is progressing normally.

▷ **Learning needs** – the school takes on a major responsibility for the learning needs of each child. Parents have the right to be informed of each child's progress and of any strengths or difficulties they may have.

The role of parents and carers in their children's welfare

Parents and carers are their child's first and most important educators. Although they may not be aware of it, they will be teaching their children from a very early age. Children will learn from their parents' routines and everyday experiences which will form the basis for their habits throughout life. All families will have their own ways of interacting, and children will pick up particular strengths and ways of doing things

▲ Parents are teaching their children at home from a very early age

from the people with whom they spend the majority of their time with. In this way, children who are from a family who are gifted in a particular way, such as musically or mathematically, may have the same aptitudes. Similarly, if the parents have bad habits, such as always being late for school and other appointments, the child will grow up thinking that being late does not matter.

Variations in family practices and cultures

All families are different, and children enter schools from a variety of backgrounds. Parents will have their own values, cultures and practices, and they may have different expectations from those of the school. You may find that in your class there are children whose parents have values that are different from yours, or those which you are used to. This can be difficult when parents' ideas do not fit in with those of the school.

Case study

You are supervising a group of children who are in the outside area in a Reception class, when you notice Ellen pushing another child over. When you go and speak to her, she tells you that she was pushed first and her mum has told her that she must always hit back if someone hurts her in school.

1 What would you do in this situation?

2 How could you explain to the parent that this might cause some problems in school?

You will need to be aware of any family practices or circumstances which parents have made known to the school, or cultural differences that make some situations sensitive for other children. This means that religious festivals which may be important to some of your children, such as Diwali or Eid, should be discussed and, if appropriate, celebrated through cooking activities, collages, musical activities, etc. and involving parents if possible. However, you should not expect all families from the same cultural group to have the same ideas and practices and you should be careful to avoid tokenism.

? Think about it

Rajiv is in a Year 1 class who are doing some Christmas work with you in a group. The subject of Father Christmas comes up and Rajiv says to one of the other children in the group that Father Christmas is not real. The other children are quite upset, but Rajiv says that in his family they do not celebrate Christmas.

What would you do in this situation? Would you, or do you think the class teacher, should say anything to Rajiv's parents?

→ Knowledge into action

How are different religious festivals and celebrations from various cultures taught in your school? Can you think of some examples of good practice where parents have been involved in showing children different artefacts or other items?

Different types of family structure

There are many different ways in which people may live together, so it is important not to make assumptions about children's home situations. Pupils may live in a variety of circumstances.

Different family circumstances

Nuclear family – this is when children live with their parents and any brothers or sisters. They may be married, or live together.

Single parent family – one parent taking care of a child or children.

Homosexual family – gay or lesbian couples taking care of children.

Adoptive family – foster or adoptive parents looking after children.

Reconstituted family – children are cared for by one natural parent and one step-parent. This may also include half brothers and sisters.

Extended family – grandparents, parents, uncles and aunts sharing the care of children.

Travelling family – parents do not live at a fixed address and travel around with their children.

Think about it

Think about the different kinds of backgrounds children in your school come from. How many variations could there be in the home life which surrounds each individual child? Think about the effect this will have on their personality and behaviour.

When families have very sensitive circumstances, for example if a parent has died, this will usually be passed on between staff verbally as well as being written down so that everyone is aware. You will also need to be sensitive with issues such as making Mother's or Father's day cards. This could also apply when children have gay or lesbian parents.

In your role as a teaching assistant, you will need to be able to establish relationships with all parents and carers. This will mean that you need to be approachable and sympathetic if you have contact with them. There may be times when this is difficult, for example if a parent is unhelpful or does not agree with the school over an issue. If you find that you are faced with a challenging situation, you must not hesitate to involve another member of staff.

End of unit test

1 What types of opportunities usually exist for the exchange of verbal information between home and school? What opportunities exist for the exchange of written information?

2 How significant is the role of the parent in their children's welfare?

3 What sort of information will your role allow you to communicate to parents and carers?

4 What difficulties might you or the school have when communicating with parents?

5 How can you reassure parents that you have regard for their own wishes for the care of their children?

6 What difficulties might you have with parents who have different values and practices from those within the school? How might you deal with this?

7 What are the different levels of care that you are expected to have for children in your school?

8 What is a 'nuclear family'?

9 How would you react if a parent asked you if they could see the headteacher?

10 What opportunities do you have for meeting with parents? Do you feel that you should have more of these opportunities?

Websites

www.dfes.gov.uk/parents

www.standards.dfes.gov.uk/parentalinvolvement

Appendix

The links between the CACHE Level 3 Certificate for Teaching Assistants (CTA3) and the National Occupational Standards (NVQ)

The CACHE Level 3 Certificate for Teaching Assistants (CTA3) aims to provide an award for candidates who work with pupils individually or in groups under the supervision of a teacher in education and learning support, or wish to work in this field. The award provides the underpinning knowledge and understanding required for the NVQ Level 3 for Teaching Assistants. Each unit has been mapped against the National Occupational Standards and is shown in the learning of each unit.

The following grid shows this mapping in more detail.

CACHE CTA3	National Occupational Standards
Unit 1 The Role of the Teaching Assistant in the School	
1 School structure and job role	3-1, 3-2, 3-3, 3-4, Set A, Set B, Set C, Set D.
2 Relationships and interactions	3-1, 3-2, 3-3, 3-4, 3-9, 3-11, 3-13, 3-15
3 Encouraging positive behaviour	3-1, 3-9, 3-10, 3-11, 3-15
4 The planning process	3-5, 3-6, 3-7, 3-8
5 The learning process	3-9, 3-10, 3-12, 3-13, 3-17, 3-18, 3-19, 3-20
6 Supporting and scaffolding the learning process	3-3, 3-9, 3-14, 3-17, 3-18, 3-19, 3-20
7 Record keeping	3-5, 3-6, 3-7, 3-8, 3-10
8 Policies and procedures	3-10, 3-11
9 Health and safety	3-5, 3-10, 3-11
Unit 2 Supporting Pupils' Particular Learning Needs	
1 The school approaches	3-21, 3-22, 3-23
2 Working with other professionals	3-21, 3-22, 3-23
3 Understanding the terminology and concepts	3-12, 3-13
4 Supporting the pupils	3-9, 3-10, 3-11, 3-12, 2-13, 3-14, 3-15, 3-16

5 Individual differences	3-9, 3-10, 3-11, 3-12, 3-13, 3-14, 3-15, 3-16
6 Factors affecting pupils	3-9, 3-10, 3-11, 3-12, 3-13, 3-14, 3-15, 3-16
7 Different approaches	3-17, 3-18, 3-19, 3-20
Unit 3 Teaching and Learning	
1 Supporting learning	3-9, 3-10, 3-11, 3-12, 3-13, 3-14, 3-15, 3-16, 3-17, 3-18, 3-19, 3-20
2 Supporting the literacy curriculum	3-18
3 Supporting the numeracy curriculum	3-19
4 Support Information Communication and Technology	3-17
5 Working with others	3-21, 3-22, 3-23
6 Working with parents and carers	3-23

Glossary

Anti-social behaviour Behaviour which harms others or destroys the property or feelings of others

Appraisal Process by which staff are required to look at their performance with their line manager and set targets for the coming year

Autism A condition which affects an individual's communication skills

Bilingual/multilingual children Children who are brought up able to speak more than one language

Children Act (1989) Legislation to ensure that children's welfare always comes first: applies to storage of information, health and safety, child protection and the rights of the child

Cognitive development The process by which children learn

Collaborative skills Skills which a team have for working together

Confidentiality Rules within the school to control the spread of information which may be inappropriate for some people to hear

Culture Way of life, beliefs and patterns of behaviour which are particular to social groups

Curriculum plans   What the teacher plans for children in the long, medium and short term in order to achieve set learning objectives

Data protection Means by which information held on individuals is protected

Differentiation The way in which the class teacher plans to teach children with different abilities

Disability Discrimination Act (1995)   Legislation to prevent discrimination against disabled people, set to include educational settings from September 2002

Early Learning Goals Expected learning outcomes for the end of the Foundation Stage in the six areas of learning

Early years settings Settings in which children are educated between the ages of 3 and 5

Educational psychologist Specialist in children's learning and behaviour

Emotional development The development of children's feelings and emotions which enables them to understand and cope with these feelings

Equal opportunities Ensuring that all individuals have the same opportunities and benefits. Some children may need to have support for this to happen

Evaluate To consider whether an activity has achieved its objectives

Fine motor skills Skills which require more intricate movements, usually with the hands, e.g. threading beads, controlling a pencil, doing up buttons

Follow-on tasks Tasks which children can be set following completion of initial learning outcomes, which will reinforce what children have just learned

Foundation Stage First stage of education, from age 3 to the end of the Reception year

Gross motor skills Skills which involve the use of larger physical skills, e.g. running, jumping, throwing

Individual Education Plan (IEP) Used to plan targets for children who have special educational needs.

Inclusive education The process by which all children have the right to be educated alongside their peers

Key Stage 1 Children's education from the start of Year 1 to the end of Year 2

Key Stage 2 Children's education from Year 3 to the end of Year 6

Language acquisition The way in which we learn language

Learning objectives What children are expected to know by the end of the lesson

Literacy Hour Daily lesson in which children work on their reading, writing and speaking and listening skills

Makaton A method of sign language

National Curriculum The curriculum for all children aged 5–16 in England and Wales

Numeracy lesson Daily lesson for mathematics; can range from 45 minutes to one hour

Observations Watching and making note of children's reactions in learning and play situations

Occupational therapist Professional who will assess and work with children who have difficulties with fine motor skills

Open-ended questions Questions which require more than a 'Yes' or 'No' answer, e.g. 'How did you work that out?'

Parent A child's birth mother or father, or adult who has been given parental responsibility by a court order

Physiotherapist Professional who will assess and work with children who have difficulties with gross motor skills or body function

Positive reinforcement Praise given to children to add weight to their achievements

Pupil records Records which are kept in school regarding each pupil. They may include a number of items such as health details, records of achievement, and parents' telephone numbers

Questioning skills The way in which children learn to ask questions during their learning

Resources Items which are available to support learning in school

Rewards Things to give children additional motivation, e.g. star charts, marbles in a jar, stickers, choices of activity

School development plan Document which sets out what the school's priorities will be during the coming year, and how they are to be achieved

School policies Documents outlining the school's agreed principles in different areas, e.g. in curriculum areas such as geography, or non-curricular areas, such as behaviour

Self-esteem The individual's own perception of their worth

Self-reliance The individual's ability to do things independently

SENCo Special Educational Needs Co-ordinator

Sensory impairment An impairment (reduction) of one or more of the senses

Settling-in procedures The way in which a school manages children who are entering school or transferring to a different class

Social development How a child learns to live and co-operate with others

Special Educational Needs (SEN) Where children are not progressing at the same rate as their peers

Speech and language therapist Professional who will assess and work with children with speech and language needs

Statement of Special Educational Needs Given to children who may need additional adult support in school for them to have full access to the curriculum

Statutory requirements Requirements which have been set down by law

Stereotyping Generalisation about a group of people which is usually negative, and based on a characteristic of one person in that group

Targets What children are expected to achieve over a specified period

Values An individual's moral principles and beliefs which they feel are important

Work teams Group of people working together with a common purpose

Index